URBAN CHANGE
AND PLANNING

A history of urban development in Britain
since 1750

URBAN CHANGE AND PLANNING

A history of urban development in Britain
since 1750

GORDON E. CHERRY

G T FOULIS & CO LTD
50a Bell Street
Henley-on-Thames, Oxfordshire

First published 1972

© Gordon E. Cherry, 1972

ISBN 0 85429 119 9

Printed in Great Britain by Alden & Mowbray Ltd
at the Alden Press, Oxford

Designed by Rosemary Harley

TO IAIN

He saw the cities of many men, and knew their mind.
HOMER, *Odyssey*, i 3

Contents

Acknowledgements

This book would not have been written without the initial enthusiasm of my publishers; in particular, John Hassell and, in the later stages of writing, Tony Feldman. Their constant interest and support while the book has been in preparation has been a source of help and encouragement.

Another reason why this book was ever taken on is that the intended coverage was very relevant to a course which I give at the Centre for Urban and Regional Studies under the title 'The Evolution of Town and Country Planning'. My Diploma and Master students have been willing participants in exploring the themes developed in this book. Frequently they have proved themselves more knowledgeable than I and they have contributed to this book to a greater extent than they realize.

The Centre Library has provided much reading matter and colleagues have drawn my attention to sources that were new to me. I am grateful for these benefits of an academic environment.

My acknowledgements for the use of illustrations are given elsewhere but my thanks are due especially to certain ex-colleagues who assisted me in gathering them. Their help was much more than I had the right to ask. They are M.J. Croft, S.N. Denney, D.G. Hayes, D. Langham and R.M.C. Shields.

I am also deeply indebted to a number of Planning Officers, Librarians and other Local Government Officers and their staff for providing me with so much useful material. A number of Planning Officers were particularly helpful and I have made grateful acknowledgement to them on the page devoted to picture credits.

To Miss D.M. Stevens, who has typed my manuscript with speed and skill, go my sincere thanks.

To my family a belated recognition of the obvious, that in operations like this, they bear all the costs and derive none of the pleasures.

Centre for Urban and
Regional Studies,
University of Birmingham,
Autumn 1971

Gordon E. Cherry

1 Introduction

This urban history is written from two closely related points of view. First, the nature and process of urban change in Britain over the last two centuries is presented against a backcloth of social, economic, political and broadly cultural affairs. Second, the course of urban change is shown from the standpoint of the town planner interested in the growth of the planning movement, the emergence and acceptance of planning ideas, and their contributory effect on the development of towns, particularly in the 20th century. It is a history, therefore, which has regard to the appearance of towns, the elements which form their main structure and the forces that promote their change and development. It is concerned with housing and housing conditions, work and places of work; with the growth of town centres, with transport, shopping and recreational facilities. It is concerned with people and the quality of life that towns offer them, and it is concerned with the work of reformers and visionaries who put forward new ideals and standards.

The book offers a general survey of urban development in Britain over the last two hundred years. Although it is 'broad brush' in style, it uses detailed examples where necessary for illustration. The development is shown in the context of a broad social history out of which the planning movement, a movement that itself influenced the development, gradually emerged. It is a book that highlights the main factors in the course of development so that we see continuity and links over a long period rather than simply a series of apparently uncoordinated events.

The chapters unfold chronologically. Chapter 2 gives an account of the 18th century instances of planned development, such as in London, Edinburgh and the resort towns, where the fine heritage of classical estate development was slow to die out. Nineteenth century development is covered in three chapters. Chapter 3 looks at the relationship between economic change and urban growth, and particularly at the major problems of the early 19th century: environment and health. Chapter 4 reviews the main factors in the development of Victorian towns: the impact of the railway, the parks and open space movement, the retail revolution and the emergence of town centres as commercial foci, the development of urban communications, and suburban growth. A number of case studies is given, including some covering holiday towns and settlements created by the railway. Chapter 5 considers the progress of housing reform, the work of social reformers and the influence which model towns exerted. The turn of the century is covered in Chapter 6. This provides us with a useful point at which to reflect on the changes that had taken place and the further developments that might occur in the years ahead. This period is particularly important for the Garden City movement and the formulation of the first town planning ideas.

The next two chapters cover the last 50 years. Chapter 7 reviews the inter-War years: housing improvement, progress in Garden Cities and planning, the impact of the motor vehicle, changes in town centres, and the question of regional shifts in industry and employment. The chapter concludes by evoking the mood of the country at this time, that of dissatisfaction and a desire for a better Britain. Chapter 8 looks at post-War changes, beginning with the emergence of planning strategies for London: containment of size and dispersal of population and employment. It goes on to consider the New Towns programme, the continuing traffic problem, the progress of slum clearance and redevelopment and the transformation of city centres. Chapter 9 is a broad summary offering certain conclusions and observations from the study. In particular it looks at the process of change as evidenced in residential cycles, and in changing urban functions.

It will be apparent from this outline of the book that architectural matters do not play a major part in it. This is quite deliberate. There is already adequate literature dealing with these fields, and repeating this coverage would divert our attention from the rather different focus intended in this book. This is not to say, of course, that matters of architecture and design are not important, nor indeed that they are not closely related to the social background which we are at pains to provide as a context. But many excellent and well-illustrated histories are already available for the general reader. For the planner, Colin and Rose Bell's *City Fathers* is a useful complementary book from the point of view of town design, and a rather more technical contribution, covering particularly the 20th century, is *Homes, Towns and Traffic* by Tetlow and Goss.

Furthermore, we might observe that in the past, the history of planning has tended to be identified with case studies of town design. The architectural approach was in accord with the planner's view of the city as a spatial phenomenon. But the planner is no longer interested solely in the physical aspects of towns and cities, but also in the social, economic and political backcloth against which the growth, stagnation or decline of towns takes place.

Another feature of this history is the relative lack of emphasis on

London. This is quite deliberate for reasons of focus and manage-ability. Land use, development and planning aspects of the history of London for our period are covered by a number of well known, authoritative works, such as John Summerson's *Georgian London*, Steen Eiler Rasmussen's *London: The Unique City*, and Donald J. Olsen's *Town Planning in London*. The problem in any general urban history is always how best to deal with London. The capital is unique, but one must discriminate against it if a balanced review of the urban process in the country as a whole is intended.

In the course of this history there is a wide range of further reading on which to draw, including standard texts, specialist works and a host of case studies. It is impossible to indicate all of these. The references given to each chapter are indications of the material available and are not necessarily the most leading or accepted sources to the particular point being made. To assist the wider reading the *Urban History Newsletter* is highly recommended for its extensive regular biblio-graphy. The planner can look at Lewis Mumford's *The City in History* as a background work. For supplementary detail of a fascinating kind, Asa Briggs' *Victorian Cities* affords wonderful insights into the development of mid-19th century Manchester, Leeds, Birmingham, Middlesbrough and London. William Ashworth's *The Genesis of Modern British Town Planning* is a standard text, informative and always useful to consult.

Once familiar with the main threads of development over the two centuries, the general reader will find the vividness of urban history at various periods evoked in a variety of sources. Testimonies from contemporary novels, tracts and reports can be particularly illumi-nating because they set the scene for a description of urban affairs and pinpoint the pressures for change. This is a book which itself draws on such evidence.

2 Early planned developments

The early growth of towns, which followed the economic transformations and demographic changes that occurred most noticeably
from the second half of the 18th century onwards, was characterized
by little consideration for orderly town building. This was particularly
so in the case of housing for the working classes; but towns as a whole,
especially the new and rapidly growing manufacturing towns of the
Midlands and North, developed to no conceived layout or plan. The
reasons for this are straightforward. Economic progress, on which the
provision of jobs, and therefore houses, depended, took place
irregularly, and investment in industrial plant and dwellings occurred
spasmodically. Boom years and depressions followed each other in
quick succession. Moreover, development took place piecemeal, both
spatially as well as over time. There was no sustained logical pattern of
building. Small building firms were the general rule and their building
plots were restricted. The opportunities for comprehensive planning
and development were rare.

While this situation was the general rule, it would be wrong to think
of urban development at the beginning of our period, from 1750
onwards, as *solely* characterized by the unplanned squalor of the new
manufacturing settlements. In this chapter we will review those
instances where a quite different form of development could be seen.
The inherited tradition of town building, where towns developed to a
conscious pattern or design, was a long one in this country, and never
quite died out from the 13th century, the time of Edward I, onwards.
Even as the Industrial Revolution gathered pace, and attention was
drawn to the plight of the new manufacturing towns, the principles of
estate development were giving character to a number of towns in the
country, and there were examples of comprehensive planning and
design achievements of a high order. This tradition was never lost and
extended into the 19th century to exist side by side with the results of
the more usual, uncoordinated urban development of the day.

Some of these examples are to be seen in the areas of town houses
surrounding Georgian squares, such as the resort (spa) towns and the
fashionable London estates. Elsewhere a paternalist influence gave
urban order to settlements that owed their growth to economic
transformations. The development of Whitehaven, Cumberland, for

example, is a product of the commercial revolution of the 17th century. Here in the 1660s Sir John Lowther first developed his estate as a coal and shipbuilding port, on a plan based on a regular grid. A century later, a descendant, Sir James Lowther, the first Earl of Lonsdale, extensively redeveloped the town on spacious lines. It was not until the 19th century that the grid was filled in with a spread of poor housing. There was a number of other instances where 18th century sea port development took place in a conscious, orderly way. For example, Helensburgh was established in 1776 on the Clyde, and Milford Haven in Pembrokeshire was restyled in 1790 to a rectangular grid design(1).

A number of ports and other towns were beginning to grow in the early years of the 18th century as commercial activity quickened. One of these was Bristol, and the building of squares, attractive streets and fine public buildings at this time makes it a good example of the dignified town design of the period. The city's Queen Square was built between 1700 and 1727, and St James's Square, a smaller venture, between 1707 and 1716. In both cases conditions in leases produced overall uniformity. Georgian taste in architecture had a widespread impact and there are many examples all over the country, ranging from main streets in country towns like Henley-on-Thames, to market places such as Newark, collegiate squares at Oxford and Cambridge, Inns of Court in London, and town design as at Blandford Forum where rebuilding followed destruction by fire in 1731.

Elsewhere, the resort town affords rather better known examples of planned development where designs of a high order were attained. Bath, for example, had already come to prominence in its transformation from a small walled town into an elegant and prosperous health resort. John Wood had built Queen Square between 1728 and 1736 in the Palladian style (one inspired by Andrea Palladio, the Italian Renaissance architect) that was to feature in many towns of Britain during the rest of the century. In the 1740s, Wood was responsible for the building of the Parades, a complex of shops, hotels and residences, and in 1754, the year of his death, he began the Circus, where 33 houses were united in three equal groups by a concave facade. His son, also called John, built the Royal Crescent between 1767 and 1775; in this instance, 30 houses were blinkered by a great Ionic colonnade, a feature which soon became a popular theme in urban architecture. With this development and its Assembly Rooms and Pump Room, Bath provided an excellent example of civic design which was to be copied in many other towns.

The first large crescent outside Bath was built at Buxton by John Carr for the Duke of Devonshire. This included a new Assembly Room and Library, but as a resort town, Buxton had keener rivals. Tunbridge, for example, was of long-standing, having achieved some prominence in the 17th century. Here the planning tradition extended into the 19th century when the development of Calverley Park to the designs of Decimus Burton took place. Equally well known was Cheltenham, and major growth took place between 1780 and 1830. The suburb of Montpellier was laid out at the end of the 18th century, and, early in the 19th, another district, Pittville, was developed on land enclosed in 1806 from the Town Field.

But the major example of a resort town being developed according to the principles of estate planning, is Brighton. The social and medical background springs from the discovery of sea water as a medicament. Dr Russell's *Dissertation on the Use of Sea-Water in the Diseases of the Glands* (1750) ultimately led to a new town, Brighthelmston, being added to the list of English spas. In 1771, the King's brother, the Duke of Cumberland, paid his first visit to the town, and in 1783 the Prince of Wales also came. The Prince enjoyed his stay so much that he made Brighton a more or less permanent residence. The town's growth accelerated and by 1820 the population was nearly 25,000. A development boom followed in the 1820s with great estates being built at Kemptown and Brunswick Town.

Thomas Read Kemp, one of the joint Lords of the Manor, began to

The Royal Crescent, Bath, built between 1767 and 1775 by John Wood. His father, John Wood the elder, was also responsible for other developments in Bath in earlier years, for example Queen Square, the Parades and the Circus. Note how the repetitive Ionic columns of the Royal Crescent give a dramatic and powerful unifying effect to the terrace of houses. This device was a popular feature of town architecture in the Georgian period.

The Royal Pavilion, Brighton. In 1786 the Prince of Wales leased a small house in Brighton which was afterwards reconstructed with a central rotunda and a dome. The house was modified still further after he became Prince Regent in 1812, and John Nash added the onion-shaped dome, the roofs to the pavilions and the many pinnacles and minarets. An astonishing building, the Pavilion adds greatly to the scenic variety of modern-day Brighton, and bears eloquent witness to the effect of Royal power and patronage of another age.

build his estate in 1823. Charles Augustus Busby was the architect and Amon Wilds (father and son) the builders; a highly successful estate of Regency design resulted. Within it, Lewes Crescent was longer than Bath's Royal Crescent and Sussex Square larger than London's Grosvenor Square. A year after the beginning of Kemptown, the development of the Brunswick Estate was begun on the other (western) side of Brighton. In the event, this turned out to be less grand, but it had the benefit of a market included in the development. Antony Dale, writing in 1947, estimated that altogether, the Wilds and C.A. Busby were responsible for three-quarters of the best existing buildings in the town erected before 1840; the men clearly exerted a profound influence on the orderly, classical development of Brighton(2).

Kemp Town, Brighton, formed part of a very successful Regency development of the 1820s on the east side of Brighton. It was the heyday of the circus with fine terraces linked in a unified design. The building boom at Brighton sprang from Royal patronage of the town together with a new social fashion which propounded the health-giving properties of sea, air and salt water. The engraving suggests this fashionable element: modishly dressed ladies strolling in front of elegant houses on the cliff top.

Besides London, there was at least one other major example where the principle of planned development and town house building on classical lines moulded the character of an entire city; this was Edinburgh. The Old Town had for centuries been restricted to a site occupying the narrow ridge extending eastwards from the Castle Rock; to the north was the Nor' Loch with open country beyond. The earliest settlement dates from the time of David I (1124–53). Houses were built outside the fortress, and markets held; at the lower end, away from the castle, the Augustinians were granted land at Holyrood, where they built their abbey, and houses were strung out along the Canongate. This plan had changed little by the middle of the 18th century, although a number of fashionable squares had been built to the south. The Nor' Loch had been made sometime in the 14th century by damming two small streams to strengthen the defences of the castle, and of this, by the 18th century, open marsh remained.

A pamphlet entitled *Proposals for carrying on certain Public Works in the City of Edinburgh* was published in 1752, largely encouraged by the Lord Provost, George Drummond. This outlined a scheme for city extension to the north, and following the construction of the North Bridge in 1765, an advertisement invited 'Architects and others to give in plans of a New Town marking out streets of a proper breadth, and by-lanes, and the best situation for a reservoir, and any other public buildings which may be thought necessary'. A plan submitted by James Craig was adjudged the best (3).

The proposals followed very much the fashion of the period. The squares of mid-18th century London were already well known, and there were impressive examples of Renaissance town planning on the continent, for example at Nancy. Elsewhere in this country, as at Bath, as we have seen, elegant Georgian development provided instances of formal layout to emulate. Craig's plan did not follow the use of curving streets, as employed by Wood at Bath, but adopted a basically simple, grid-iron pattern, with two squares (St Andrew's and Charlotte Square), formed centrally by a straight street (George Street), with a flanking street on each side. The two outer streets, Princes Street and Queen Street, had houses on one side only. Initially, as the plan was put into effect, a single unified frontage to a set of houses was not achieved, but the magistrates of the city passed Acts and resolutions laying down the lines on which building was to proceed, and some uniformity was eventually attained.

The eastern-most of the two squares, St Andrew's Square, was complete by the 1780s. Running across George Street at right angles, Hanover Street was largely built up by 1790, and before the end of the century Frederick Street was too. At this time there was a departure from the piecemeal development of Craig's plan, and Robert Adam, a

successor to the Woods in Bath and noted for the building of Pulteney
Bridge there (1769—74), was commissioned to design Charlotte Square
as a whole. With the completion of that square in 1820, the plan was
complete, but the regular and geometric style continued to influence
the development of Edinburgh, particularly in the neighbouring estates
of the Earl of Moray, of Heriot's Hospital, of Sir Francis Walker and of
Henry Raeburn. By this time the population of the city was increasing

rapidly; at the turn of the century it was 162,000 and major areas of
growth had to be planned adjoining the New Town. The land to the
north and east was the subject of the first extension on land largely
owned by the town and Heriot's Hospital. Between 1804 and 1806
Robert Reid planned and laid out the land between Heriot's Town and
Fettes Row in the north. A number of crescents and circuses, Randolph
Crescent, Ainslie Place, Moray Place and Royal Circus compensated for
the regularity of Craig's plan. In 1814 a plan by William Playfair,
covering the whole area between the Calton Hill to the east and Leith
on the coast, was adopted.

New Town, Edinburgh in the 1830s,
seen from Ramsay Gardens. The
engraving shows the line of Princes
Street in front of the Royal Institution, now the Royal Scottish Academy.
St Andrew's Church, George Street,
is behind. While it is not a very
accurate drawing – the appearance
of the Firth of Forth in the background, for instance, is rather
idealized – the scene indicates
plainly enough the distinct separation
of the New Town from Old Edinburgh
by open land.

But the prime examples of planned development belong to London. The story has been well covered (4, 5, 6) and we can in no way attempt to review adequately the full range of developments which took place. But there are certain projects to which we should refer and a number of observations which we should make for the context of this chapter to be complete.

Grosvenor Square, London, 1789. The Square was a typical example of estate development in the first half of the 18th century, the form of which established the pattern for estates later in the century. Such squares of commodious houses facing on to private gardens set a high note of fashion and quality in urban design. Notice the terrace of houses, a distinctive form of building in this period.

Estate development in London had begun in the 17th century, with the Earl of Bedford laying out Covent Garden and nearby streets in the 1630s. Thereafter, London spread westward in an irregular succession of building booms. The first was in the 1660s following the Great Fire of London and the Plague, when the Earl of St Albans developed St James's Square and its neighbourhood, and the Earl of Southampton began to grant building leases on his Bloomsbury estate. A new impetus was given to building in the early 18th century, and Hanover, Cavendish and Grosvenor Squares appeared before 1730. In the middle of the century there was a quickening of building activity in the fields north of Oxford Street on lands of the Portman family, which produced Portman and Manchester Squares, and Portland Place.

In the 1770s even greater expansion took place, particularly in Bloomsbury. The Duke of Bedford's estate lay within the rectangle formed by Tottenham Court Road, Euston Road, Woburn Place, Southampton Row and New Oxford Street. Before 1776, development was largely to the south of Great Russell Street, but in that year development began to the north with the granting of articles of agreement for Bedford Square, a phase of building which did not end until the completion of Gordon Square in 1860.

Bedford Square and the building of the nearby streets led to the transformation of the fields of northern Bloomsbury into an upper-middle-class suburb, the whole being laid out as a district of big town houses. On the other hand, Fig Mead, another estate of the Duke of Bedford lying north of Euston Station, bounded on the west by Hampstead Road and on the north by Crowndale Road, was designed for the lower-middle-class. This area became known as Bedford New Town and was an effort to create a model suburb for the artisan and the successful clerk.

Adjoining the Duke of Bedford's Bloomsbury estate was that of the Foundling Hospital to the east, and systematic development took place there from 1790, producing Mecklenburgh and Brunswick Squares. On land leased from the Skinners' Company, Russell, Tavistock, and Euston Squares were developed; later, the Southampton estate between Russell Square and the New Road was developed.

Elsewhere the planned design of London's peripheral development continued on a wide front, planted between main roads at locations selected by landowners and builders. These estates were sometimes called 'new town' or had the word 'town' added to the family name or title of the freeholder. Somers Town, for example, was begun on land of Lord Somers of Evesham in 1786. Camden Town came in 1791 on property of the Lord Chancellor Camden. There were estates in Islington, including Barnsbury Square which was to achieve fame, if not notoriety, for the rehabilitation proposals which were to attend it in the 1960s when plans were considered for the improvement of the area.

Early in the 19th century, the Crown began to develop its lands around Regent's Park. North of Portland Place, Marylebone Farm was due to revert to the Crown in 1811, and for some years before this John Fordyce, Surveyor-General of His Majesty's Land Revenue, tried to encourage the drawing up of a plan for its comprehensive development. Fordyce died in 1809 and his Department was merged with that of Woods and Forests, where John Nash and his assistant James Morgan were architects. For the next twenty years, Nash's proposals dominated the development of central London: Regent's Park, the cutting of Regent Street, Waterloo Place, St James's Park and the Carlton House Terrace, and finally Trafalgar Square and proposals to link Whitehall with the British Museum and Bloomsbury.

The spread of building in 18th-century West London. John Rocque's *Plan of London* (1769) reveals how far the built-up areas had spread by the latter part of the 18th century. Particularly noticeable is the sharp distinction beteen the city and the adjoining countryside. The approximate boundaries of some of the principal estates mentioned in the text are superimposed on the plan. Already developed were the Grosvenor Estates, south of Tyburn Road and Oxford Street, and, in part, the Cavendish-Harley Estates to the north. But around Marylebone, across Lambs Conduit Fields and towards Pancras, virtually open fields owned by wealthy families or institutions in large, compact holdings permitted the rapid spread of well laid-out estates during the rest of the century and beyond.

Rocque's Plan was also altered later by John Nash's improvements between 1811 and 1835, with his designs for Regent's Park (on Crown land north of Islington New Road) and St James's Park, linked by a number of streets and squares, including the new Regent Street. The scale of the plan is approximately 8 cm to one kilometre (5 in. to one mile).

The personal histories of some of the men involved in these great town planning schemes enliven the account of this period. There is the story of Nash, for example, and his probably scandalous relationship with the Prince of Wales; also of James Burton, the dominant builder who was responsible for much of Bloomsbury in the early 19th century and who made a large fortune thereby. But suffice to say that, while under the stimulus of the Industrial Revolution the first new manufacturing towns were spawning their wretched areas of working class housing and growing generally haphazardly, in central London a major contribution to town design was being made with a succession of town improvements and highly fashionable residential estates incorporating the common elements of square, circus, crescent, street, market and church.

Projects did not cease with Nash and Metropolitan improvement went on. We can only hint at the extent of this work, but to make the point we might note that Nash's assistant, James Pennethorne, continued to prepare plans and succeeded in cutting New Oxford Street through the slums of St Giles under the Improvement Act, 1839. Much later in the century, the Metropolitan Board of Works assumed responsibility for improvement, and there followed such developments as the building of the Thames Embankments (1862–74), and new roads Shaftesbury Avenue (1886) and Charing Cross Road (1887). On the residential front, the speculations of Thomas Cubitt, and his younger brother Lewis, influenced early 19th century development widely in North London. Thomas Cubitt laid out Pimlico and a great part of Clapham. Bayswater and Notting Hill were built up by builder-speculators; Hyde Park Gardens (1836), Leinster Square and Princes Square (1856) and Lancaster Gate (1857) were among the most imposing sections.

The reasons why London was able to benefit in this way concern its distinctive pattern of land ownership, characterized by the existence of great estates, not a collection of tiny freeholds. This meant that before the formation of the Metropolitan Board of Works in 1855, and to a great extent thereafter, the primary planning unit in London was the landed estate. The enormous size of land holdings gave the ground landlords great power. The Duke of Westminster had the whole of northern Mayfair together with what is now Belgravia and Pimlico. Lord Portman and the Duke of Portland had nearly the whole of Marylebone between them. The Duke of Bedford had Bloomsbury and Covent Garden. The Marquis of Northampton had Clerkenwell and Islington to work with.

The significance of this situation was that estate planning could proceed without continual preoccupation with immediate financial returns. The landowners were either men of wealth or social position or were public bodies or charitable institutions, and could therefore afford to ignore immediate profits and concentrate on enhancing the long term value of their estates. Neither of these factors, uniform land ownership and realization of long term financial benefits, was generally present in other towns, and especially the new manufacturing centres. The lack of orderly town building can be attributed to these differences.

Only a portion of London's growth could, of course, be accounted for by estate development of the kind we have described, with its distinctive domestic architecture and regularity of suburban layout. Much of the rest of the capital's expansion was dependent on the unplanned and irregular mushrooming of the village centres which London swallowed up during the century, as at Hampstead, Peckham, Hammersmith and Fulham. The planned estates could not cater for all upper-middle-class demand and the search of the townsman for a semi-rural foothold was also evidenced by the building of small country villas. More noticeably, growth took place through the ribbon development of house building following long stretches of roadside; this had been a ubiquitous form of natural expansion since the Middle Ages when 'fore-streets', a term retained occasionally in street names today, extended from the principal gates. Roadside development could be very varied in character, comprising the large private house, the group of cottages, nursery-garden, brickyard and factory, but the speculative terrace, built particularly after 1851, began to be a chief feature. One of the earliest ribbons, even in the 18th century, was the road to Islington; another was in Southwark, leading south from London Bridge, but in the 19th century, ribbons extended in every direction.

The purpose of this chapter has been to put in perspective the general nature of early urban development in our period, the tempo of which quickened in the second half of the 18th century. We should be giving a misleading impression if we pictured solely the evidence of unplanned, sporadic development which produced such an unsavoury result in wretched housing and sanitary conditions for the working class. The next chapter gives an ample description of the state of many of our new manufacturing towns in the first half of the 19th century, but this has to be set against the quite different urban traditions in other parts of the country (and in the case of London, in the same city). The exercise of conscious town building was never quite forgotten and the principles of estate development, for residential and other purposes, were taken up from previous generations and handed on.

As we shall see, settlements which were the product of the most aggressive, commercial enterprises, could still embody elements of orderly planning. Railway towns and the creations of the philanthropic manufacturer are cases in point, as are also various town improvement schemes, either redevelopment as at Newcastle, or town establishment as at Birkenhead. Much depended on enlightened land ownership. At Ashton-under-Lyne, for example, the Earl of Stamford owned the town and made building conditions when he granted leases. Similarly, Sir John Ramsden, who owned Huddersfield, enforced wide streets and good housing, and at Glossop, the Duke of Norfolk laid out his land in regular form and his agent superintended satisfactory development (7). But enlightened paternalism was not enough, and for at least half a century, a number of British towns had to withstand unbridled forces of expansion and growth while waiting for the restraint of community intervention to become practical politics. These towns were the first casualties of an urban revolution, and it is to them that we must now turn.

References

(1) Bell, Colin and Rose, *City Fathers: the early history of town planning in Britain*, The Cresset Press, 1969.
(2) Dale, Antony, *Fashionable Brighton 1820—1860,* Country Life Ltd. 1947.
(3) Youngman, A.J., *The Making of Classical Edinburgh,* Edinburgh University Press, 1966.
(4) Summerson, John, *Georgian London*, Pleiades Books, 1945. Pelican 1962, 1969.
(5) Rasmussen, Steen Eiler, *London: The Unique City,* Jonathan Cape, 1948.
(6) Olsen, Donald J., *Town Planning in London,* Yale University Press, 1964.
(7) Hammond, J.L. and Barbara, *The Bleak Age*, 1934, revised, Pelican Books, 1947.

3 Economic and demographic changes: urban environment and health

The Industrial Revolution was a complex period of economic and social change. It is difficult to unravel the interrelated strands of causes and effects in the transformations of the time. There can be no attempt here to fully review the major events, but in order to attempt to explain the growth of towns as a related phenomenon, we might highlight a number of economic and demographic issues. Of economic changes, those in technology and in communications were particularly significant. The first advances on both fronts were made in the 1760s and 1770s, and quickened over the next half-century. They provided a grounding for the 19th century economic transformations that took Britain from a largely agricultural and rural country to one that was industrial and urban.

At the same time, the population increased significantly and, due particularly to the migration of labour in search of job opportunities, there was a perceptible shift in geographical distribution. Urban populations expanded, and severe environmental and sanitary problems were created in the growing towns where local authority powers were inadequate to deal with safeguarding standards of working-class housing and questions of public health.

ECONOMIC CHANGES

The early technical advances were in the cotton industry and in the harnessing of steam power to drive machinery. Both had major repercussions for industry and town growth. Arkwright's steam frame (1769) for spinning enabled factory production on a larger scale. Watt's steam engine, dating from the same year, but later (1781) developed with rotary motion, led to the building of mills in towns; a steam engine was first used to operate a spinning mill in 1785. The power loom was invented in 1787 and became a feasible proposition in the cotton industry at the beginning of the 19th century. Cotton was, in fact, the industry in which technical innovation was most sought and most achieved, and it made a leap forward that had profound social and urban implications. The first wave of factory settlements in the North West, Clydeside, Derbyshire and elsewhere, marks one of the first identifiable stages of the urban revolution.

The discovery of the new power of steam stimulated the demand for coal and annual production, estimated at somewhat less than five million tonnes in 1750, had more than doubled by the end of the century. Early coal mines were, of course, small and relatively scattered, and contributed only little at first to urban growth. But where coal mining was associated with other industries, such as iron manufacture and brick making, then a complementary stimulus to town development was afforded.

The iron (and coal) industry was greatly stimulated by Henry Cort's puddling process which made cheap wrought iron available from the 1780s. Cort's invention, patented in 1784, consisted of exposing pig iron, as obtained from the blast furnace, in a reverberating furnace until it was decarbonized by the action of the oxygen circulating through the furnace, and converted into malleable iron. This method enabled fifteen times as much iron to be produced by the same amount of power in the same period of time. Timber gave way to coal, and coal and iron became a foundation not only for national prosperity but also for a rash of small-scale settlements, particularly where the products were found together — for example, in Lanarkshire, the West Midlands and the West Riding. British production of pig iron rose from 62,000 tonnes in 1788 to a quarter of a million tonnes in 1806. Nielson's hot blast invention followed in 1828 and production soared.

Changes in communications complement this initial picture, contributing directly to the quickening of economic life. The beginning might be marked with the opening of the Sankey Navigation in 1757, constructed from St Helens to the Mersey with the objective of transporting coal more cheaply to Liverpool. It was immediately followed by a much more important canal, built at the expense of the third Duke of Bridgewater to transport coal from his mines at Worsley to Manchester. It was a great work of engineering master-minded by James Brindley. It opened in 1761 (1).

The canal was later linked with the Mersey at Runcorn. Later still, two other groups of investors constructed two canals connected with the Duke's: the Trent and Mersey running from Wilden Ferry in Derbyshire to Preston Brook and Runcorn, and the Staffordshire and Worcestershire from the Trent and Mersey canal at Great Haywood to Bewdley on the Severn. This was the Grand Trunk, completed in 1777, offering a continuous navigable waterway across England. The Birmingham canal as a branch feeder of the Staffordshire and Worcestershire was opened in 1772. Birmingham, the Black Country and the Potteries all benefited from these waterways; significantly Josiah Wedgwood, the great pottery manufacturer, acted as treasurer of the Grand Trunk canal.

Bewdley had been a flourishing river port for some centuries, but because of local objections the terminus of the Staffordshire and Worcestershire canal was diverted to reach the Severn six kilometres down stream at its junction with the River Stour. A mushroom town, Stourport, grew up, the first canal-created settlement. A port and dockyards were built and a market established. By 1795 it had about 1,300 inhabitants (2).

The West Midlands was not the only part of the country where canal construction stimulated economic development and town growth. In Scotland, the Forth and Clyde canal was begun in 1768, and completed in 1775. In Southern England canals focused on London. For example, there was the Thames and Severn, the Kennett and Avon, and, most important, the Grand Junction from Brentford to Napton in Warwickshire where there was a link with the Midland system. There were canals in South Wales, and in the 19th century, canals crossing the Pennines were constructed in Northern England.

It was in the North, in fact, that a second canal-created town was built, at Goole by the Aire and Calder Navigation Company, for the export of South Yorkshire coal. A new canal also for coal export was built from Knottingly to Goole, first by John Rennie and, after his death in 1821, by George Leather who went on to lay out a Company town adjoining the new port (3).

The locomotive emerged swiftly as an alternative form of communication. The railway's effect on urban growth and development was startling, as we see in the next chapter, but at this stage we need only note early background events. There was nothing essentially new about the railways as tracks for wheeled carts for carrying coal from pits to navigable water: as such they had existed since the early 17th century in Tyneside, Shropshire and Nottinghamshire. But in the early 19th century, striking innovations were made. Richard Trevithick built a steam locomotive for the Penydarren Ironworks near Merthyr Tydfil in 1804 and there were additional experiments elsewhere, for example by George Stephenson who advocated the Stockton-Darlington Railway in 1825. The kind of interrelationships existing in the Industrial Revolution at this time is illustrated by the availability of cheap wrought iron, following upon Henry Cort's new process, directly stimulating railway expansion.

In the 1820s the Stephensons, father and son, George and Robert, built the Liverpool and Manchester Railway. It opened in September 1830 and such was its success, not only for freight but for passengers too, that within two years only one horse-drawn coach remained travelling between the two towns. The transport revolution had entered a new phase, and urban development everywhere was dramatically affected.

DEMOGRAPHIC CHANGES

Changes in technology and systems of communications combined in a quickening of economic tempo. At the same time an increasing population sought employment in towns where new job opportunities were to be found.

The rise in population began to occur in the 18th century. The years 1751 to 1781, for example, witnessed a population increase of nearly 1.4 million in England and Wales, compared with less than a quarter of that total in the preceding fifty years. London, of course, was already growing rapidly, but the rise of Liverpool and Birmingham, numerically small in comparison, was becoming noticeable. Liverpool's population trebled between 1700 and 1740 and then increased five times by the population census of 1801. In the forty years between 1760 and 1801, Birmingham doubled its population, and that of Glasgow trebled, a rate of expansion which took Manchester even fewer years.

An east view of Birmingham in 1779. The results of two centuries of urban development can be seen by comparing this illustration with the photograph on pages 194-5. Birmingham before the close of the 18th century was a small compact settlement on a hillside above the River Rea, crowned by what is now the Cathedral Church of St Philip. Note the closeness of the countryside to the built-up area, the sharp demarcation between town and country, and the absence of any obvious manufacturing establishments.

As part of the process of urban growth national shifts in population distribution began and substantial changes in population densities took place. At the beginning of the 18th century there was a very even spread of population throughout the country. By the beginning of the 19th this even distribution had been broken up into noticeable clusters, and by the beginning of the 20th century the clusters were the dominant feature of the national population map. The growth of particular towns has to be seen in this context. In 1700, the first five counties in order of population density were Worcester, Somerset, Devon, Lancashire and Gloucester, and of all counties the one with the lowest density had 0.2 people per hectare (54 per square mile) and the one with the highest, 0.5. In 1801 the first five counties in order of density were Lancashire, Warwick, the West Riding, Stafford and Gloucester, and the densities in the counties ranged from 1.4 to 0.2 per hectare (353 to 55 per square mile). The lowest density was virtually the same, but the highest had grown two and a half times (4).

By the second half of the 18th century, then, there were noticeable increases of population. These were in areas associated with cotton manufacture, such as Lancashire, Cheshire and Nottinghamshire, with coal mining and iron manufacture, as in the Midlands, and with the woollen industry, noticeably in the West Riding, this area taking over from East Anglia and the West Country as the major centre of production. The 19th century saw the accentuation of these trends with unmistakeably quickening growth. Later, Durham, South Wales and Central Scotland emerged as additional clusters of population. By 1815 more than one third of the total population of Great Britain was living in 70 towns of more than 20,000 population. Moreover, they were of increasing relative importance as they were growing more quickly than the population of the country as a whole. Decennial rates of growth, measured from census returns, were high and persistent with the highest for the larger towns being in the period 1821–1831.

The mechanics behind this increase were a complex amalgam of birth rates, death rates, migration rates and social and economic factors, particularly those which had an influence on the effective child bearing years of the mother. Significant increases in birth rates began after 1780 but fell away after 1820. There was a progressive decrease in the death rate to about 1820, the fall being greatest in the towns, particularly among children. Public health measures had an especially powerful effect in reducing mortality among newly born infants.

These factors apart, it was labour migration which had the biggest impact on town development. It was not until the census of 1851 that detailed information was collected about people's birthplaces. By this time, of course, almost all the large towns had passed their maximum rate of growth, and the first wave of migration to manufacturing areas had slackened. But earlier census reports were still of some use in that for the period after 1811 certain information about aspects of movement of population was given in the local notes to successive census returns. In 1821, and at succeeding censuses, the local enumeration officers were asked to account for any remarkable increase or decrease of population in their respective areas during the preceding decade. A general, but fairly consistent pattern of impressions was given.

There was no cataclysmic transfer of population from south to north as the manufacturing districts expanded. The movement was much more a regionally-based drift, composed of a large number of short

Above: a plan of Newcastle upon Tyne, 1788; *below:* a plan of Newcastle upon Tyne, 1830. These two plans show evidence of the quickening pace of urban development during the early 19th century. The reliance on the single river crossing is clear. Gateshead grew relatively slowly, but in the 1830 plan a number of new streets can be seen in Newcastle, some in consequence of the first of Grainger's schemes. The empty spaces which allowed the next projects to take place in the 1830s were on the site of the Nuns, south of the newly built Blackett Street.

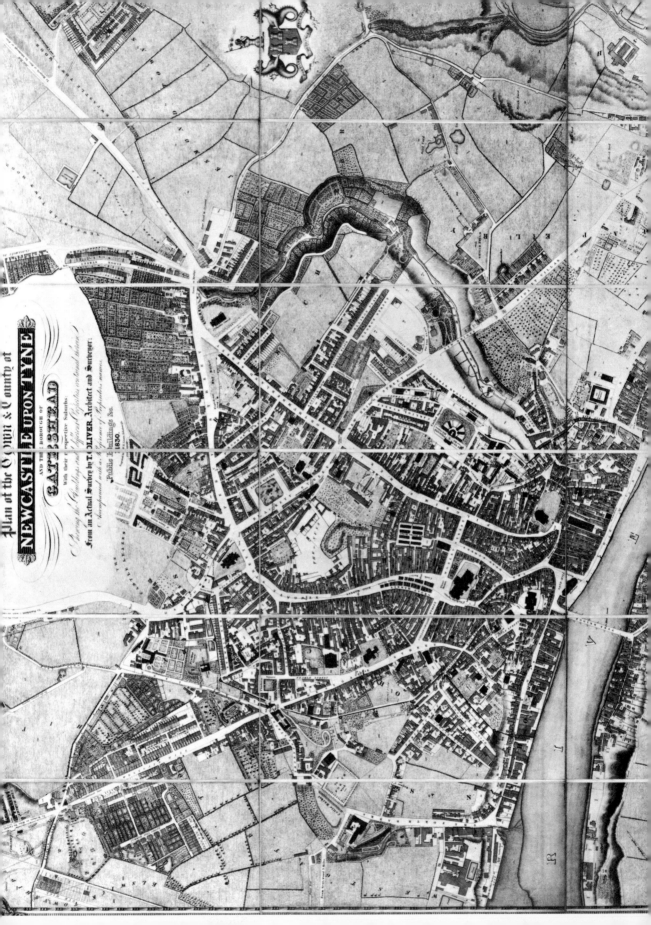

Plan of the Town & County of

NEWCASTLE UPON TYNE

AND THE BOROUGH OF

GATESHEAD

With their respective Suburbs

Shewing the Buildings and different Objects contained therein

From an Actual Survey by T. OLIVER, Architect and Surveyor;

Accompanied with a Reference of Respective names.

Public Buildings &c.

1830.

hops to the rising towns from the rural areas of surrounding counties. Arthur Redford, writing on labour migration, describes the situation thus: 'They were a mixed company, in which cobblers and tailors rubbed shoulders with starving handloom weavers and gawkey husbandmen; but the workers coming from agriculture far out-numbered the rest' (5).

Increases in population in particular areas due to migration had already been noted in the second half of the 18th century, and a broad regional pattern of movement in recognizable catchment areas had probably existed for many years. During the early 19th century the trends were dramatically accentuated. Redford observes that 'the parish registers of Manchester, for example, show that even from the 17th century there had been a gradual influx of population from all the surrounding counties, and that it had been quite common for the yeomen of North Lancashire, Yorkshire and Cumberland to establish their sons in Manchester as clothworkers, haberdashers, glovers, linen-drapers, woollen-drapers, and felt-makers' (6). Before 1815, both Manchester and Liverpool were drawing population from the eastern counties of North Wales, and Liverpool from Anglesey. The histories of Oldham, Ashton-under-Lyne and Stalybridge show that practically all the migrants came from either the west or north of Lancashire, from surrounding counties or from Ireland. Similarly, towns in the West Riding of Yorkshire received labour from the rest of Yorkshire and Lincolnshire; Birmingham drew population from rural Staffordshire and Warwickshire, Shropshire and Northhamptonshire; Glasgow from the rural Lowlands and the Highlands.

A significant aspect of migration to towns was the Irish element. This was not a sudden matter, but in the 1840s the inflow assumed dramatic proportions. The result was that by the middle of the century there were nearly three quarters of a million Irish-born people in Great Britain, excluding the unknown number of persons born in Great Britain of Irish parents. Irish settlement had been on a sizeable scale since at least the end of the 18th century (with some immigration for many years before that) and there were well established Irish colonies in Manchester and Liverpool. Alongside this Irish influx there was also Scottish and Welsh migration which affected particular parts of the country, but its extent was much less.

In the 19th century the Irish influx grew, with an increased movement of beggars and vagrants. The failure of the Irish potato crop of 1821, followed by famine and epidemic a year later, encouraged emigration. But the peak years were 1841–51 when a new potato famine caused 700,000 deaths and resulted in an exodus of over a million people. Liverpool, Glasgow, the South Wales ports bore the brunt of the movement: in 1846 over 280,000 immigrants arrived in

Liverpool from Ireland, 123,000 eventually sailing on to foreign countries. Lancashire, Glasgow and London emerged at this time as the main areas of Irish settlement (7).

Population migration has been a well studied demographic phenomenon. A characteristic usually observed is the counter current in population flows: in any particular area there are a large number of total movements in which one stream (say inward) usually exceeds the other (outward) by only a small proportion. So the consistently maintained net inward migration into the growing towns was the product of a very complex pattern of total movements, both inwards and outwards. The slowing down of urban growth later in the century was partly due to changes in migration flows. Much later in the century there was a real check for some towns when emigration to overseas countries became popular.

URBAN CHARACTERISTICS

With the economic and demographic context now set, we can refer to the quickening of urban development that took place during the years on either side of the turn of the 19th century and, in particular, to the nature of the towns that grew so rapidly. Particularly important are the environmental and housing deficiencies which characterized these towns and the halting steps of public intervention that were taken to remedy them.

By the early 1800s cotton manufacture became established as a factory industry. By 1831, over 800,000 persons were employed in textile manufacture in Britain, and certain towns in particular were associated with this and other related industries such as textile machine making and engineering. Manchester represents a prime example: a population of 24,000 in 1774 rose to more than 70,000 by the time of the first census in 1801. In the 1820s a quarter of the cotton spindles in the United Kingdom were to be found within the boundaries of Manchester, and in 1827 Manchester and Stockport together accounted for half the power looms of the country (8).

Rates of population growth varied between different towns, much depending on the nature of the particular industrial base. Some manufacture favoured concentration of activity and people, such as the textile trade with its new large mills, but some industries, notably the iron, coal and metal working trades, permitted a looser dispersal in smaller settlements. At the same time there were the thriving commercial centres whose prosperity was already developing strongly in the 18th century; Liverpool and Bristol were expanding ports for example. Overshadowing all, of course, was the unique example of London which was continuing to grow apace.

Not every town could match the rise of the new Manchester and, in any case, it would be quite wrong to imagine that the early 19th century town elsewhere resembled this particular model. There were, in fact, many types of urban development with their own characteristics and phases of growth. The Potteries, for example, with a population of 6—7,000 in the 1760s, had risen to more than 20,000 by the turn of the century; any centrality was lacking until the mid-1840s when the railway made Stoke an important focus, although it had participated least in the pottery industry of all the six towns (9). On the other hand Leeds grew outwards from its old site, nearly doubling its population in the last 30 years of the 18th century, reaching 30,600 by 1801, and more than doubling it again in the next 30 years (10). In Glasgow, a formerly dispersed textile industry in a number of urban centres became concentrated when cotton replaced linen, and machinery was introduced. Paisley and Greenock remained important, but Glasgow became supreme, and remained so even when the exploitation of local coal and iron resources led to urban growth elsewhere in Central Scotland as at Coatbridge, Motherwell and Wishaw (11).

The Black Country is an example of an area of diffused urban growth (notwithstanding the early centrality at Birmingham); moreover it exemplifies the nature of the complex relationship that existed between town development and the vagaries of economic change, particularly in the metal trades (12). For at least two centuries the area had been the home of scattered communities of smiths and miners. In 1700 it was noted for its nails, locks, bolts, saddlers' ironmongery, buckles, guns and swords. By 1800 the production of all these items had greatly increased and the hardware trades very much expanded. There was brass and brassware trades, ironfounding, glassware manufacture and the jewellery, tinplate, enamel and pinware trades. Birmingham was the centre for the production of light finished metal goods and famous for its achievements in engineering. South Staffordshire began an important phase of iron production.

The next 60 years saw a continuing industrial development and the population of Birmingham and district rose from 187,000 in 1801 to 819,000 in 1861. We should note that this was accompanied by no rapid transition from small to large scale industry and, in many ways, the area possessed the same industrial character in 1860 as it had done at the turn of the century. But the Black Country benefited from a number of influences: the increased demand for iron, the introduction of steam power, the availability of more extensive markets through railway development, and the widening of the domestic market because of population growth and increased prosperity. We see the Black Country, therefore, with its own characteristics, distinct from Manchester or Glasgow or indeed from virtually everywhere else. There was, in fact, a wide range of manufacturing or commercial towns, all developing as an integral part of the economic growth of the regions to which they belonged.

The West Midlands were particularly favoured by a large number of complementary industries where the rise of one trade could compensate for the demise of another. But in single staple-trade towns, such as those dependent on textiles, economic depression could be extremely serious. Economic progress tended to be made in a series of leaps, followed by troughs of temporary stagnation when there were many social casualties unprotected by adequate welfare legislation. Rapid industrial development encouraged a quickening of migration of people to the towns; this was accompanied by an initial shortage of houses, but before brick production or the release of capital for house building could be geared to meet it, an economic slump would probably take place and result in widespread unemployment and distress for the poorer classes.

The difficulty of matching population increase with house construction was always a problem. From a national viewpoint and over a period of a number of years, the situation appeared to have been in hand. In the first decade of the 19th century, for example, the number of houses in the country increased by 216,000 (14 per cent), which was in step with population increase of the period. But within the country there were marked regional variations. In Lancashire, for instance, the population rose by 25 per cent, outpacing the supply of houses (13).

The 1820s was a typical period of boom and depression. A peak in house and factory building came in 1825 and the upswing is reflected in the number of cotton mills constructed or blast furnaces erected, or in the increase in dock building. The decade 1821–31 saw a net increase of 444,000 houses in England and Wales, equivalent to an increase in housing stock of over one fifth, and in fact the number of houses increased at a faster rate than the population. In St Helens, to take one example, we read that the high demand for housing had made house building a profitable form of investment and, in 1824, the first St Helens Building Society was formed. In Bolton 1,500 houses were built in and around the town in the period 1820–25. But bad times were just round the corner, and in the same town 1826 was a year of distress when widespread unemployment caused poverty and acute family hardship.

An important element in the house building industry and in the history of towns at this time was the availability of funds for local house building (14). In a number of towns the building society movement became of substantial importance by the mid-19th century, the movement having originated in Birmingham about 1775. The first building societies were terminating societies. That is to say, they received subscriptions from members and, as the money accumulated, it was used to provide houses for the same people; once this task had been accomplished, the society terminated its activities. Subscriptions varied between five and ten shillings a month, and the funds were invested. The usual procedure was a draw, those selected first having the first house, built with an advance from the communal fund, although they themselves had paid very few subscriptions. The person continued to pay his subscription together with interest on the sum borrowed from the date of the advance to the date of the winding up of the society. Consequently those selected later in the draw for houses paid out less; the last in the queue paid out less than the actual cost.

Ketley's Building Society was the first in Birmingham and others followed, particularly in the north. The Greenwich Union was London's first, in 1809. In 1836 the movement received encouragement from legislation which exempted societies from stamp duty on shares. With the provision of model rules, the number of societies grew rapidly. By 1846 nearly 2,000 societies were registered, some of them with as many as 250 members. Permanent societies followed as media for channelling saving into a permanent supply of new houses. Previously it had been a case of persons providing their own money for their own houses. Now people in various districts (local to begin with, but growing to national coverage eventually) provided their own markets for housing finance. By 1854 there were over 400 building societies in London and over 500 in the provinces, including 85 in Manchester, 61 in Liverpool, 22 in Birmingham and 12 in Sheffield. All these gave new and specific sources of funds which were very important in the housing development of these towns.

But these indications of sustained progress and suggestions of regularity in house building should not blind us to the evidence to which we have already referred: economic conditions were prone to wide fluctuations with consequent social distress. For example, the boom of the 1830s broke and the textile industry slumped. There were many unemployed and in November 1839 Greater Bolton, for instance, had over 1,000 empty houses. The 1840s were also very hard and difficult, especially at the time of the collapse of the railway boom; in 1848 the proportion of iron founders unemployed rose to one third. J. Parry Lewis has described the nature of building cycles throughout the 19th century and it is useful to have this as a context in which to trace urban development generally and the history of certain towns in particular (15).

While economic instability was an important backcloth for a number of towns, the ill-adjusted structure of local government, causing over-lapping activity and waste, was equally significant for most. Sheffield, for example, was incorporated in 1843 when its population was over 100,000. By 1850 it still had several separate Authorities responsible for its sanitation. The Police (later, the Improvement) Commissioners were responsible for cleaning, lighting, watching and other improvement, excluding street improvements, drainage or sewering, and even then only to a distance of just over a kilometre from the parish church. An ancient body of Town Trustees was responsible for street improvements; highway repair was the responsibility of Highway Boards; and there were two Poor Law Unions and a Sanitary Committee of the Guardians. Other sanitary duties were shared by magistrates, vestries and the Cutlers Company (16).

The Municipal Corporations Act of 1835 was intended to remedy the weakness of municipal government. It certainly gave to the reformed boroughs a more liberal constitution, but, although there was less corruption as a result, it achieved little in the way of administrative efficiency (17). In any case, responsibility for public services was usually shared with other bodies, such as the Improvement Commissioners. Another weakness which was not tackled was the failure to relate urban areas with realistic local government boundaries. This meant that large parts of growing towns were excluded from effective local government, reliance being placed on parish authorities. Finally, we should note that many large towns had not even been incorporated and were exposed to out-dated government machinery. Major reform of London government came in 1855, but elsewhere it was not until the Public Health Act of 1875 that a realistic national structure of urban and rural sanitary districts with clearly defined responsibilities was provided.

With regard to London, the situation in the 1840s was even more chaotic and prejudicial to effective action than in provincial centres (18). In 1847, London, outside the walls of the city, was governed by 300 local bodies including seven Commissions of Sewers, 172 vestries, and almost one hundred paving, lighting and cleansing boards. The Royal Commission on Municipal Corporations concluded in its second Report, in 1837, that London should have a uniform government, but did not decide whether this should be in the form of a Government Commission or a new municipality. Not until the reform of London government in 1855, and the setting up of a Metropolitan Board of Works, did the Capital have an administrative body responsible for the planning and construction of public works for the whole metropolitan area outside the City. This permitted a comprehensive scheme for main drainage to be prepared, and within ten years a gigantic scheme involving 134 kilometres of intercepting sewers had been completed.

But the chief characteristics of the early 19th century towns to which we should refer concern the low standard of housing for the poorer classes and the poverty of general environmental conditions.

The important Reports of the 1840s provide abundant evidence on which the urban historian can draw. The story is horrifying enough and made J.L. and Barbara Hammond call the thirties and forties of the last century 'the Bleak Age' (19). Independent surveys in a host of different towns provide supplementary information and a political interpretation is given in the work of Frederick Engels.

Speculative building and the virtual absence of building regulations produced housing of a very low standard. In Bradford one reads of superficial dwellings, rapidly erected, with no cellars or foundations, with walls only half a brick thick; and houses built back-to-back, without ventilation or drainage, double rows forming courts with common pumps and privies. Overcrowding was especially severe in Manchester, Liverpool, London and Leeds. The Window Tax (even though since 1825 houses with less than eight windows were exempted) and the high duty on window glass served to discourage access to light and air. Living conditions were probably at their worst with cellar dwellers, and there were at least 18,000 in both Manchester and Liverpool.

Back-to-back houses were a notorious feature of certain towns, especially Leeds, where, for every decade after the 1790s, this form of building was prevalent. It was so marked, in fact, that by 1886 back-to-backs formed 71 per cent of the total dwellings in the borough. Indeed, this type of building continued and there was no year between 1886 and 1903 when back-to-back houses formed less than two-thirds of the plans passed by the local Authority Building Surveyor for new houses in Leeds. Back-to-backs continued to be built until 1937, although elsewhere, as in Bradford, Manchester and Liverpool, they had long been in disrepute, and in some industrial towns had never been built at all (20).

Professor M.W. Beresford (21) suggests that historical factors of plot shape were instrumental in this form of development. Enclosure by agreement during the later Middle Ages, for example, had given Leeds a pattern of long narrow fields. These were largely in separate hands and were turned into building plots only spasmodically. The alternative use was as 'tenter grounds', used by the domestic clothier and by the finishing trades. Long cul-de-sac streets tempted builders to develop two further rows of back-to-backs behind the main street, adding to the number of interior courtyards.

In most towns provision for sanitation was quite inadequate and arrangements for the disposal of refuse were abysmal. The demand for human manure on the nearby farms soon declined as towns grew and the cost of cartage increased. Furthermore, the spread of water sanitation exacerbated the problem through a consequent increase in the number of cesspools. An inordinate number of soak-aways contaminated much of the subsoil of the larger towns and spring water was polluted. In due time, house drainage was discharged into sewers originally constructed for surface water, and water courses became heavily polluted. In manufacturing towns rivers dammed for water power became cesspools; in London the Serpentine became an open sewer. An additional town hazard was the escape of sewer gas which found its way through gratings into the streets.

Street cleansing was originally considered to be an obligation of the householder, but gradually became a municipal duty. For long it was incompetently carried out and at irregular intervals; moreover, only a proportion of streets were swept at all, with courts and alleys omitted. In Leeds, for example, in 1842, only 68 out of 586 streets were under any regulation as to paving, draining, sewering or cleansing.

Water supply was seldom laid on to areas of working class housing. The usual arrangement was a standpipe, one to fifteen or more dwellings, with an intermittent supply at that. In Preston and Nottingham, however, the water was always on and in Nottingham two-thirds of the houses were supplied. But if it was difficult to wash at home, it was rarely possible to wash elsewhere, public baths and wash-houses being provided in very few towns.

Conditions were, of course at their worst in those areas of towns given over to working class dwellings. Far more salubrious environments existed for the more prosperous. The early Victorian town was extremely close-knit, as the evidence of overcrowding suggests. Liverpool, for example, covered only 750 hectares (1,860 acres) in 1831 when the population totalled 165,000. An important consequence of this was the juxtaposition of social classes, residential districts of very different quality existing almost cheek by jowl, and this probably had important consequences for the success of the public health reform movement. This is a question raised by B.D. White, who, in his *History of the Corporation of Liverpool* wonders 'whether the prosperous citizens of the forties, if they had been living in Heswall or Hoylake, or even in Mossley Hill or Wallasey, instead of in Abercromby Square or Everton, would have been sufficiently affected by, or even acquainted with, the conditions under which the poor were living, to have been willing to support such sanitary legislation as they did' (22). We hear similar views today concerning the effective divorce of the middle classes, because of distance, from the social problems and environmental squalor of some of the inner areas of our cities.

Comprehensive evidence of the state of certain 19th century towns is given by Engels, who worked on his book *The Condition of the Working Class in England* during 1844–45 (23). As well as being a general analysis of the evolution of industrial capitalism, it was a survey of working class conditions drawing on first hand observation and a wide range of available sources of information. He knew industrial Lancashire well, particularly the Manchester area, and visited the main industrial towns of Yorkshire.

His chapter 'The Great Towns' reviews the situation in London, Dublin, Edinburgh, Glasgow and many provincial English towns, with particular attention paid to Manchester. The descriptions are arresting. In London he writes of the 'rookery' of St Giles, 'a disorderly collection of tall, three or four storeyed houses, with narrow, crooked filthy streets', and the slums close to Portman Square and in the neighbourhood of Drury Lane Theatre where there were 'some of the worst streets of the whole metropolis'. He singled out the plight of the homeless for special attention. In Dublin he found the poor quarters 'extremely extensive, and the filth and the unhabitableness of the houses and the neglect of the streets, surpass all description'. He quotes evidence of atrocious conditions in the narrow courts (wynds) of Edinburgh and Glasgow, the cellar dwellings of Liverpool and the courts of Birmingham. He confirms bad reports from the West Riding.

He knew parts of Lancashire somewhat better than these towns and he knew Manchester best of all. His analysis of Manchester indicates his detailed knowledge: 'All Manchester proper, all Salford and Hulme, a great part of Pendleton and Chorlton, two-thirds of Ardwick, and single stretches of Cheetham Hill and Broughton are all unrivalled working people's quarters, stretching like a girdle, averaging a mile and a half in breadth, around the commercial district. Outside, beyond this girdle, was the upper and middle bourgoisie, the middle bourgoisie in regularly laid out streets in the vicinity of the working quarters, especially in Chorlton and Ardwick, or on the breezy heights of Cheetham Hill, Broughton and Pendleton, in free, wholesome country air, in fine, comfortable houses, passed once every half or quarter hour by omnibuses going into the city'.

Engels' knowledge of the working class districts in Manchester was extensive. The courts which led down to the River Irk 'contain unqualifiedly the most humble dwellings which I have yet beheld', he wrote. With regard to the Old Town, he wrote that his description was 'far from black enough to convey a true impression of the filth, ruin and unhabitableness, the defiance of all considerations of cleanliness, ventilation and health which characterize the construction of this single district, containing at least twenty or thirty thousand inhabitants'. In the New Town, 'Single rows of houses, or groups of streets stand, here and there, like little villages on the naked not even grass-grown clay soil; the houses, or rather cottages, are in bad order, never repaired, filthy, with damp, unclean, cellar dwellings; the lanes are neither paved nor supplied with sewers, but harbour numerous colonies of swine penned in small sties or yards, or wandering through the neighbourhood'. Ancoates, by comparison, was a mixed district of mill hands, and in the worst streets, of hand weavers. In the newly built-up streets 'the cottages look neat and clean, doors and windows are new and freshly painted, the rooms within newly white-washed'. His graphic portrayals continue, but he reserves his greatest condemnation for a district known as 'little Ireland', in a meander loop of the River Medlock, where not only the cellars but the first floors of the houses were damp, and where 'for each one hundred and twenty persons, one usually inaccessible privy is provided'.

From the point of view of the country as a whole, Engels concluded that in the great towns, 'The dwellings of the workers are everywhere badly planned, badly built, and kept in the worst condition, badly ventilated, damp and unwholesome. The inhabitants are confined to the smallest possible space, and at least one family usually sleeps in each room. The interior arrangements of the dwellings is poverty-stricken in various degrees, down to the utter absence of even the most necessary furniture'.

Engels described the living conditions of the poor: 'They are drawn into the large cities where they breathe a poorer atmosphere than in the country; they are relegated to districts which, by reason of the method of construction, are worse ventilated than any others; they are deprived of all means of cleanliness, of water itself, since pipes are laid only when paid for, and the sewers so polluted that they are useless for such purposes . . . If the population of great cities is too dense in general, it is they in particular who are packed into the least space. As though vitiated atmosphere of the streets were not enough, they are penned in dozens into single rooms so that the air which they breathe at night is enough to stifle them. They are given damp dwellings, cellar dens that are not waterproof from below, or garrets that leak from above'. Historians will differ on the question of the reliability of Engels' work, but because he based his book on first-hand observation we must regard this publication as an important primary source for our knowledge of certain industrial towns.

Fortunately, there is abundant evidence elsewhere to confirm the deplorable environmental standards in the big cities. Statistics giving the average age at death are particularly revealing. In 1844 in the Metropolis (*i.e.* Kensington, Strand, Whitechapel and Bethnal Green Unions) the age was 26½ years; in Leeds it was 21, Manchester 20, Bolton 19, and Liverpool 17 (the figures include infant mortality). The sanitary conditions were so primitive that the prevalence of water-borne diseases caused repeated health problems on a major scale. In Liverpool, for example, in 1847, in the midst of the Irish potato famine when immigrants crowded into the cellars of the poorest districts, and epidemics followed, the mortality rate ranged from one out of every

seven of the population in the crowded Vauxhall district, to one in
twenty-eight in the then outer areas of Rodney and Abercromby (24).
But Liverpool was not unique and conditions described in all the big
towns from the various official Reports of the 1840s, all bear a
remarkable similarity, pointing to appalling sanitary deficiencies.

SANITARY REFORM

As we have seen, for the poorer classes, urbanization during the early
part of the 19th century, particularly in the new manufacturing towns,
frequently had distressing consequences. The combination of rapid
economic expansion, with towns subject to extreme fluctuations in
fortune, unmanageable influxes of local and Irish population, the
inability of the building industry to meet housing needs, failings in the
organization of public services, and low standards of crowded living
conditions, led to instances of the most squalid urban living conditions.
In addition to this, there was no effective organizational structure of
local government to fall back on. Many years had to pass before
municipal reform could begin to rescue the casualties of unparalleled
urban change.

With hindsight it is easy to say that the situation demanded
governmental intervention to protect the weaker members of the
community, to up-grade standards of accommodation, to provide
public services, and to bring some measure of coordination to related
economic activities. But it was to take a century or more of political
change to evolve a governmental system that could begin to achieve all
these things. The 19th century began with the tradition of widespread
objection to Government interference and unnecessary Government
expenditure, a view that was to be eroded only very slowly. It was a
legacy of the previous century that people thought Government
interference was likely to be incompetent and Government expenditure corrupt.

The early 19th century history of our towns has woven into it
increasing demands for intervention. Because of the evident squalor of
living conditions and the facts of disease affecting vast numbers, the
first attack was on housing and health, and the role of the public health
reform movement assumed great importance.

A growing concern for public health can be seen dating from the
1830s. In 1833 there had been the Report from the Select Committee
on Public Walks, a body 'appointed to consider the best means of
securing Open Spaces in the Vicinity of Popular Towns as Public Walks
and Places of Exercise calculated to promote the Health and Comfort
of the Inhabitants'. Concern was stimulated by collection of data
which illustrated the urban conditions of the time. William Farr was
appointed compiler of abstracts in the Registrar General's office in

1838 and became an important source of information on sanitary conditions. Edwin Chadwick is better known. He was particularly influential in amassing documentary evidence that was collected between 1840 and 1845 about the state of British towns: the *Reports of the Select Committees on the Health of Towns* (1840) and on *Intra-Mural Interments* (1843); Chadwick's own *Report on the Sanitary Condition of the Labouring Population* and the *Report to the Poor Law Commission* (1842); and the two *Reports of the Royal Commission on the State of Large Towns* (1844 and 1845). All these were carefully documented investigations which provide valuable source material for an assessment of the condition of our towns at that time. Important legislation, namely the Public Health Act, ultimately followed in 1848.

During the 1830s, Chadwick was in uneasy conflict with the Poor Law Commission, gaining a reputation for painstaking investigations and increasing power, but both then and in later years his own obdurate personality led him to be regarded with suspicion and even hostility. The most important stage of his work began in August 1839 when the Bishop of London proposed in the House of Lords that an enquiry be made into the sanitary conditions of the working classes. This was agreed and, in spite of the fact that no money was vested and no arrangements made to facilitate any investigation, work began that year. The scene had already been set: the *Report of the Select Committee on the Health of Towns*, published in 1840, contained ideas which were to crop up repeatedly in the next few years. Important points included a general Act to apply to all future building, a general sewerage Act, the appointment of boards of health in towns above a certain size, and the appointment in large towns of an inspector to enforce sanitary regulations.

The Sanitary Report was presented in July 1840 and more copies of it were sold by the Stationery Office than of any previous Government publication. Subsequently, a Supplementary Report on interments in towns was prepared, a subject excluded from the Sanitary Report by virtue of its size and subject matter. Within a year the sanitary question assumed greater political importance and the Home Secretary set up a Royal Commission to extend the enquiry. This was a notable advance by the public health campaign and a success for Chadwick's continued pressure (25).

The fifty towns in the country with the highest death rates very soon received a letter with an appendix of 62 questions. Replies gave the first evidence from the largest manufacturing towns and ports of the country, in all having a combined population of three millions. The Commissioners, comprising doctors, engineers, and politicians, went to see the conditions in the towns themselves. At the same time, a number of Chadwick's supporters in the movement reported on the state of certain provincial towns with which they were acquainted. The first Report of the Commission, published in July 1844, was brief and made little impact on the public. It contained a few dramatic passages about the state of drainage and water supply in provincial towns, but it was largely a general outline of interim conclusions.

The second Report contained a host of important recommendations which read almost as a kind of charter for the public health campaign. The main points concerned new powers for local Authorities: it was recommended that these powers should be wider in sanitary matters than previously granted either under Local Acts or by the Statute of Sewers. Local Authorities should be responsible for the paving of all streets, courts and alleys, and for the construction of house drains as well as the sewers; they should be invested with the rights to all the dust, ashes and street refuse; and they should have powers, subject to approval, to buy out mill owners and others whose property rights were an obstruction to proper drainage, and to purchase property for the purpose of opening thoroughfares, improving ventilation, and increasing the general convenience of traffic.

Equally important were the recommendations on water supply. The Commission considered that it should be obligatory on local Authorities to procure an adequate and constant supply of water, not only for the domestic needs of the population (and this meant all dwelling houses), but for fire fighting, street cleaning and the scouring of drains and sewers. Competition between private water companies was to be discouraged and such companies were to be required to comply with the demands of the local Authority.

Chadwick had agitated for several months for the appointment of Officers of Health. In the event, the recommendation was rather muted, namely that the local Authority should have the power to appoint, subject to the approval of the Crown, a properly qualified Medical Officer, whose function it would be to inspect and report on the sanitary condition of his district.

The Health of Towns Report had immediate results and the Government promised a Public Health Bill in its legislative programme. But the Government were not to be bound by the conclusions of Chadwick's enquiry. The preparation of the Bill was entrusted to the Earl of Lincoln, First Commissioner of Woods and Forests, perhaps suggesting that this was to be a relatively unimportant measure of a small Department. Moreover, perhaps because anti-Corn Law agitation dominated Westminster at this time, there was considerable delay; the Corn Laws, which imposed a protective duty on imported corn, were repealed in 1846. But there were encouraging signs elsewhere, and the 'sanitary idea' had effects in other directions. The Baths and

Wash-houses Act, 1846, enabling local Authorities to provide public baths, and the Nuisances Removal Act of the same year empowering Boards of Guardians in rural areas to indict nuisances to public health before the Justices of the Peace, were both relevant to sanitary legislation. Meanwhile the founding of the Health of Towns Association in 1844 by Southwood Smith, with branches in a number of provincial towns, promoted pressure for reform.

Deep seated resistance to public intervention in community affairs led to both delay and opposition to public health legislation; indeed, in July 1847 the Public Health Bill was thrown out and Chadwick's career seemed in jeopardy. But already a plague of cholera had broken out in Asia and was shortly to reach Britain. Originating in Afghanistan in 1845 it swept through the north west provinces of India, Persia and Asiatic Turkey the following year. In 1847 the epidemic spread through Eastern and Central Europe. In September 1848, cholera was at Hamburg and for the second time in a generation the disease had visited Western Europe. In October it appeared in Edinburgh.

Many people still remembered that a few months of cholera in 1831–32 had caused considerable panic. There were 700 deaths in Leeds between May and November 1832, and Exeter suffered equally. In both towns most deaths were in areas of slum housing. Cholera was by no means, of course, the only killer at this time, but its attack was sudden and no respecter of social position. Typhus, for example, claimed thousands of victims every year but primarily in slum housing conditions; the disease was essentially a poor man's illness. But as R.A. Lewis, a historian of the public health movement, has pointed out, 'the *comma bacillus* was a social climber; excreted by some lowly sufferer in Fore Street, Lambeth or Hairbrain Court, it might penetrate the half-hearted filter defences of the water companies to poison his betters in the broad squares of the West End' (26).

The outbreak of cholera was just as the Sanitary Commission had predicted — in neglected districts where plagues and fevers bred successively. In Leith, the first case was in the same house in 1848 as in 1832; in Bermondsey it was near the same ditch; in Pollockshaws the first victim died in the same room and even the same bed as sixteen years before. The relationship with contaminated drinking water was revealed by Dr John Snow who was practising in the Golden Square area of Soho when the epidemic broke out. He mapped the exact house where deaths occurred and also the stand pumps which were the only supplies of drinking water. He found that the deaths were clustered round a manual pump in Broad Street, and when the handle of the pump was removed the incidence of new cases fell dramatically. Perhaps the epidemic had passed its peak anyway, but the sure role of contaminated water had been exposed (27).

London experienced two waves of cholera, the first from September 1848 to March 1849 with nearly 1,000 deaths, and the next in the second half of 1849 when the highest weekly mortality rose to almost 2,300. In one ten-day period between August and September 1848, 500 people died in Soho alone.

Chadwick regained his influence and it is against this tangled background of personality conflicts, political horse-trading between vested interests, the ineffective but jealously guarded privilege of a myriad of local *ad hoc* bodies and Authorities, a national plague and a renewed determination by the reformers that something must be done, that we should see the passing of the Public Health Act, 1848. Although the Act established a Central Commission it was the new local powers that were to be particularly important. In those districts which already possessed municipal institutions, the Town Council was to be the public health Authority. A new Authority, known as a Local Board of Health, was given to non-corporate districts and officers were to be appointed, namely a clerk, a treasurer, and inspector of nuisances and a surveyor. They were also permitted to appoint a Medical Officer of Health.

The powers to be exercised by the new local Authorities were extensive, covering cleansing, sewering, paving and the provision of a water supply; forty five clauses dealt with these powers. Six years' pressure by Chadwick and such bodies as the Health of Towns Association had had their result. In addition to the provision of extensive powers, the 1848 Act was of great importance in considerably widening legislative measures to many more local Authorities. The Act met the particular situation of the day whereby only twenty nine English Municipal Corporations possessed Local Acts which conferred powers of drainage, cleansing and paving on the Mayor and Corporation. Sixty two corporate towns possessed no Local Act which enabled either the Corporation or a body of *ad hoc* Commissioners to undertake these vital services. A further sixty six corporate towns did exercise such powers jointly between Corporation and Commissioners. The position was unsatisfacotry, therefore, in corporate towns and even more so in non-corporate towns. Of such towns in England, with a population of more than 5,000, only 175 had Local Acts and 296 were without.

Those Authorities, corporate and non-corporate, which possessed Local Acts, had of course striven for many years to improve the sanitary conditions which existed in their areas. A number of improvements, albeit slight, were effected in certain towns before the 1840s. The first Liverpool Improvement Act of 1784, for example, secured various street widenings and extensions. Indeed, in the late 18th and early 19th centuries, Liverpool Corporation had its own

Select Committee of Improvements. A further Improvement Act in 1826 gave powers for street widening, their rebuilding and the improvement of the cemetery. Additional powers for control over the condition of streets and buildings were secured in 1842. In 1847 it obtained a Sanitary Act (28).

Further legislation produced sanitary improvements later in the century, but the 1840s marked a watershed in this aspect of urban development. From this time on, there was widespread and positive progress in the paving, lighting and sewerage of towns and cities. The next decades were to provide substantial evidence of the contribution of public engineering to the appearance and health of the urban parts of the country. This indeed was a remarkable technical achievement of Victorian Britain, one on which subsequent improvements were to be based.

References

(1) *See,* Simmons, Jack, *Transport: a visual history of modern Britain,* Vista Books, 1962.
(2) Bell, Colin and Rose, *City Fathers: the early history of town planning in Britain,* The Cresset Press, 1969.
(3) *Op cit.,* Bell, Colin and Rose.
(4) Smith, Wilfred, *An Historical Introduction to the Economic Geography of Great Britain,* G. Bell & Sons, 1968 (reprint).
(5) Redford, Arthur, *Labour Migration in England 1820–1850,* Manchester University Press, 1926. (2nd edition edited and revised by W.H. Chaloner, 1964).
(6) *Op cit.,* Redford, Arthur.
(7) *Op cit.,* Redford, Arthur.
(8) Chaloner, W.H., *The Birth of Modern Manchester* in 'Manchester and its Region', British Association for the Advancement of Science, 1962.
(9) Beaver, S.H., *The Potteries, a Study in the Evolution of a Cultural Landscape,* Transactions, Institute of British Geographers, 1964.
(10) Sigsworth, E.M., *The Industrial Revolution,* in 'Leeds and its Region', British Association for the Advancement of Science, 1967.
(11) Tivy, Joy, *Population Distribution and Change,* in 'The Glasgow Region', British Association for the Advancement of Science, 1958.
(12) Allen, G.C. *The Industrial Development of Birmingham and the Black Country, 1860–1927,* Allen and Unwin, 1929.
(13) Lewis, J. Parry, *Building Cycles and Britain's Growth,* Macmillan, 1965.
(14) *Op cit.,* Lewis, J. Parry.
(15) *Op cit.,* Lewis, J. Parry.
(16) Pollard, Sydney, *A History of Labour in Sheffield,* Liverpool University Press, 1959.
(17) Ashworth, William, *The Genesis of Modern British Town Planning,* Routledge, 1954.
(18) Lewis, R.A., *Edwin Chadwick and the Public Health Movement, 1832–1854* Longman, Green & Company, 1952.
(19) Hammond, J.L. and Barbara, *The Bleak Age,* 1934, revised Pelican Books, 1947.
(20) Beresford, M.W. *From Tenter Grounds to Building Grounds,* mimeo, Urban History Conference, University of Birmingham, 1969.
(21) *Op cit.,* Beresford, M.W.
(22) White, Brian D., *A History of the Corporation of Liverpool,* Liverpool University Press 1951.
(23) Engels, Frederick, *The Condition of the Working Class in England,* 1845, Panther Books with an introduction by E.J. Hobshawm, 1969.
(24) *Report of Royal Commission on Distribution of Industrial Population,* Cmd.6153, HMSO 1940.
(25) *Op cit.,* Lewis, R.A.
(26) *Op cit.,* Lewis, R.A.
(27) Stamp, Dudley L., *The Geography of Life and Death,* Fontana, 1964.
(28) *Op cit.,* Ashworth, William.

4 Factors in the development of Victorian cities

This chapter looks at some of the changing elements in the land use structure and composition of the Victorian city. It reviews the introduction of the railway and the growing provision of urban parks. It examines the developing commerical function of central areas and looks particularly at changes in retail trading. Transportation improvements and the complex forces behind suburban expansion are examined. Finally it looks at a number of general developments as well as specific factors in the growth of individual towns. In the next chapter other changes, notably those regarding housing and social questions, will be examined.

THE RAILWAY

The railway was a revolutionary factor in the pattern of change in Victorian towns and cities; it affected the very appearance of towns; it had a great impact on urban structure, and from it flowed many social consequences (1). From the physical point of view it was a most powerful intrusion into an existing, tightly-knit, urban fabric, due in part to the fact that from the outset the railway companies were granted two unusual public privileges: notably, corporate form and the power to acquire property by compulsory purchase. It is true that these privileges were also extended to public utilities, planning and improvement projects, canal and turnpike companies and other large scale undertakings which were in the public interest, but we shall see that with the railway they were to have particularly far-reaching effects.

The railway burst upon the urban scene after 1830. From a historical point of view, this form of transport in cities introduced a new element into the built-up area in that it required a completely new transport net: lines, terminals, sidings and marshalling yards, as well as new generating points in the form of railway stations. In other words it did not use the existing framework of social overhead capital as the profitable omnibus and carting businesses could do. These manifestations of a new system had made their appearance largely by the 1860s, but of course we should note that other consequences of the railway continued to shape the development of towns for many decades afterwards.

The railway cut great swathes into the tightly built-up area of the

Victorian town. Frequently the central-area stations were approached on viaducts, a major reason being to avoid street closures. It was inevitable that the poorer housing districts in congested areas near town centres suffered the most because of either the necessary removal of dwellings, or the construction of the line and its subsequent daily traffic for the occupants of the houses which remained. The very act of population disturbance and house removal was an important factor in the evolution of any town; residential upheavals were not necessarily novel situations, but the scale of the enterprise could be a new experience. At first, when towns, at least in the provinces, were relatively small the impact was manageable and drew no unfavourable comment. Indeed the sudden implanting of railway development may have been salutary from a physical point of view and correct from the moral standpoint of the age. Clearance of undesirable property could usefully disperse concentrations of social problems, hotbeds of vice and trouble spots. In Birmingham, for example, Robert Stephenson's New Street Station removed 'a certain class of the inhabitants' (2) adjoining the principal and best streets of the city by choosing a route through the slums and brothels behind Navigation Street.

The displacement of people for railway improvement was often on a very large scale indeed, and, because it was relatively easy to secure eviction, this expulsion could be both violent and sudden. One thousand two hundred and seventy-five people in 255 cottages made way for Manchester Central Station; 540 in 135 houses for the Liverpool Central; 6142 in 443 of the larger Glasgow tenements were required for St. Enoch's Station; and 2178 people in 141 houses for the Caledonian Central. Eight hundred families were dispossessed by the construction of a viaduct linking Central Station, Newcastle, to nearby Manors. Such estimates of displacement were frequently very conservative and thoroughly understated, and in the case of London termini or major line developments, it was probably of a very much higher order. Disturbing evidence of demolition and eviction meant that after the 1860s the railway was not so enthusiastically received as had been the case in the 1830s and 1840s, when it had been seen as a welcome symbol of technological progress. This is perhaps very similar to the first public reception of the motorway a century later. At the threshold of the 1970s it seems that in view of the intolerable living conditions that they can bring to those unfortunate enough to be housed near to them, the urban motorways in the inner areas of our major cities will no longer be looked upon as simple devices for relieving problems; they are mixed blessings with attendant disadvantages.

The dramatic impact of the railway on the urban fabric can also be seen in its effect on land use. The railway's hunger for land was striking, and everywhere made a big impact on town development. The estimate of J.R. Kellet, who has written on the influence of the railway on Victorian cities, is that between 5 per cent and 9 per cent of the central area of towns was devoted to railway land in the form of lines, marshalling yards, locomotive sheds and terminals (3). In Glasgow the land demands were particularly pronounced. In 1900 the urban lines, terminals and the railways skirting the city together with associated yards and sidings totalled 332 hectares (820 acres), three-quarters of the built-up area of the whole city in 1840. This was bigger than in either Liverpool or Manchester where the equivalent proportion was half, and certainly bigger than Birmingham and London, but in all these cities the proportions were large enough to reflect the heavy land use requirements for railway purposes.

Fresh buildings followed in the wake of the railway. The railway station was a new feature and, as a symbol of advance in a technological world, was often afforded architectural prestige. Victorian railway stations are, a century later, high on the list of impressive buildings for retention and preservation. John Dobson, for example, the architect for Newcastle's central area redevelopment in the 1830s, produced a magnificent Central Station in 1850 for the York, Newcastle and

Temple Meads Railway Station, Bristol. The original part by Brunel dates from 1839–40, and the curved train shed by Matthew Digby Wyatt from 1856–78. The Gothic ornament applied to this building is typical of railway Victoriana. It was a period when even tunnels were flanked by embattled towers to suggest the gateways of medieval castles. Railway stations were some of the most important new buildings in mid-19th-century towns and in the larger centres every effort was made to reflect the power and prestige of the Company to which they belonged.

Berwick Railway Company when they transferred their offices from York to the north east. There are many other examples of architectural importance: Bristol Temple Meads, the original part by Brunel dating from 1839—40; the classical portico at Cheltenham Lansdown (1844); the Gothic design at Great Malvern; and the classical facade by John Dobson at Monkwearmouth, Sunderland, a station built to commemorate the election of George Hudson, the railway magnate prominent in the boom of the 1840s, as local M.P. The classical facade at Huddersfield is important, as indeed is the building as a whole, forming as it does a central feature in the town. In London, St Pancras and Kings Cross are particularly noteworthy.

Railway hotels followed station development somewhat later and, together, they exercised a good deal of local influence in land use activity. Railways tended to emphasize the attractive pull of town centres. Land values rose around the stations and as retail shops and transit warehouses were attracted, residential properties were repelled. Where stations were on the edge of town centres there was a strong tendency for an adjoining warehousing district to become established. Around the stations themselves a good deal of street traffic was generated, particularly cabs and heavy cartage traffic. In London, street congestion was particularly severe and in the 1860s was only relieved by the building of the Metropolitan underground line.

But the impact of the railway was not confined to town centres or the changes in land use they wrought. The railway represented the superimposition of a dynamic element in town growth as a whole, and it had an effect both in the inner areas and in the expansion of outer districts.

In the inner areas, change resulted most obviously from the displacement of people. Most frequently the persons who were moved were those who could least resist the effects of this form of dramatic intervention and they tended to be pushed into adjoining areas. This had the effect of then concentrating human and social problems in the under-privileged belt of the inner districts, already areas of poor housing and environmental squalor. At the most extreme the flotsam of human life concentrated in the viaducts of the railway arches. Charles Dickens' Mr. Dombey (*Dombey and Sons*, 1869) describes his view from the viaduct as his railway journey came to an end: 'Everything around is blackened. There are dark pools of water, muddy lanes and miserable habitations far below. There are jagged walls and filthy houses close at hand, and through the battered roofs and broken windows, wretched rooms are seen, where want and fever hide themselves in many wretched shapes, where smoke and crowded gables, and distorted chimneys, and deformity of brick and mortar prising up deformity of mind and body, choke the nearby distance'.

A view of the inner areas of some of our modern cities from the railway might well be sketched in similar terms. The backs of decaying Victorian properties, with evidence of occupation by many families in areas which obviously have few play areas and open spaces, or of cleared plots of land strewn with building materials and the disposed gadgets of domestic rejects, are reminders of the very different environmental qualities which exist today between the inner and outer districts of major cities.

The impact of the railway on inner areas had many indirect consequences — for example, because of the railway and its ancillary developments which covered vast areas, the area within walking distance of city centres was noticeably compressed. This had its effect on industrial location and in due time encouraged the re-siting of larger premises in suburban or outlying districts where one of the advantages was an immediate labour force. Conversely, of course, while there was some encouragement for industrial dispersal, more obviously the railway provided an extended system of public transport which enabled people to travel to fixed locations. In terms of activities in a spatial sense, therefore, the railway was a loosener of links, aiding the dispersal of industrial plant as well as homes.

Railways in inner areas, whether at ground level or on a viaduct or in cuttings, seriously interrupted communications between particular residential districts. Great loops of railway and junction land resulted in surviving residential districts becoming seriously ill-shaped. This sometimes created social ghettoes in backwater territories.

The effect of the railway in outer areas is bound up with the story of suburban expansion, to which we have just referred. It was largely in London, because of its disproportionate size, that this development was most in evidence, but none the less there are some factors of wider applicability that we should mention. From the 1860s the middle classes widened, embracing proportionately more people than before, and, for many, rail travel was a necessary link between job and home. Even in London, however, regular suburban rail travel was restricted to a relatively small section of people until well into the century. In the mid-1850s there were 27,000 rail commuters a day entering London; this compares with the total of 244,000 daily foot and omnibus passengers entering the city. But expansion did take place and in some instances it is possible to see a particular relationship between railway development and suburban growth. Cheaper rail fares began to be introduced in the 1870s, and the Cheap Trains Act of 1883 introduced workmen's fares. Extremely cheap fares were offered by the Great Eastern Railway, a particular stimulus to the area of Edmonton and Walthamstow, which increased its population ten-fold in the last four decades of the century.

Another impact of the railway on suburban development was the stimulation afforded to the movement of certain industries, larger ones in particular, to suburban locations. Canal-side location had been important earlier in the century, but the availability of private sidings to main lines, which were increasingly valuable for the delivery of raw materials and transport of manufactured products, was particularly attractive. It was not until the alternative of road and motor transport in the 20th century that this particular trend in industrial location was reversed.

The traffic generating capacity of the railway in Victorian cities was to reflect a rapidly growing service industry and the railways themselves provided a new range of urban employment during the century. In London, for example, between 1861 and 1891 the number of people employed in regular service for the railways (clerks, porters, guards, drivers and officials) trebled. In addition there were cabmen and carters in horse drawn traffic; those engaged in the urban transport of passengers and goods became one of the largest occupational groups.

The impact of the railway on the Victorian city, therefore, was extensive. It was also complex because it led to consequences which were felt throughout the physical urban structure and in a variety of social questions. The makers of the railway and those concerned in the railway companies moulded Victorian cities in a decisive way and the history of particular towns is indissolubly bound up with issues in the history of railway development. The question of land ownership over which the routes were to pass, or decisions by railway companies as to routes and timings of development became crucial factors in the history of certain towns.

Some small provincial towns, which for one reason or another missed a rail connection, were condemned to economic stagnation until the development of road traffic could rescue them. Stamford, for example, was denied a rail link by the Marquis of Exeter, owner of the land across which the line was to run, and Peterborough was selected by the Company instead. Some towns, which already had clear nodality by virtue of geographical factors and had been small market or regional centres, had their centrality emphasized by the railway; Carlisle and Derby are instances of this. Some towns were actual railway creations, with railway companies providing perhaps 25 to 30 per cent of the total employment — Crewe, Swindon, Wolverton and Redhill are cases in point. Many towns owe their development, if not their actual creation, to railway companies, the facilities they afforded and the capital they invested. Barrow, for example, owed much to the Furness Railway which financed the construction of the docks, provided gas and water, and built the Town and Market Halls. Similarly, the Manchester, Sheffield and Lincolnshire Railway provided Cleethorpes with its amenities as a seaside resort, including promenade, gardens and shopping arcade (4). The North Eastern Railway invested heavily in docks at Middlesbrough and Hartlepools; the Caledonian Railway did the same at Grangemouth, and the London and South Western Railway made a spectacular investment when it acquired the Southampton Docks in 1892.

In all these instances, the powerful impact of the railway can be seen; an excellent example is the development of Swindon (5). In 1831 it was a small market town of less than 2000 people, a much smaller population than, say, nearby Marlborough with nearly 3500, or Warminster with more than 6000. In December 1840 the Great Western line from Paddington reached Swindon and there was a decision within the next few months to set up an Engine Establishment including large repair shops. Swindon station was opened in 1842, the railway works in 1843, and the first houses of a new town followed. Between 1851 and 1911 the population of the town soared from 4800 to more than 50,000.

The railway village built by the Company a small distance from the old market settlement became known as Swindon New Town. The estate comprised terraces of one and two-bedroomed houses laid out on a regular grid. In due time a range of social facilities, including a library, reading room and mechanics' institute (a popular mid-century institution aimed at technical education), a park and cricket ground, baths and a school, and a church, were provided. Nikolaus Pevsner, the art historian, praises it as 'one of the few planned Victorian estates, small and modest and laid out without ingenuity, but planned all the same, and architecturally as orderly as in the design of the streets'. Not everywhere was the railway as benevolent as in Swindon, but its impact was usually massive.

Other examples can be given (6). Wolverton was rather like Swindon in that a new railway colony over-powered an existing settlement. The Midland Railway Carriage Works were opened there in 1838, when the London-Birmingham line was built, and a small township of red brick houses was developed. Eastleigh, on the other hand, was an even more original creation. Bishopstoke Junction had been built as a station only, in 1839, in open fields. Connections to Gosport and Salisbury were provided later, and a permanent railway colony grew up, taking its name from a neighbouring farm – Eastleigh. Rapid development followed at the end of the century when it acquired the Nine Elms carriage works (1891), the Southampton engine repair sheds (1903) and the Nine Elms locomotive workshops (1910).

While the Great Western Railway boasted its model colony at New Swindon, and the London and Birmingham Company had its Wolverton, the London and North Western Railway, formed by amalgamation in 1846, created its model town, Crewe. Already by 1842 Crewe was the focus of four lines of railway and further lines were attracted later. From 1837 to 1840 Crewe was merely a station on the Grand Junction line and the engine sheds and repair shops of the Company were at Edgehill, Liverpool. But Crewe's central position on the network was a locational advantage when removal became necessary. A decision was taken in 1840 and the Company's Engineer, Joseph Locke, drew up plans for a new township. The first houses were completed in 1842, and the Company, with railway paternalism, built up a new community in what had previously been the rural township of Monks Coppenhall.

PARKS AND OPEN SPACES

An important ingredient of a successful Victorian town was the public park, and while, from a land-use point of view, its implications for urban structure were less than those of the railway, it is still an urban feature to which we should give some attention (7). At local level the existence of a public park usually enhanced residential property values and was frequently associated with the success of a fashionable housing area, but compared with the railway its broader consequences on land use activities were of less importance.

The idea of the park attracted the financial support of many a Victorian benefactor, and the open space movement to which it was linked took firm root throughout the middle classes with the result that towards the end of the century there was widespread support for measures for improving health, reducing overcrowding and preserving open air amenities. This was a complex amalgam, but the Victorian public park was part of a total concern, including the improvement and enhancement of urban landscape, the question of health and morality of the masses, attitudes towards public recreation and belief in the natural benefits of air and sunlight in overcrowded cities. All these factors were ultimately connected first with the question of reducing densities, and then the form and size which towns and cities might take.

The whole idea of creating landscapes within towns for public use and enjoyment began very largely with the Victorians. Previously a 'park' had meant a private area of land adjoining a gentleman's house. These were frequently in the countryside, but even when landscaped areas were provided in towns, as in the Georgian development at Bath or in the London squares, they were for private use — the sole enjoyment of those resident in the houses surrounding them.

There was, however, the urban tradition of the pleasure garden and the public walk, and in London, for example, the public for a considerable time enjoyed access to the Royal Parks. The development of Regent's Park as one of the Metropolitan improvements of the early

19th century should be seen in this context. But elsewhere the park movement needed special stimulus, and this was to come from two main sources: first, the energies and products of individual landscape gardeners who set new trends and fashions, and second, the increasing concern over public health.

Humphrey Repton was an important early figure, active as a professional landscape gardener between 1788 and 1811. He advocated a system of gardening rather different from that of the previous dominant figure, Lancelot Brown; it was on a smaller scale and marked the end of the grand style of the mid-Georgian era. Repton laid out the gardens in Russell Square and in Cadogan Place, London, but his influence was seen more extensively in the work of John Nash, first at Marylebone Park and later at St. James' Park. Another important early figure was John Claudius Loudon, who, like Repton, was concerned with the smaller scale landscape of suburban gardens, squares and crescents. His 'gardenesque' system, as it became known, was based on a developing interest in new plants which were introduced from abroad for the first time as overseas tropical countries were explored.

With regard to the concern for public health, in 1833 there was an important report from the Select Committee on Public Walks, a body appointed to consider the best means of securing open spaces in the vicinity of popular towns (see page 34). Their findings reflected the situation of the day, namely that certain towns had some open space for public walks, for example Liverpool, Bristol, Norwich, Nottingham and Shrewsbury, but that inadequacies were the general rule. The Committee favoured the provision of Public Walks and Open Spaces, suggesting legislation to facilitate the exchange and dedication of land for the purpose.

During the 1840s there were a number of Acts which gave power for the provision of public parks, but not until the Recreation Grounds Act of 1859 was there a public general Act. A good deal of impetus, therefore, remained with private benefactors, local societies, the energy of individual gardeners of repute, as well as with local authorities who blazed a pioneering trail. The development of Victorian cities benefited from the activity of all these.

In many ways the forerunner of the public park was the botanic garden, usually laid out and maintained by a local society. Kew Gardens dates back to 1759, but the great expansion in numbers came in the 19th century. Botanic gardens in Birmingham, Liverpool and Sheffield date from the 1830s. The public park as such was somewhat different, but in 1830 a Victoria Park was laid out in Bath, the first of many Victoria Parks and Queen's Parks throughout Britain by the end of the century.

Joseph Paxton was the great designer in the middle of the century.

His first park was Princes Park in Liverpool which he designed in 1842. But perhaps his greatest creation was two years later at Birkenhead, a town then being developed as a rival to Liverpool by the Improvement Commissioners. The Third Improvement Act of 1843 provided for land to be purchased for a park to be set aside for the free recreation of the people. Fifty hectares (125 acres) were ultimately dedicated for public use. After the Great Exhibition of 1851, where Paxton designed the Crystal Palace, he designed parks at Glasgow, Halifax, Dundee and Dunfermline. His influence continued and extended through the men he trained and employed, such as Edward Kemp, who laid out Hesketh Park, Southport (1868) and Stanley Park, Liverpool (1870), and John Gibson and Edward Milner.

By this time the urban park had become a distinctive and invaluable feature of most Victorian towns. In 1868 Henry Bölckow, a steel magnate of Middlesbrough, founded Albert Park. In the same year Alexander Park was opened in Manchester, and in Liverpool in the late 1860s and early 1870s three additional parks were opened to form a ring of parks on the edge of the city. Manchester had been prominent in the mid-1850s for the provision of parks and recreation facilities; one of them, Peel Park, even boasted a gymnasium for girls.

But, on the other hand, London's parks were slow to appear. Victoria Park in the East End dates from 1845, Battersea Park from 1856 and Finsbury Park and Southwark Park, developed by the Metropolitan Board of Works, in 1869. Other parks remained in the hands of Her Majesty's Commissioners of Woods and Forests and the

Paxton's Pavilions, Sheffield. The Botanic Gardens in Sheffield were one of the earliest examples of this form of park development. There was a widespread interest in plants, particularly new species from abroad. Paxton, who designed these Botanical Pavilions, was one of the greatest park designers of the early Victorian period.

Office of Works until 1887 when they were transferred to the Metropolitan Board of Works (subsequently the London County Council).

Design fashions changed slowly. First there was the elaborate Italian Garden, followed by the gradual trend to an axial and geometric design as found in parks later in the century at Leicester (Abbey Park, 1877), Wolverhampton (West Park, 1879) and Crewe (Queen's Park, 1887). Battersea Park is probably the most notable. An Act was passed in 1846 to enable Her Majesty's Commissioners to form a Royal Park in Battersea Fields. £200,000 was authorized for this purpose to cover the purchase of the land, laying out and planting, and the forming of an embankment along the Thames. It was opened in 1858 and contained features which were to characterize the Victorian Park: an 'Old English garden', plants and shrubbery, playing fields, broad avenues as walkways, a bandstand and an ornamental fountain.

By and large, urban park development continued with no major break in style. The Victorian tradition had become successfully established: the park was a valuable open area in the urban fabric, patently valued by the town dweller.

It is equally important to note other aspects of the park and open space movement because of their consequences for town structure. In 1865 the Commons Preservation Society had been founded to protect the great natural heritage of commons and woodlands in the London area and was to wage successful battles during the next decades (8). Until the 1860s there had been little public attention directed to commons, but this was the time of significant enclosure of common land. Opposition was roused, the view being that commons within reach of the large towns, particularly London, were of greater value to the public as open space for health and recreation, than as cultivated land or building sites. Support for this view came in connection with Wimbledon Common, when Earl Spencer, Lord of the Manor of Wimbledon, announced his intention to dedicate the greater part of his common to the public. But elsewhere many commons were seriously threatened. In Epping Forest hundreds of hectares were fenced off by various Lords of Manors who claimed rights there, and other commons were enclosed. It was against this background that the Commons Preservation Society was founded. In 1866 the Metropolitan Commons Act was passed which gave the Inclosure Commissioners (later the Board of Agriculture) power, under certain circumstances, to outline a scheme for the regulation of a common and its management by a Board of Conservators. In 1883 the Metropolitan Public Gardens Association was founded under the chairmanship of the Earl of Meath, which was responsible for promoting the Disused Burial Grounds Act of 1884 and Open Spaces Acts of subsequent years. This Association was particularly influential in directing public attention to the evils of over-crowding and the great need to provide play and recreation spaces in densely populated districts.

RETAIL TRADING

During the century the combination of the growth of population, ever increasing economic activity and the expanding sizes of towns resulted in an enhanced commercial function for central areas. We should recall that whereas in 1801 there had been no other city than London of above 100,000 persons in England and Wales, and only fifteen above 20,000, by 1891 twenty-three centres were in the largest category and 185 in the other category. The essential force attending urban growth in the 19th century was a centripetal one, concentration at the centre being an essential characteristic. The commercial functions of the central area flourished, therefore, as insurance, banking and other services expanded. At the same time retail trade was transformed, and town centre shopping was changed out of all recognition. Except where street improvements were undertaken, perhaps creating new thorough-fares out of a warren of slum housing, much of this new activity was crowded into an existing street pattern which was to remain unchanged in most cities until the blitz of the 1940s and post-War redevelopment. In the 19th century the basic form of central area land uses was laid down, with, in the largest towns, distinctive banking districts, quality shopping areas and mixed commercial areas. Business activity followed the radial roads into the adjoining areas. Central land values rose consistently and may have increased by something of the order of 75 – 100 per cent in 30 years after 1840; values in the more favoured streets may have increased by three to five fold.

Change in the Victorian city and in day-to-day life for families was very marked with regard to shopping habits (9, 10). From early emphasis on market trading there developed the multiple and the department store. But in addition to alternative forms of trading we should note the sheer scale of activity because of more people and greater purchasing power. A closer look at the retailing revolution is useful because the important changes that were taking place in the city centres helps us to recognize the important social transformations that were also taking place at that time. The heart of the matter was that the industrial wealth of Britain was creating a new spending population, and, in a widening middle class, great importance was attached to signs of prosperity: clothes, household furnishings and the trappings of a large family. The family, indeed, was all important and tradesmen readily called themselves Family Drapers, Family Butchers or Family Furnishers, or set up Family Mourning Warehouses.

In the first half of the 19th century, finished consumer goods were purchased in four main ways. First, there were the retail units proper, such as grocers, drapers, haberdashers and so on. Second, there were producer-retailers, such as boot and shoe makers, tailors, cabinet makers and butchers. Third, there were itinerant tradesmen. Fourth, there were the markets, usually weekly but sometimes daily, and in the new industrial towns market halls took on the same function as market places in the country towns. Liverpool led the way in providing a spacious, gas-lit municipal market hall in 1822.

Until the middle of the century the shops were still small, independently owned and run by the shopkeeper on the premises. One master, one shop was the rule and the opening of a branch was rare. A host of minor trades of the craftsman/retailer persisted. Milk, for example, was sold by dairymen who kept their cows in cellars or at the backs of their shops, but 'railway milk', brought in overnight from the country and retailed in quite a different way, ended this particular trade. There was no large-scale organization in shopping, and shop-keeping was still structured to the needs of a largely pre-industrial society. This broke down, gradually at first, but then rapidly with the growing class of weekly wage earners and a rapid increase in the real income per head of the population. The demand for a widening range of goods transformed the distributive trades, bringing new techniques of selling, new methods of wholesale and retail trade, producing new consumer goods (cheap, imported food and new products of concerns such as the boot and shoe industry and the men's clothing industry for example), and creating new forms of retail units.

The new shopkeeping organizations took on a number of different forms: co-operatives, multiples, department stores and bazaars. They were all demanded and made possible by the growing numbers of population and their prosperity and the growing standardization of merchandise. There was an increasing range of basic necessities and a large and stable demand existed for the first time. For example, one of the first consequences of Victorian prosperity in towns was that people, particularly the working class, ate more food.

A basic transformation came with large-scale organizations for retailing. It needed a new type of retailer to exploit the potential of importing foreign provisions cheaply and selling them to the working class. The growth in the last quarter of the century of the multiple, selling grocery and provisions, was particularly spectacular (11). Thomas Lipton, for example, started a one-man grocery shop in Glasgow in 1872 and had 245 branches all over the country by the end of the century. In the late 1880s they were handling over 10 per cent of national tea sales. A more impressive market slice was taken by the Maypole Dairy Company which in 1913 was selling about one-third of all the margarine in the country. The spending habits of millions were being rapidly changed. As the flood of cheaper food entered the country, the small holding which provided milk, butter, cheese and bacon had had its day. The prices of staple imports, such as tea, sugar, grain, ham, bacon, lard and cheese, fell and the multiple retailers prospered. Tea consumption rose from 1.3 kgm per head in 1861 to 2.8 kgm per head in 1910; sugar from 18.7 kgm to 40 kgm; cocoa from 50 gms to 550 gms; rice from 2.6 kgm to 7.2 kgm. For middle class and upper class trade, tea-blending and coffee roasting were the foundations of sales and status, but it was the working class residential district which supported most of this multiple trade.

Other multiple shop organizations were equally successful and made their mark on the shopping districts of the day. Chains of book stalls were built up after the 1880s by W.H. Smith & Son and by J. Menzies in Scotland; the Singer Manufacturing Company also entered the market, to be followed by the footwear trade and others. Co-operative shopping also developed rapidly between the 1890s and the First World War; co-operative societies increased from some 400 in 1862 to 1043 in 1882, and 1453 in 1903. Central area co-operative trading, later organized on department store lines, was supported by large numbers of branch grocery shops.

The department store was another important development and was found particularly in central areas. Following the example of the Bon Marché and the Louvre in Paris in the 1860s, there was rapid development, particularly in London, during the next two decades. Several existing drapers (for example Debenhams, Swan and Edgars and Dickens and Jones) and an existing grocer (Harrods) were joined by new arrivals such as Whiteleys, The Civil Service Stores and the Army and Navy. Outside London, there were the examples of Lewis's of Liverpool, House of Fraser (Glasgow), Binns (Sunderland), Robinson and Cleaver (Belfast), Kendal Milnes of Manchester and many others.

These catered especially for the middle class customer and aimed at providing comfort, or even luxury, in very large buildings. These new multi-storey shops became commercial show places and the pride of expanding towns. Well before the flamboyant example of Selfridges' opening in Oxford Street in 1909, there was a host of other shopping extravaganzas with huge plate-glass windows for display and, inside, novelties like lifts and pneumatic cash tubes. In Newcastle, as one example, the elegant and exclusive Fenwicks was opened in 1882. The shop front, designed by a local architect, was striking. Alison Adburgham describes it as follows: 'two large display windows each had seven graceful supporting pillars with fluting picked out in gold leaf. The windows were advanced from the building, and curved round to the centre entrance in which stood a metal statue supported by a large gas lamp. Above, there was an elegant balustrade' (12).

Right: St Mary Street, Cardiff, 1890; *below:* High Street, Southampton at the turn of the century; *opposite:* Briggate, Leeds, 1890. These three photographs reveal marked similarity in the features of the main shopping streets in provincial cities in the late Victorian period. The main concentration of commercial power had been established. The essential form of town centres was in being, and, with the exception of bomb damage and post-1945 redevelopment, they have not changed greatly since. The main thoroughfares were shopping streets; they were busy and congested with wheeled traffic. Cobbled streets, trams and horses' hooves created a cacophony of noise. The streets were well lit, major shops were established and had become important foci of social life.

Another feature of the Victorian shopping centre was the arcade, an intimate pedestrian route for small shops, where frequently quality trades were assembled. They provided fashionable areas of concourse in the days of leisurely shopping; sometimes ornate cast-iron arches supported roofs of glass in the style of the Crystal Palace.

The next development was in the rise of the variety chain store, but this belongs to a later chapter. Suffice to say at this stage that after a beginning in the 1890s with the penny bazaars that Michael Marks had established in the North, there was a very rapid growth in the 20th century, all of which further enhanced the commercial prestige and attractive power of the city centre.

Right: Market Street, Manchester, 1847, looking toward Market Place; *below:* Market Street, Manchester, 1902, also looking towards Market Place; *below, right:* Market Street, Manchester, 1933, looking towards Picadilly. These three illustrations cover almost a century of central area development and the progressive concentration of shopping interests can be seen quite clearly. In a sense, little has changed over the period. Certainly the scene in 1847 suggests a relatively leisurely way of life, the scene in 1902, bustle and vigour, and the 1933 scene, the growing domination of the motor car over the pedestrian. But otherwise, the continuity of the location of retail trade in this short stretch of Manchester's central area has not altered significantly and is an important general feature of urban development over the last 150 years.

URBAN TRANSPORT

The concentration of economic activity and of people in towns of ever growing size demanded an improvement in facilities for urban circulation, and, during the 19th century, dramatic transport revolutions concerning road and railway were to have their impact on the character of urban life and the physical appearance of towns. The repercussions of this development continued into the 20th century in an even more extreme form when the need for urban surgery for the accommodation of road traffic has gone still further to influence the very form and shape of cities. Urban history in the last two centuries is intimately concerned with the transport revolution. Canal development belonged largely to an earlier phase and had its own impact, particularly on the stimulation of certain forms of economic activity where reduction in the cost of cartage was critical; by and large, apart from the visual aspect of their introduction into the urban scene (sometimes dramatic when associated with flights of locks), they did not have any serious implications for the circulation of people. This was left to road and rail improvements.

For a number of years the significance of the railway was in *inter*-urban, rather than *intra*-urban communications. After the opening to public traffic of the Liverpool and Manchester Railway in September 1830, major developments soon took place (the Stockton and Darlington Railway had not been designed primarily for carrying passengers). During the later 1830s the construction of the first main lines leading from London began. The first main line in the world was constructed from Camden to Birmingham with a double track throughout, by the two Stephensons — father and son — in 1837 and 1838. This inter-city travel innovation marked the end of the golden age of coaching, and, for something like 90 years, the road was in relative eclipse. At its peak there were probably 3000 coaches on the road, employing 30,000 men in the form of coachmen, guards, horsekeepers and others. But although there would be a resurgence of road traffic with the coming of the motor car, the coaches were gone forever (13).

The early role of the railways was that of trunk routes, and in their initial stages they did little to stimulate suburban traffic. The first station on the London-Birmingham Railway when it was opened was at Harrow, 18½ kilometres out. It is true that other stations were added later at Willesden, Sudbury and Pinner six years later, but the local service was very limited. For a long time the great main line companies seemed to regard a heavy suburban traffic as a nuisance, and it is significant that of the five Home Counties, Middlesex, which depended most for its railway services on the main line companies, was the least developed in Victorian times (14).

There were, of course, exceptions. The Greenwich and Blackwall Companies in London and certain provincial companies like the Newcastle and North Shields, later, began to exploit suburban traffic. These were the companies which had no great long-distance traffic in passengers or freight, and together with others, such as the Great Eastern or the London, Brighton and South Coast, they began to do most for suburban development.

Within the cities considerable attention was paid, therefore, to roads and road traffic. London had its Hansom Patent Safety Cabs, invented by Joseph Aloysius Hansom in 1834. The national carriage of the mid-Victorian period, the Brougham (named after a popular Lord Chancellor, Henry Brougham) was first built in the 1830s. But as the century unfolded, the transport demands of an expanding middle class, the growth of commercial activity in city centres and the widening distance between residence and work place, led to experiments and development in the field of public transport.

As early as 1829 public vehicles had appeared in London. Following experiments in Paris, George Schillibeer operated a service between Paddington and the Bank, four times a day at one shilling a time. His two vehicles called *The Schillibeer* and *The Omnibus* were each drawn by three horses abreast. There were improvements with steam carriages developed by Walter Hancock who ran a number of services in the 1830s in London. The largest vehicle was a 22 seater and, over the years, many thousands of passengers were carried. But by 1840 the first generation of steam carriages had come to an end, in most cases the mechanical problem being machine parts which were unable to withstand the strain of long or repeated journeys.

Meanwhile, horse omnibuses improved in service and comfort and, as a sign of social change, it soon became respectable for ladies to travel this way. In 1856 a number of small omnibus companies were absorbed by a French Company with offices in Paris and London, the Compagnie Génèral des Omnibus de Londres. The fleet was rapidly expanded offering more regular services, and the Company was registered as an English concern under the name of the London General Omnibus Company. In 1856, 800 omnibuses were on the streets of London.

But city centre congestion increased rapidly and could only be resolved by other forms of transport. The Metropolitan Railway development and the construction of the Inner Circle saved the day for London in the 1870s. The building of the first underground railway had been sanctioned in 1854. Twenty-one miles long, it was to be of basic importance in maintaining the concentration of activity in the heart of the city. An obvious contrast is with Paris, for it was precisely at this time that much of the French capital was being demolished to accomodate traffic and highway improvements. In 1862 Paris con-

This photograph of the overhead railway in Liverpool was taken in 1952, a few years before the railway was dismantled. The line was a prominent and rather ugly structure running parallel to the waterfront. The Liver Building can be seen in the background.

tained 66,500 houses, and when the construction of the boulevards planned by Napoleon III and Baron Haussmann was carried out, 27,000 of them were removed (15).

We should also note the part played by horse drawn trams which appeared in the 1860s. The first line opened in London from Marble Arch to Notting Hill Gate and subsequent improvements were to offer a very cheap service to the city worker. But London remained primarily a bus city and it was the provincial towns which became more notable for tramway services: Leeds, Plymouth, Hull, Glasgow, Liverpool and Bolton all had tram services dating from the 1870s.

We should naturally look to London for the most dramatic urban transport developments on account of the congestion and circulation problems presented by such a huge city. The 1890s proved to be the decade for the inauguration of the tube railway and the coming of electric traction. The Metropolitan Railway had opened in 1863 and the Inner Circle was completed in 1884; it had extended west to

Hammersmith, north to Harrow, and east to Whitechapel and New Cross. But the shallow tunnel construction disturbed streets and property and deeper tube tunnels were necessary. Engineers P.W. Barlow and J.H. Greathead had already demonstrated the possibilities of building a railway in a continuous underground tunnel. Their Tower Subway, opened in 1870, conveyed passengers by cable traction under the Thames in a tube 2 metres in diameter. Their new method became known as the 'Greathead Shield', which allowed circular tunnels to be built comparatively easily beneath London. The City and South London Electric Railway was constructed from the Monument to Stockwell and inaugurated in 1890 by the Prince of Wales. In 1898 the Waterloo and City Railway terminating at the Bank was opened. The Central London tube (Bank to Shepherds Bush) was opened in 1900 (16).

Outside London, spectacular railway developments extended to Liverpool and Glasgow. In Liverpool an overhead railway opened between 1893 and 1896, carried above the streets on viaducts and an iron framework. The line closed at the end of 1956. In Glasgow an underground railway opened in 1896 running on a circular route in tube tunnels and operated by cable haulage.

Developments were taking place, too, with regard to trams. Until 1877 all tramway motive-power was provided by horses; but in that year, after a number of experiments, a regular service of steam trams was begun by the Vale of Clyde Tramways at Govan. Another system of mechanical haulage was by cable, successfully employed in Edinburgh from 1889. The city became unique in Britain for adopting cable working for its whole (city and suburban) tramway system (17).

In addition to horse trams, electric power came into use. Short stretches of electric railway were built at Brighton, Blackpool and Ryde in 1884–5, and other stretches were introduced in Leeds in 1891. The innovation spread rapidly in all the great cities and municipalities followed the lead given by Bradford in 1889 when the town established its own electric power station for its own tramways and other public services. Visually, in the urban scene, a new feature was introduced: fixed equipment such as poles and wires, which sixty years later a host of amenity socieites was only too glad to remove.

In the meantime, developments in private transport began with the bicycle. The first cycles appeared on the road in 1869. They had wooden wheels and iron tyres and were soon replaced by a type known as the Ordinary — the high bicycle with the seat 1½ metres from the ground. This in turn was displaced by the Safety Cycle, with rubber tyres, following work by H.J. Lawson of Coventry. But it was the internal combustion engine which was to create the real revolution in urban road traffic. In the 1880s bearers of now famous names such as

Panhard, Peugot, Benz, Daimler and others, were experimenting with the early motor car and producing viable prototypes. The passage of the Locomotive and Highways Act, 1896, which repealed earlier legislation, removed speed restrictions (there had been no need for cars to be preceded by a person carrying a red flag for some years) and allowed engineering enterprise to flourish in the search for faster and more reliable machines. We shall see the enormous changes that were to take place in a later chapter.

SUBURBAN DEVELOPMENT

The cycle, tram and bus, and increasingly the train, allowed people to live further from their work than ever before. As population numbers increased, the geographical spread of towns became a marked urban feature of the second half of the 19th century and beyond. The leap-frogging suburban cycle of selection, settlement and later partial rejection, by a widening band of middle class people, was the process by which a growing urban population was redistributed. A comparable activity still sustains the growth dynamics of the city today.

In London, suburban growth was spectacular, and the outer ring of Greater London suburbs grew by about 50 per cent in each of the three intercensal periods between 1861 and 1891, and by 45 per cent in the decade 1891 to 1901. In the provinces too the same pattern was revealed, although the impetus came at different times in different towns. Asa Briggs has catalogued the changes in his history of Birmingham. For example, Moseley changed from 'a pretty little village with a green, low-roofed old fashioned houses, and a parish church dominating the landscape' to 'an exclusive suburb with large villas of red brick, regular train services into Birmingham, and trams'. On the other hand, nearby Small Heath changed within a generation 'from a scattered hamlet into a town as big as the Oxford or Worcester of its day'; the building of the B S A factory there encouraged rapid urbanization. Rapid growth was the feature in other Birmingham suburbs: Handsworth expanded its population from 11,000 in 1861 to 70,000 in 1911; Erdington from 2,600 in 1881 to 32,500 in 1911 (18).

Suburban spread was associated with social motivations. The right suburban address was a social requirement. 'The momentous but purposeful recital of Debrett—Burlington, Montague, Addington, Melbourne, Devonshire, Bedford and so on', as H.J. Dyos puts it in his study of Camberwell, had been a characteristic of pre- and early Victorian suburban addresses (19). The later Victorian period was no exception in the search by a widening section of the middle class for accommodation of style and size in an acceptable district. The forces behind suburban development were complex, the consequences of

Left: Bellefield Avenue, Dundee, 1895. The Scottish cities produced some very distinctive examples of robust, good quality residential apartments for the middle class. The apartments were generally spacious and, if well maintained, provided quite desirable accommodation. The property shown in this photograph is still in use today.

Below: Park Circus, Glasgow. At the most fortunate end of the housing and social spectrum was accommodation for the well-to-do. The larger cities with their sizeable business groups all had districts devoted to fashionable residences: the sea captain's houses in Plymouth, the jute magnate's mansions in Dundee, and the fine houses in Edgbaston (Birmingham), Headingly (Leeds) or Sefton Park (Liverpool). These properties in Park Circus, Glasgow, were and still are houses of distinction. Today they are included by the City Council in conservation plans.

many interrelating factors, but one of the mainsprings was a powerful social dictate. This was largely concerned with first, the quest for social exclusiveness, and second, with the growing convention of the single-family dwelling. Socially distinctive property and equally distinctive neighbourhoods represented important attractions in suburban development.

The speed and nature of suburban development was naturally conditioned by the growth of population, both by natural increase and inward migration. Where population increase was most rapid, so too was suburban spread with a leap-frogging situation developing with people moving from one growing suburb to another. London was the one city of the country where suburban development was most marked, but all provincial towns, where growth was to be seen at all in terms of new building to house more people, showed evidence in some degree of the phenomenon.

Residential expansion was only made possible, however, through a wider availability of capital and land, and, in order to meet the demand, the 19th century saw important changes in this direction. With regard to capital we should mention in particular the importance of building societies and freehold land societies. Building societies had been in existence since about 1775. First they were concentrated in the Midlands and North, but by the middle of the century, when they numbered about 2000, they were more equally distributed throughout the country. They were to have immense importance in making capital for private house building available for an ever expanding section of the community.

Freehold land estates were also important for housing development. After the Reform Bill of 1832 the country franchise included all people holding a £2.00 freehold. For some time freehold land societies were political weapons as, for example, during the anti-Corn Law agitation of the early 1840s, but after mid-century they became important means of providing cheap freehold building plots in the suburbs.

Towards the end of the century there was also an influential movement for co-partnership housing. The first example was the Tenant Co-operations Ltd founded in 1888, but real progress was only made after the turn of the century in association with interest in the garden city movement.

At the same time there were significant changes in legal circumstances affecting the tenure of land and the development of estates. From the 1840s onwards, the number of land owners who could legally consider the granting of building leases was increased by changes in law relating to settled estates and to church and ecclesiastical land. Additionally, the law relating to building development was being clarified by both general Acts and by a number of judicial decisions.

The pace and scale of suburban development was also facilitated by the rise of the speculative builder. The Census of 1851 published data on employers, the only census of the century to do so. It was clear that the large contracting firm had made its appearance: nine firms in London, for example, described themselves as 'builders' employing 200 or more men each. But, on the other hand, only 57 out of 739 building firms employed 50 persons or more. As H.J. Dyos remarks, the most impressive feature of the situation was 'not that the few were so large, but that the many were so small' (20). But the building boom of the late 1870s and early 1880s in London encouraged a rise in size of firms and in the last decade the really large firm came into its own: Watts of Catford, for example, built over 400 houses in south east London in 1899 alone.

It is important to recognize however that, whatever the new circumstances of the 19th century, there were some essential features of suburban spread which had characterized the growing city for many centuries. Indeed, Lewis Mumford asserts that 'the suburb becomes visible almost as early as the city itself, and perhaps explains the ability of the ancient town to survive the insanitary conditions that prevailed within its walls' (21). Throughout history there have been individual people or groups of communities who settled on the outskirts of towns, with the attractions of hygenic superiority and the possibility of relative isolation. However, it was the *mass* movement of people into suburban areas that characterized the 19th century. This remains a feature of our own times, a process of development that has broken up old urban forms, giving spatial looseness, so much in contrast with the former compactness.

We have mentioned the drive for social distinction and manifestation of social status. This was underlain throughout the 19th century by the very practical consideration of regard for health. To escape from smoke, dust and the prevalence of disease became imperative and showed itself in the demand to get away from the overcrowded town centres. An additional urge was to escape from surroundings of poverty and crime, the undesirable social features of the inner city.

The early suburbs produced a new domestic landscape of large villas which afforded restricted private solutions to the disorder of an unwholesome town. Early in the 19th century fashionable inner suburbs were developed in all the important provincial towns. Dates vary and locations differ according to terrain and the influence of land ownership, but where possible, elevated, airy districts were sought out. These have tended to determine the distribution of good quality residential districts ever since. For example, in Sheffield the higher western land was attractive: here, building leases for good houses were granted on the Broom Hall estate from 1829, the fashionable Endcliffe

Crescent dates from 1830, and from 1835 the tree lined streets of Sharrow were laid out (22). The prize, everywhere, was space, sunlight and air.

Much later in the century, more extensive building took over and the age of the middle class suburbs had arrived. The story of the development of any one is quite fascinating: how a way of life emerged from the unplanned and uncoordinated labour of many men, now long dead and forgotten; how an intricate street pattern was forced together in jigsaw style, reflecting the divided ownerships of land; how the community vested itself with its churches and chapels; how suburban shopping centres grew under the stimulus of an increasing mass market, greater affluence, the availabilty of standardized merchandise, and new methods of retail organization; and how they gained their own employment with local industries (it would be naïve to consider that suburbs simply existed on a journey to work to city centres). The growth of Camberwell has been studied by Dyos and he presents these and other aspects as part of one case study of the development of Victorian London (23). It is in such studies that we can trace the broad characteristics that governed the urban spread of the day. As an unusual example, there was the creation of Bedford Park (1877) in West London, to the design of Norman Shaw; this was a planned private experiment in suburban development which attracted considerable attention at the time, but was quite out of the mainstream of typical suburban growth.

In all the complexities of suburban development, associated transport improvement was usually a feature. Working hours were falling and daily travelling time could extend accordingly. At the same time wages and incomes were rising and the cost of daily travel could be better met. The introduction of relatively cheap public transport by tram, horse-omnibus and railway made possible suburban development at increasing distances from town centres or other places of work. The growth of Edmonton and Walthamstow in north east London was particularly associated with cheaper rail fares for workmen. The overall consequences could be seen dramatically in London by a comparison of the night and day populations of the city. Between 1871 and 1881 the night population of London fell by 32.5 per cent (74,900 to 50,500), while from 1866 to 1881, the day population rose by 53.4 per cent (170,100 to 261,000). The number of passengers carried by local railways, tramways and the two principal bus companies rose from 269,600,000 in 1881 to 847,200,000 in 1901, an increase in the average number of journeys per head from 56.6 a year to 128.7 a year. In London, artisans moved out to North Paddington, Hammersmith and Fulham, and the middle class further afield to Highgate, Hampstead, Putney, Wimbledon, Wandsworth and Brixton.

It is in the pattern of suburban expansion during the 19th century that we can detect one of the important keys to an understanding of the evolution of the Victorian city. The move to the suburbs was first taken up by the upper middle classes and last of all by the working classes, but there was no simple migration flow. Generalizing to a degree, one can see a common rationale behind the emergent pattern whereby once fashionable suburbs failed to maintain their reputations, being subject to invasion and occupation by successive inflows of lower class communities. In detail, however, the pattern is confused.

D.A. Reeder (24) has described the general pattern of development in West London during the 19th century, and, while it can be claimed that London is always unique, this sort of population movement applied to all the larger provincial cities where rapid growth was being experienced. At the beginning of the century, some of the villages that lay to the west of the built-up area of London, were already fashionable places of residence; Paddington and Kensington were particularly renowned, the latter with the added advantage of royal patronage. But other districts were more representative of solid middle class; for example, the Ladbroke district of North Kensington. But the professional and merchant classes moved west during the century, leaving pockets of very fashionable quarters behind. In this movement Ealing became a middle class residential suburb from the 1850s, but Acton had a lower social standing. The lower middle class gathered round suburban commercial centres such as Hammersmith. New transport lines encouraged the formation of communities of tradesmen, clerks and better paid artisans, as at Fulham, South Acton and Ealing. Finally, working class settlements expanded into sub-centres of employment: colonies of pig-keepers, labourers, laundry workers and railway workers became nuclei of working class districts.

Factors which affected the fortunes of particular Victorian suburbs were many and varied. There were two possible extreme situations — one where a fashionable reputation was maintained, and the other where in the space of two or three generations a cycle from new building to obsolescence was accompanied by a radical change in social occupance. Between these two, all sorts of variations were possible as successive invasions of social classes gave a certain district or estate particular characteristics.

Edgbaston, Birmingham, is a good example of a well-to-do garden suburb which has kept its style and social reputation. The owner of the Edgbaston Estate, Sir Henry Gough Calthorpe, determined to defend the area from possible industrial development, which was likely to follow from the construction of the nearby Worcester/Birmingham canal. Edgbaston became a gracious suburb, systematically developed over a lengthy period of time. It was fashionable and built for the wealthy, an image which was perpetuated by careful estate development in such a way that the long term value of the land was protected. Important instruments of control became the convenants in the building leases; these included regulations about building materials, the distances of frontages from the main road and prohibitions on the use of property which might in any way be offensive or detract from amenity. A suburban élite emerged which the Calthorpe estate office sought to protect, and the physical character of the garden suburb persists to this day.

The example of Edgbaston has not been frequently repeated, but the other end of the suburban spectrum is common enough; this is the suburban estate which has experienced a full cycle of physical life, where ageing houses are passed down through the social scale, until, through neglect and obsolescence, the area becomes ripe for redevelopment. The story of post-1945 slum clearance in almost every provincial town and city has origins in this situation.

GENERAL DEVELOPMENTS

As we have seen in this chapter, there were a number of trends during the 19th century that gave a broadly common pattern of urban development. We have considered the railway, parks and open spaces, retail trading, urban transport and suburban development. There are a number of other common features which we should also mention.

We should not, for example, forget the continuing fight for public health measures. Rather surprisingly, Chadwick's reforms did not lead to a substantial fall in crude death rates until the 1870s. The infant mortality rate, a critical expression of social health, remained more or less constant until the 20th century. But deaths from zymotic diseases, fever, smallpox, cholera, diarrhoea, all due to filth, fell sharply. The Public Health Act of 1875 compelled local Authorities to build sewage works and, as a consequence, smallpox, typhoid, typhus and cholera virtually disappeared.

An improved water supply aggravated the sewage problem because there was now more liquid waste to dispose of. But impressive progress was made. In London, from 1855 onwards, Joseph Bazalgette, Chief Engineer to the Metropolitan Board of Works, constructed 83 miles of sewers to drain the 100 square miles of the Capital. Equally important, an enormous contribution was made everywhere to aspects of urban life which we now regard as common place, by sanitary engineers such as Thomas Hawksley, Angus Smith and others (25).

It was a great step forward to move from the well and the water cart to a piped supply of drinking water. It was a development, however, not without implications; there followed, for example, a rapidly increased demand for water. Private water companies were replaced by local authorities, and by 1855 more than a dozen towns in the North were empowered to set up water undertakings. This was an aspect of 'municipal socialism' which was later followed with regard to gas. Private gas companies were more profitable than water companies and resisted longer, but by 1870, 33 towns had their own gas undertakings.

Environmental improvements continued to be made on a wide front, especially in England. In Scotland, however, the situation was noticeably different. The legislative framework which controlled Scottish cities was not the same as that controlling English ones. As a consequence of this and other factors, Geoffrey Best, writing on the Scottish Victorian city, observes that 'only in the 1860s did the general government of Scotland attain, in respect of public health, the state which England had been in since 1848, and that only in the 1890s did the Scottish laws of public health really catch up with the English' (26).

But there were surprising exceptions to this. Glasgow's Loch Katrine water scheme, completed in 1859, was with the possible exception of Liverpool's the first of the great municipal long-distance water projects. Again, Glasgow bought out the two existing private gas companies in 1869, and in 1893 was supplying a higher yielding gas than any other city except Liverpool. With Dundee, it pioneered the public lighting of private courts and common stairs. The city was also prominent in tramway development in the 1870s. The three big Scottish cities led the way in slum clearance. Their own Improvement Acts gave to Dundee in 1871, to Edinburgh in 1867 and Glasgow in 1866, powers to purchase, clear and redevelop central slum areas which only in 1875 were the Cross Acts to make generally available (see bottom of this page and also page 88).

Local municipal action was of course very much responsible for improvements of all kinds. Action taken by Birmingham, particularly during the years of Joseph Chamberlain as Mayor (1873–76), was impressive and set the pace for many other cities in the country. Asa Briggs, in his penetrating study *Victorian Cities,* has shown how the Civic Gospel was made in Birmingham. A positive radicalism emerged, based on economic and social alliance within the Town Council and the town, stimulated by religious idealism and shaped by a dissatisfaction with narrow concepts of the former scope of local government. There was a marked effect on the town's affairs. A Central Reference Library was opened in 1866. The Council purchased the Birmingham Gas, Light and Coke Company in 1874 and later the Birmingham Water Works Company. The new Council House was opened in 1884, and a new Central Reference Library the year following.

It was in this context that in 1875 Chamberlain's great improvement scheme was started. Richard Cross, the Home Secretary, formulated the Artisans' Dwellings Act of 1875 which provided for the compulsory acquisition by specified local authorities of insanitary areas within their boundaries. After acquisition, properties could be demolished, new houses built and general improvements carried out. In Birmingham, 38 hectares were scheduled, of which the Corporation acquired 17. Building began in 1878 and an imposing new street, Corporation Street, was created, significantly altering the layout of the centre of the town.

The improvement scheme should be seen very much in the context of a general desire, not only in Birmingham but in many of the other large cities, of Victorian Corporations for projects of civic grandeur. Town Halls were show pieces of civic pride and occasions for royal openings and great jubilation, as Asa Briggs describes in Leeds, for example, in 1858, and Sheffield in 1897. The Leeds Town Hall in particular is an impressive architectural monument by any standards, covering an area of 4680 square metres, on which all the riches of Victorian England were lavished (27).

Of quite a different type from the Birmingham scheme was the much earlier improvement of the centre of Newcastle where a fruitful combination of the activities of three people, rather than a political or a reforming party, had been instrumental in town centre development. The Town Clerk, John Clayton, an estate developer, Richard Grainger and an architect and builder, John Dobson, combined to set a new

Grey Street, Newcastle upon Tyne. One of the imposing streets of the Grainger-Dobson period of planned redevelopment in Newcastle in the 1830s. This photograph, taken in 1971, brings out the fine curve of the street and the unified elevations of the buildings; the projected portico of the Theatre Royal helps to frame the column and statue of Earl Grey which commemorates the 1832 Reform Act. The buildings in Grey Street are being progressively cleaned and careful control is being kept of new shop front design and advertising. One building was even demolished and rebuilt to its original design to preserve the unified street scene.

pattern for Newcastle's central streets (28). Groups of remarkably fine buildings were built; Grey Street, where residential and commercial buildings designed with classical proportions are set on a slight curve on a steep hillside, is particularly renowned.

By 1825 Blackett Street had been erected by Grainger from the designs of another architect, Thomas Oliver, and Eldon Square from John Dobson's designs. After some delay the Common Council of the City approved Grainger's plans for what was virtually the redevelopment of the central area of the town, utilizing existing open ground and aiming to link the river side and northward extension of the town centre. The plans gave Newcastle a planned central area, with the accent not on residences, but on improved shopping facilities, an imposing market, the whole co-ordinated by fine street architecture. The work was completed by 1839.

Other striking urban features in towns throughout the country were concerned with industrial development. A good deal of manufacturing was disseminated in craft workshops and it was only in particular trades that large buildings and their chimneys exerted such a dominant visual impact. The early textile towns were cases in point. The cotton industry, for example, employed 450,000 workers by 1830, making it the biggest industrial employer in Britain. Seven mills alone employed over a thousand persons, a further twenty-three employed over 500, and another thirty-six over 250. These were large scale establishments and the towns of the north-west and elsewhere were to have a distinctive townscape. Even larger sized mills were built later in the century and in the early part of the next century. Woollen manufacture and hosiery likewise produced characteristic buildings for the local urban scene.

Coalmining, metal manufacture and chinaware also produced distinctive urban townscapes through their buildings, associated industrial plant and other visual aspects. Contemporary writers referred repeatedly to noise, smoke and dirt as well as the glare of furnaces. Other new industrial establishments marked the later Victorian city: the metropolitan laundry at the turn of the century, factories for the production of food, new style breweries, chemicals and soap factories, gas works and so on. In addition, as we have mentioned elsewhere, there were considerable changes in occupational structure as the century wore on, with marked increases in secondary manufacture, service industries — such as those dependent on communications or the retail trade — and in clerical occupations.

In certain parts of the country there were other dramatic events which moulded particular Victorian townscapes. For example, it was a major period for dock development. At Liverpool, throughout the century, the largest interval between the opening of successive docks

The harbour and docks of Dundee in 1888. Port development was the foundation of prosperity for many Victorian towns and cities. The forests of masts, the intimate scale of the docks and the close juxtaposition of water within the heart of the town created a rich variety in urban landscape. These docks in Dundee have now been closed and filled in as part of the Tay Road Bridge development.

was only twelve years, and soon a vast system of major docks and warehouses transformed the Merseyside frontage. Manchester became a major port literally overnight when, in January 1894, its ship canal was completed. At Bristol, a cramped site for the docks in the heart of the city led to new port construction downstream at Avonmouth. At Southampton, dock building was stimulated by the growth of liner traffic. At Hull, the concave bank of the Humber provided an ideal area for dock construction. At Glasgow, the canalization of the Clyde led to a distinctive landscape of docks and shipbuilding yards, as also at Belfast, Newcastle, Birkenhead and Sunderland. At London and Thames-side, a complex dock system spread down river from the original Western Dock (1805) and St Katherine Docks (1828–29) in an attempt to accommodate larger ships and a different type of trade.

Another common feature of urban development during the century was the new emphasis given to leisure pursuits in towns, and this accounted for the rise of spa towns and seaside resorts. As early as the 16th century there had been a revival of exploitation of thermal waters, first used for bathing in Roman times. Thereafter, health resorts catered for the leisured classes and increasing attention was given to medical treatment. Tunbridge Wells and Epsom had been fashionable in the 17th century and Bath in the 18th. Cheltenham and Leamington flourished in the Regency period and Buxton and Harrogate in Victorian times when they were reached by railway.

The actual development, and subsequent fortunes, of some of these towns make interesting studies in urban and social history. Physically, much depended on the detailed location of the springs because it was these that most affected the layout of the settlement. At Cheltenham, for example, the springs were widely scattered and as many as seven separate spas gained prominence with no single centre emerging. This dispersion made the town open, spacious and varied in focus. It was later growth which concentrated activity into a small area immediately north of the medieval High Street. At Leamington, the old town, with a cramped and irregular layout, lay south of the River Leam, but after 1808 a new town was constructed on the north bank with a rectangular layout incorporating squares and parades. Pump rooms and baths were sited near to the river where a number of springs were discovered in close proximity. Hotels were built in the new town and gardens laid out immediately north of the river. Harrogate, on the other hand, was quite different. There was a High and a Low Harrogate, two villages which remained quite separate until after the opening of the railway through open land between them in 1862. The former was the social and commercial centre; the latter, with a provision of springs, the medical centre.

The 19th century also saw the rise of the seaside holiday town. Sea bathing took on a new popularity. Virtues were seen in fresh sea air. Outdoor leisure centred on the beach, the seaside promenade and the pier became the base of a new industry. Seaside towns catering for mass enjoyment became the expression of a new age and changing society just as the assembly rooms of the spa towns had been in their provision for elegant leisure for a privileged minority. The Victorian pier was the most obvious urban feature. What was initially the product of the pleasure steamer, with its need for a landing place, grew, in fact, into a recreation street with its complement of pavilions, restaurants and theatres. The individual fortunes of the seaside town bore a direct relationship to the whims and fashions of the day, but, more generally, we can see the development of the resort as a consequence of the extension of leisure time in Victorian society and the growth of family incomes. The holiday trade for the masses was one of the most obvious products of a rising standard of living. More dramatically the seaside town depended on the arrival of the railway, which provided the possibility of day excursions from the inland towns to the coastal resorts (Thomas Cook's first organized excursion, in 1846, from Loughborough to Leicester, was the fore-runner of this sort of activity). Some seaside towns rose from virtually nothing, apart from a natural resource such as a dune coast or a fisherman's hamlet. As an example of the former, Southport in Lancashire became an early favourite and in 1851 had a population of more than 4,000, twice that of Blackpool. On the other hand, on Thames-side, Southend grew from the little settlement of Prittlewell. Other resorts were larger; for example, Scarborough (13,000 in 1851) with its old established spa trade.

Hamilton Terrace, Leamington Spa. A scene of Regency leisure in a flourishing spa town. Notice the private park and the setting of the fashionable houses.

Waterloo Place, Leamington Spa, 1970; an example of how the architectural treasures of an earlier age are being preserved in a 20th-century setting.

Above: Valley Gardens, Harrogate, about 1850, before the railway reached the town. Notice the relative simplicity in the life of the people of Low Harrogate suggested in this engraving.

Below: The Royal Pump Room and Sulphur Well, Harrogate, 1890. After forty years there is a very different 'feel' about Harrogate, both socially and in terms of the town's physical appearance.

Above: A Victorian photograph of the Pier, Southend on Sea. The Victorian pier was a seaside recreation street catering for very different social needs from the days of the Regency and early Victorian spa towns. This photograph, taken towards the end of the 19th century, shows the full complement of late-Victorian pier attractions: the seaside walk, the pavilions, seats, slot machines, refreshment kiosks and landing stage.

Left: This photograph of the sands, Southend on Sea, taken towards the end of the 19th century, shows how mass, seaside-oriented Victorian leisure had come into its own. Most activity was focused on the promenade and the sands.

PARTICULAR HISTORIES

We have reviewed some of the broad, underlying trends which gave a common pattern to urban development throughout the century. Nevertheless, each town or city possessed its own characteristics and there were always particular circumstances or situations to take into account. Hence many individual courses of events ensued. Much of the fascination of urban history comes from unexpected turning points, perhaps associated with particular people or companies, or with quirks of land ownership. A few examples will suggest their variety.

The development of Llandudno in North Wales, shows the part played by an enlightened developer, anxious to maintain the good value of his estate. Before 1840 there existed simply a straggling village below Llandudno Mountain and Great Orme's Head. The bulk of the surrounding land was owned by the Mostyn family and when the common land fronting the broad sweep of Llandudno Bay was enclosed during the 1840s, 344 out of 385 hectares went to Edward Mostyn as Lord of the Manor. A new town was laid out as a resort, in grid form. Building regulations were enforced by the Town Commissioners, of whom the first chairmen were the Mostyns. Much of the town's present character stems from this time, particularly the paternalist efforts to maintain land and property values. Overcrowding and congestion were avoided and courts and cellars ruled out; new streets were to be at least 11 metres wide. Llandudno evolved as a town built to the specifications of a prosperous Victorian suburb (29).

Another example of town development following, over a number of years, the ideas of an original designer, is Bournemouth. The new Lord of the Manor of Christchurch prepared plans for the development of his Westover estate at Bourne Mouth shortly after succeeding to the title in 1835. To add to the momentum at the time, a local architect published plans in 1838 showing a proposed layout of a 'New Marine Village of Bourne'. The Lord of the Manor died in 1842, but his attempts to create a seaside town were not forgotten. His successor was a minor, but Trustees in 1846 obtained authority by Private Act to extend their powers of sale and exchange and of granting building licences. What became the town of Bournemouth rapidly outgrew the administrative capacity of the parish of Holdenhurst in which it was first situated. The Bournemouth Improvement Act of 1856 overcame this by providing for Commissioners empowered to carry out improvements and to build a pier. In due time the Commissioners' boundary was extended to Boscombe Chine and virtually the whole of the Bournemouth sea front was brought under the control of one Authority. Bournemouth was, in fact, under the control of the Commissioners for 34 years until a Municipal Borough Charter was granted in 1890. During this time the railway came to Christchurch in 1862 and to Bournemouth in 1870, and the success of the resort was assured (30).

Such single-minded development presents a fairly straight-forward story. Rather more complicated are the instances of towns which grew from a number of different influences. The history of Barrow is a case in point (31). A very influential person in the area of Barrow was James Ramsden who was associated with all major development proposals over the first thirty years or so of the town's history. Ramsden came to Barrow in 1846 at the age of 23 as Manager of the Engineering Department of the Furness Railway. He became Secretary, General Manager and then Director of the Railway Company. His vision was of a prosperous town of 100,000 people, and he found backing from the Dukes of Devonshire and Buccleugh and other wealthy land-owners. Over the years he persuaded them to finance dock extensions, the manufacture of iron and steel, shipbuilding and jute manufacture.

High-grade iron ore was discovered nearby in 1850, and blast furnaces were erected in 1859. Under Ramsden's influence a grid-iron of uniform streets grew up. The houses were soundly built, there was adequate sanitation and the streets were wide. In the 1860s, Barrow became a centre of immigration with labour for the iron industry arriving from Cornwall, Staffordshire, Scotland and Ireland. After 1870, the emphasis was on shipbuilding and heavy engineering. Vickers developed Walney and a new suburb, Vickerstown, was built as a marine garden city. In 1851 the population of Barrow was 448; Old Barrow and Hindpool were other small settlements. By 1881 the population had reached 47,000, but by then the tide of immigration had stopped as industrial expansion came to an end. The future, because of Barrow's geographical isolation and its economic dependence on vulnerable industries, was never quite as rosy as Ramsden had hoped. But he left his mark on the appearance of the town as well as on its economic history, not so much from attention to housing, but rather because of his grandiose notions concerning avenues and squares. Ramsden's plan for the town laid great emphasis on wide roads, imposing facades, dignified buildings and noble vistas. Some of this grand design was accomplished, but later development failed to match earlier intentions.

The early development of Barrow, then, has a common persistent thread from the contribution of one person. Other towns have experienced the contributions of many people and a range of economic stimuli. Middlesbrough, for example, is another instance of a 19th century creation where the urban record has similarities to Barrow, but the results are quite different.

The success of the Stockton and Darlington Railway had suggested the likely profitability of the export of coal from Tees-side. In 1828

Joseph Pease of the Railway Company selected Port Darlington as a
new dock terminus, 9½ kilometres downstream from Stockton (32). In
1830 a grid-iron town was built on 13 hectares, centred on a church and
a market, and in due course development of no great quality filled in
the available plots. In 1850 the first iron quarry was opened in the
nearby Cleveland Hills, and rapid urban growth began to take place
under the stimulus of iron manufacture. By this time the old town had
grown to a population of 5,500, but with the arrival of the iron masters
a dramatic rise occurred. By 1871 the population was 40,000. The old
town was engulfed in a sea of shoddy development. Subsequent
industrial development has continued to expand Middlesbrough, and
the new borough of Tees-side, of which the old town is part, includes
industry from steel to chemicals, in areas far removed from Pease's old
estate. The contrasts with Barrow are striking: one town has expanded
greatly, the other has not; one town embodied a reputation for quality
of planned development, but the other failed in this direction.

Llandudno, Bournemouth, Barrow and Middlesborough were
essentially 19th century towns where the pattern of development
conformed remarkably to the effects of particular contributions, either
personal intervention or economic fortunes. In already established
towns with a dynamism of their own from a variety of influences, it was
less usual for the pattern of change to be radically affected by single
events or episodes. But there were examples of sudden transformations, as for instance when land tenure changed dramatically.

Belfast in the middle of the century reflects this situation. The city's
largest land-owner, the second Marquis of Donegal ran up great debts
during his extravagant lifetime. Three years after his death the full
extent of his debts became apparent and his estate was encumbered by
£408,000. To meet this liability the leasehold reversions on his
property throughout Belfast were sold through the Incumbered Estates
Court to the people of the city. Belfast was converted almost overnight
from a town of tenants with short leases to one of freeholders, and
these transformed tenures increased the rapid rate of building in the
city over the second half of the century (33).

A rather different example can be seen in the peculiarity of
Nottingham. By 1831 the town had reached a population of more than
50,000. It was severely overcrowded because only limited extensions
of the built-up area had been possible by virtue of the persistent
opposition of the burgesses and freemen of the city to the enclosure of
the surrounding common lands. These comprised the Sand Fields and
Clay Field to the north, and the East Croft, the West Croft and the
Meadows which lay to the south; in addition there was the Forest and
the Duke of Newcastle's park. These were formidable barriers to urban
growth, only broken following the Nottingham Enclosure Act of 1845,

which permitted the rapid spread of the town (34).

As another example, Coventry had expanded from 16,000 people in 1801 to 27,000 in 1830, but was almost encircled by pasture lands that could not be enclosed save by Act of Parliament. The principal obstruction was the Common and Michaelmas land, covering 400 hectares, over which the freemen of the city had a right of pasture; linked with this were commons covering 120 hectares as well as Cheylesmere Park belonging to the Marquis of Hertford. The freemen were a minority of the population and those freemen who actually exercised their rights were a minority again, but they held sufficient political power to prevent for many years all attempts at enclosure and the extinguishing of pasture rights (35).

Coventry from the park, 1850. The skyline of the city, with the occasional chimney, shows the beginnings of industrial development; the really striking feature, however, is the small, compact nature of the town, a sharp demarcation from the surrounding countryside and the numerous church spires that dominate the scene. But the town was to change rapidly: this drawing was made from the site of what is today the railway station, and the more modern photograph on pages 234—5 emphasizes the city's total transformation over the past 120 years.

These are some of the examples which provide the individual background to particular towns. But we can repeat a previous observation, namely that in spite of the effect of individual and perhaps unique situations, the processes of urban change during the century followed remarkably similar patterns forged by trends and developments, the most important of which we have outlined in this chapter. It was a period when the basic urban structure took shape, fixing commercial uses in central areas and selecting broad distributions of

residential and industrial uses and open spaces, a structure frequently
little altered even today.

The growth of Leeds suggests a typical course of events (36, 37).
Its population of 16,000 in 1771 was almost doubled by 1801 and
then more than doubled in the next thirty years. Old Leeds, for long
almost completely confined to the north side of the River Aire, began
to lose its physical identity, and neighbouring townships were linked
by continuous development. By the first quarter of the 19th century
three main areas were expanding: a congested area of yards and streets
formed an eastward extension; westwards, the developments of the old
manorial park, with designs for elegant squares and terraces, had been
succeeded by houses for the well-to-do on the hill slopes of Little
Woodhouse; southwards, the land towards the townships of Hunslet
and Holbeck was gradually filled in with housing.

During the rest of the century the basic structure of Leeds evolved.
The area covered by the late 18th century town, with its rectangular
street pattern, gradually emerged as a compact shopping and market
area. Industry became concentrated in three areas: heavy engineering
by the river and canal and near the railways; in the Meanwood Valley,
tanneries, dyeworks and wholesale clothing factories developed; there
was heavy and light engineering in Hunslet and Holbeck and
engineering and textile mills in Armley and Wortley. Good class
residential areas spread to high ground to the north, for example,
Headingly, Chapletown and Roundhay where there was a popular
urban park. Working class housing spread west, east and south, with
particular housing areas interwoven with factories and warehouses
along the Meanwood Valley and in south Leeds.

It was during these formative years of the 19th century then that
towns and cities in Britain assumed a form that we readily recognize
today. There were substantial environmental improvements as part of
sanitary and public health reform. Central areas had their shopping
streets, banking and commercial districts, and public buildings
including libraries and town halls. Overall, the structure of land use was
developing into a settled pattern — residential, industrial and open
space in the form of the occasional park or cemetery. Congestion,
reflected in high population densities, overcrowding and traffic
dislocation, was a key note. But the pattern was never static, and the
forces behind suburban expansion indicated the likely characteristic
for the next century — dispersal instead of centrality.

References

(1) *See* Kellett, John R., *The Impact of Railways on Victorian Cities*, Routledge, 1969.
(2) *Op cit.* Kellett, John R.
(3) *Op cit.* Kellett, John R.
(4) Simmons, Jack, *Transport: a visual history of modern Britain*, Vista Books, 1962.

(5) Hudson, Kenneth, *The Early Years of the Railway Community in Swindon*, Transport History, 1968. Reprint David & Charles, 1969.

(6) *See* Simmons, Jack.

(7) *See* Chadwick, George F., *The Park and the Town*, The Architectural Press, 1966.

(8) Eversley, Lord, *Commons, Forests and Footpaths*, Cassell & Co., 1910.

(9) Davis, Dorothy, *A History of Shopping*, Routledge, 1966.

(10) *See* Jeffreys, James B., *Retail Trading in Britain 1850 — 1950*, Cambridge University Press, 1954.

(11) Mathias, Peter, *Retailing Revolution*, Longmans, 1967.

(12) Adburgham, Alison, *Shops and Shopping*, Allen & Unwin, 1964.

(13) Copeland, John, *Roads and Their Traffic 1750–1850*, David & Charles, 1968.

(14) *Op cit* Simmons, Jack.

(15) Rasmussen, Steen Eiler, *London: The Unique City*, Jonathan Cape, 1948.

(16) Sherrington, C.E.R., *100 Years of Inland Transport 1830 — 1933*, Reprint, Frank Cass, 1969.

(17) *Op cit.,* Simmons, Jack.

(18) Briggs, Asa, *History of Birmingham* Vol.II, Borough and City 1865–1938, Oxford University Press, 1952.

(19) Dyos, H.J., *Victorian Suburb: a study of the growth of Camberwell*, Leicester University Press, 1961.

(20) Dyos, H.J., *Speculative Builders and Developers of Victorian London*, Victorian Studies, Vol.XI, No. 4, Summer 1968.

(21) Mumford, Lewis, *The City in History*, Secker and Warburg, 1961, Pelican, 1966.

(22) Walton, Mary, *Sheffield: its Story and its Achievement*, Sheffield Telegraph and Star, 1949.

(23) *Op. cit.,* Dyos, H.J., (*Victorian Suburb*).

(24) Reeder, D.A., *A Theatre of Suburbs: some patterns of development in West London, 1801 — 1911*, in 'The Study of Urban History' (Ed.) H.J. Dyos, Edward Arnold, 1968.

(25) *See* Armytage, W.H.G., *A Social History of Engineering*, Faber, 1961.

(26) Best, Geoffrey, *The Scottish Victorian City*, Victorian Studies, Vol. XI, No.3, March 1968.

(27) Briggs, Asa, *Victorian Cities*, Odhams Press 1963, Pelican, 1968.

(28) Wilkes, Lyall and Dodds, Gordon, *Tyneside Classical*, John Murray, 1964.

(29) Carter, H., *A Decision-making Approach to Town Plan Analysis: a case study of Llandudno*, in 'Urban Essays: Studies in the Geography of Wales', Carter H. and Davies W.K.D., Longman, 1970.

(30) Young, David S., *The Story of Bournemouth*, Robert Hale Ltd, 1957.

(31) Barnes, F., *Barrow and District 1951*, 2nd edition, Barrow-in-Furness Corporation, 1968.

(32) Bell, Colin and Rose, *City Fathers: the early history of town planning in Britain*, The Cresset Press, 1969.

(33) Brett, C.E.B., *Buildings of Belfast*, Weidenfeld and Nicolson, 1967.

(34) Edwards, K.C., *The Geographical Development of Nottingham*, in 'Nottingham and its Region', British Association for the Advancement of Science, 1966.

(35) Prest, John, *The Industrial Revolution in Coventry*, Oxford University Press, 1960.

(36) Sigsworth, E.M., *The Industrial Revolution*, in 'Leeds and its Region', British Association for the Advancement of Science, Leeds, 1967.

(37) Fowler, F.J., *Urban Renewal, 1918–1966*, in 'Leeds and its Region', British Association for the Advancement of Science, Leeds, 1967.

5 Housing improvement and social concern

In this chapter we look at other forces which helped to shape the Victorian city, particularly in the second half of the 19th century. We must look at housing and the continuing search for improved conditions, at the increased attention to social problems, and the work of the social reformers, especially in their contribution to what became known as 'model villages'. All can be conveniently examined together. It was, after all, through the search for better housing and a better urban environment that social problems were first brought into the open, stimulating the great social reforms of the age.

Town planning stems from two main sources: the work of the architect and designer in their search for the ideal city, and the work of the community builder in his search for an ideal society (1). Both these human drives have been in evidence throughout man's history and have contributed to the creation of many beautiful urban settings, and the stimulation of ideals of social progress. In the town planning movement these two came together in a continuous and positive attempt to shape an urban environment and provide for community needs. Town planning, as we know it in its comprehensive form today, has its most obvious antecedents in the last two decades of the 19th century. This was the period when a number of community issues coincided: concern over housing conditions led to a recognition of the need to intervene more positively on behalf of the working classes to provide better housing; there was a renewal of social enquiry and agitation; there were hosts of practical experiments by reformers, and the ever-increasing size of cities, particularly London, showed no signs of abating. Out of this maelstrom there emerged a positive shift of direction in housing and urban affairs.

HOUSING

It is important to remember that, by and large, the vast majority of builders during the second half of the 19th century operated on a very small scale indeed (see page 65). The smaller, cheaper types of houses were usually built by men who had saved a little money and who bartered their labour for materials. The bricklayer, the joiner, the glazier and the painter combined to speculate in cheap house construction. Not until the 1870s onwards were there large scale operations by speculative builders, and these were on open sites in middle-class suburbs.

It is true that the 19th century produced a number of people who were famous for building, but they were confined to the builders of warehouses and mills like Rennie and Fairburn, and a few master-builders like Thomas Cubitt, for example, who were exceptional in their organization and deployment of vast resources.

During this period, the rise in dwelling standards (house construction, provision of essential services, environmental setting and space allocation) was accompanied by a rise in standards of household comfort. In passing, it is worth reflecting on the changing demand for furniture and fittings, as this puts into context the standard of living at the time. Sydney Pollard affords useful evidence of the situation in Sheffield (2). In that city, by the middle 1860s, the top ranks of the skilled local artisans had become accustomed to having carpets and wallpaper; some possessed a piano, pictures or statuettes; a well stuffed hair cloth sofa and chairs to match were thought indispensable. By the 1890s most of these items had diffused among all but the poorest people. Floor coverings and curtains became notable additions. The flock or feather bed had replaced the palliasse; cheap sofas or couches were usual possessions and leather covered chairs were becoming popular. Sewing machines and pianos could be bought by instalment payments.

But more importantly, the main features of the mid-century concern the increased public intervention in the question of housing standards and the provision of working class housing. It is necessary to pay some attention to progress on these fronts. A Royal Sanitary Commission was appointed in 1868. It issued its Report in 1871, criticizing the permissive character of the provisions of the existing sanitary code, the lack of adequate inspection, the friction caused by the presence of numerous *ad hoc* bodies, and the absence of a strong system of central control. Immediate reforms came with the creation of the Local Government Board in 1871, and the passing of the Public Health Act, 1872, and the Sanitary Law Amendment Act, 1874. Both these Acts and others were repealed and consolidated by the Public Health Act, 1875, which was to form an essential foundation for public health legislation for sixty years.

Of immediate relevance was the fact that the Acts of 1872 and 1875 gave a public health service administered for the first time over the whole country. England was mapped out into sanitary districts, urban and rural. Powers were provided for the proper regulation of the construction of buildings: urban authorities were empowered to regulate the construction of new streets and new buildings by making and enforcing byelaws. Some cities already had their own byelaws limiting street widths and such matters as the heights of buildings, but it was not until the 1875 Act that general permission to make building byelaws was extended over the whole country (in the provinces that is, as this power already applied to the metropolis). But even as a result of later legislation, the Public Health Acts Amendment Act, 1890, it still did not become *compulsory* for all local Authorities to make building byelaws, and the situation, because of local laxity, was far from perfect. But nevertheless the 1875 legislation did have an important impact on the urban scene because of the strict requirements for building which standardized appearances: the monotonous byelaw street is now a symbol of late Victorian residential areas.

While progress was made on this front there were particular problems still largely outstanding, such as the increasing difficulty of providing houses for those critically in need. By the middle of the century it had become clear that building houses for the working class was an uneconomic venture for capital, and, as a result, the rate of interest charged on building loans was very high. The proper housing of the working classes was an increasingly pressing problem and its solution came to be a major feature of housing policies.

A recent photograph of 19th-century housing in the Green Lane district of Bradford. A good deal of late 19th-century housing was solid and well built giving new standards of open space and sanitation for skilled artisans (perhaps working at the mill in the distance), shopkeepers and clerks. Notice the front gardens and the slight touch of distinction given by the small canopies over the doors.

In the private sector, philanthropic housing associations were formed to meet the problem. These were established chiefly in London where the problem numerically was most pressing, but they appeared in the provincial cities too, for example, in Manchester, Leeds, Bristol and Newcastle (3). The Metropolitan Association for Improving the Dwellings of the Industrious Classes had been founded in 1841 and the Society for the Improvement of the Condition of the Labouring Classes in 1844. These provided dwellings which ensured certain minimum standards with rents lower than prevailing market conditions would have permitted. Numerous other bodies followed, for example the Peabody Trust founded by George Peabody in 1862 and the Improved Industrial Dwellings Company founded by Sir Sydney Waterlow in 1863. Other societies operating in London at this time included the Marylebone Association, the London Labourers' Dwelling Society Limited, the Highgate Dwelling Company and the Strand Building Company. Many of these were small; at the end of the century the largest housing association was the Artisans', Labourers' and General Dwellings Company Limited, which had begun operations in 1868 and was building on sites of from 16—40 hectares. Although their numerical contribution to the total housing problem was relatively small in terms of families actually housed, and while they failed to tackle some of the residual housing problems, for example in their failure to house the very poor, the societies and associations were nonetheless important in drawing attention to an ever present problem. Reformers such as Octavia Hill were prominent in exerting personal influence, and political opinion was gradually shaped towards recognition of the need for intervention.

Action remained almost entirely in the private sector until the last decade of the century. The Labouring Classes Lodging Houses Act of 1851 permitted borough councils and local Boards of Health to build lodging houses for artisans, but in the first thirty years, only Huddersfield, Liverpool and Nottingham made any use of the powers and then only in a very reluctant way. It was not until 1890 that this legislation was re-enacted with amendments; this was the Housing of the Working Classes Act of that year.

A related aspect of residential improvement was the clearance of unfit housing. Some local Authorities had novel powers from private Acts of Parliament, but by and large there was little concerted action for redevelopment until the last two decades of the century when new legislation provided powers of compulsion to clear unhealthy areas. There were two sets of measures. First there were those which permitted local Authorities to compel the owner of an insanitary house to demolish or repair it at his own expense. These were known as the Torrens Acts, from the name of the private member who promoted the

Fish Street and Coutties Wynd, Dundee, 1886. The four Scottish boroughs had markedly worse housing conditions than was normal in England. Poverty and squalor went with a harsh and depressing urban environment.

first of the series, the Artisans' and Labourers' Dwelling Act, 1868. Secondly there were the Cross Acts which permitted local Authorities to prepare reconstruction schemes for areas of insanitary housing. These were named after the Home Secretary who was responsible for the first of them, the Artisans' and Labourers' Dwellings Improvement Act, 1875.

Both sets of legislation, entirely permissive until 1885, had as their object the maintenance of an adequate standard of working class housing. From the point of view of present day town planning they are of some significance because with the Cross Acts came the possibility that local Authorities could prepare new layout plans for certain areas.

Today this function is commonplace. Nationally, only limited achievements were recorded; we have already noted Birmingham's improvement scheme under Joseph Chamberlain (see page 70). In addition to these projects, there was also the rehousing of displaced persons following public and private constructional projects which affected densely populated districts. Vexed questions of compensation arose, and some authorities prepared plans only to withdraw them on learning of the cost of the exercise. But it was a start, and the vast reconstruction schemes of Britain in the post-1945 period can be traced to these modest beginnings.

While it is, therefore, true that important improvements to housing conditions were recorded as the century went on, deplorable conditions persisted in the larger towns, and especially those which had seen rapid growth earlier in the century. A description of Dundee, for example, at the time of the Public Health (Scotland) Act, 1867, makes far from pleasant reading (4). The town was wholly devoid of sanitation and there was no proper supply of water for domestic, culinary or flushing purposes. The water supply was limited and derived entirely from natural springs. There was appalling overcrowding and between 200 and 300 underground cellars were being used as homes. Piggeries were scattered throughout the town, even bedrooms, cellars and attics being used as stys. Smallpox, typhus and typhoid or gastric fevers were serious menaces. Conditions in Scotland were, in general, worse than elsewhere, but even so, in England, urban sanitary improvements were necessary, and new legislation was demanded.

Overgate, Dundee, 1898. In the tightly knit 19th-century city the poorest residential quarters were cheek by jowl with the central commercial and shopping district. The Overgate has now been demolished to make way for a newly redeveloped shopping precinct.

An examination of death rate statistics over the last century gives some indication of the tremendous improvements which have taken place in medical health. Attention to better housing conditions has played an important part. In 1870 the death rate in England and Wales expressed as deaths per thousand persons was 22.9 Consistent reductions have taken place since: a fall to 18.2 in 1900 accelerated to 13.5 in 1910. Since 1930, apart from fluctuations in the war years, the figure has fallen below 12, almost half what it was in the middle of the 19th century. Similar improvements are recorded in figures of infant mortality. In 1870 there were 160 infant deaths per thousand live births. In 1900 the figure was still as high as 154, but from then on substantial reductions were achieved: 1910, 105 per thousand; 1920, 80 and 1960, 22 per thousand.

The Public Health Act, 1875, was one of the landmarks in the second half of the 19th century in housing legislation and urban affairs. But this was overshadowed by the Royal Commission on the Housing of the Poor, appointed in 1884 to enquire, as its title suggests, into the housing conditions of the working classes. The Commission, under the chairmanship of Sir Charles Dilke, reported in six volumes in 1885. It recommended a wide extension of local Authority powers and duties, including inspection of the sanitary conditions of houses for the working classes, prevention or removal of sanitary defects, powers of compulsory purchase of land for workmen's dwelling houses, and provision of Government loans for municipal housing schemes.

These recommendations led to the Housing of the Working Classes Act, 1890. There were three main sections: one was concerned with the removal of unhealthy groups of dwellings; a second provided means for the closing and, if necessary, the demolition of separate unhealthy dwellings; and a third gave powers for new dwelling houses for the working classes to be built at the cost of public funds. This was major legislation in its effect on the course of residential development. Twentieth century housing legislation was for long built up from these three approaches.

SOCIAL REFORMERS AND VISIONARIES

The changing physical, economic and social conditions of the 19th century stimulated social agitation and the growth of radical reform movements on many fronts, including industrial, political and housing. The growth of a comprehensive movement which embraced housing improvement, the quality of town life and criteria of social justice in terms of equality of opportunity for the masses, was one which we might broadly recognize today as town planning. It was affected by an evangelical revival of religion and influenced a wide field of social activity, stimulating the activities of philanthropists in housing reform, manufacturers in the improvement of living and working conditions, and reformers in exposing various social evils of the day (5).

This was a time when individuals of conviction and drive could make tremendous achievements. Hence, in our study of 19th century urban change, we have to consider the influence of important personalities in a number of reform movements who analysed conditions, exposed injustices, agitated for improvement or experimented with new possibilities. One might ascribe this activity to a basic groundswell of humanitarianism, or democratic stirrings associated with the search for social equality, or the re-discovery of religious insights. In this complex interrelationship the catalyst for action could well have been the economic problems of the period and industrial unrest which focused attention on poverty and unemployment. Equally likely was the inevitable recognition of urban problems at this time, which were getting worse and needed radical attention; these varied from financial impoverishment of households, to the prevalence of crime and disease, and the fear in people's minds of the ever-expanding city.

Much of the social agitation was directly relevant to changing ideas about the form of cities and the nature of the urban environment. It fostered a particular attitude concerning the size of big cities and the social problems which they produced, and in so doing contributed substantially to an emergent town planning view. In this brief section we can only mention some of the more important figures. First there were those who made their contribution in the housing field; we have already noted the context of these and we shall trace the work of industrial philanthropists later. Second, there were the social enquirers, people who by patient objective study provided the raw material for more flamboyant popular figures to act upon. Finally there were the interpreters of decades of social concern: the intellectuals, the visionaries and the agitators.

The search for an improved urban environment, and particularly a higher quality of housing, was very much bound up with moral judgements of the day. James Hole was an interesting mid-Victorian writer on housing and the following passage of his from a publication of 1866 summarizes much of what was at stake for the improvement of society: 'In a dark, dirty, crowded, ill-ventilated court or back street, common sense perceives, what is confirmed by the longest experience, that it is as difficult for health or virtue to exist as for the vegetation of the tropics to thrive amid the snows of Iceland. The improvement of the material circumstances of the working classes is the condition precedent for all other efforts for raising their moral character' (6). The search for sunlight, pure air and clean water was given expression in a philosophy of environmental determinism, and this continued to be a particular driving force throughout the period.

Hole was largely concerned about working class housing conditions and naturally praised those who had secured achievements in the absence of government intervention in this field: the housing associations in London, the enterprise and energy behind Saltaire and the model dwellings of Halifax. He was quick to point out the deteriorating quality of standards which statistics of his day suggested. From the *Seventh Report of the Medical Officer on Public Health* (1864) he could point out that 821 parishes or townships in England received in 1861, as compared with 1851, a population 5½ per cent greater into house room 4½ per cent less. While newly erected dwellings among the middle and upper classes were improving in convenience, there was not at this time a corresponding improvement in dwellings of the working classes. Hole proved to be a forceful agitator concerning such questions as prevention of overcrowding and the requirements of good drainage, constant supply of good water and the abolition of back-to-back houses. From our point of view, the force of his plea is his concern for housing expressed in a wider environmental context. His uncompromising summary was that 'our manufacturing towns and villages are masses of ugliness — rows of houses with no architectural feature to please the eye; the only glimpse of nature being the narrow strip of murky sky overhead, dull and saddening' (7).

Octavia Hill was a popular figure who made her influence on the century and beyond it, through personal involvement in a number of issues which had a bearing on town life. Quite apart from her contribution to the education of girls in the later 19th century, she had particular influence in housing, the provision of social facilities and the open space movement. Important influences on her own life were F.D. Maurice, one of the leaders of the Christian Socialists, and John Ruskin who trained her to be an artist. Some details of her life show just how important her personal activites were in developing popular movements of social agitation (8).

She acquired houses and personally managed them, relieving overcrowding, and keeping contact with her tenants as part of her social work. She became involved in The London Association for the Prevention of Pauperization and Crime, later to become known as the Charity Organization Society, and reports of an enquiry by this society played a large part in the drawing up of the Artisans' Dwelling Act, 1875. She became interested in the provision of open spaces for town people and served on the executive of the Commons Preservation Society, instrumental, as we have seen, in saving important commons and woodlands in the London area (see page 50). She was concerned with the founding of the Kyrle Society, which took over the business of collecting flowers for poor homes, planting small gardens and providing entertainment for poor parishes; sub-committees were concerned with smoke abatement and the re-use of churchyards for playgrounds. During 1884 and 1885, having become a recognized authority on housing and social problems, she took over the management of property owned by the Ecclesiastical Commissioners, in Southwark. Here she was to open a community hall and later, with the foundation of Settlements (centres for social experiment) in the poorer parts of great cities, she was to become connected with the Women's University Settlement in Southwark. In her later years she was a member of the Royal Commission on the Poor Law (1905–8).

Personal involvement by committed people such as Octavia Hill was accompanied by an increasing emphasis on social enquiry and three names in the second half of the century stand out: Henry Mayhew, Charles Booth and Seebohm Rowntree. They were to confirm in horrifying detail the depth of social problems which the Victorian city had thrown up.

On Monday, 24 September 1849, an article appeared in the *Morning Chronicle* entitled 'A Visit to the Cholera Districts of Bermondsey', written by Henry Mayhew. It was to be the first of a series of articles devoted to the atrocious conditions of London's underprivileged. The *Chronicle* continued to describe the social iniquities which were rife both in England and abroad; three journalists covered northern industrial centres, the Continent and London. Mayhew's 'precise and compassionate delineations of the lives of the flotsam and jetsam of a great city' culminated nearly fifteen years later in a four-volume study, *London Labour and the London Poor*. In all he contributed 76 'letters' to the *Chronicle* during 1849 and 1850, each, in the words of John Bradley, a recent commentator on Mayhew's work, 'a grim and frequently poignant picture of deprivation and despair as Mayhew extracts tale after tale from coal whippers, shop tailors, food sellers, needle workers, sawyers, furniture workers, street performers, coopers and others who lived on the extreme periphery of life' (9).

While Victorian pride basked in the marvels of the Great Exhibition, this recorder of mid-century urban squalor gave undoubted impetus to social reformers in their search for improvement in housing and environmental conditions. But what was achieved was clearly not enough, and it needed Charles Booth's work, together with others, to further agitate public opinion. Mayhew's writings had been essentially impressionistic, and popular variations were to follow in the form of publications by General William Booth, of Salvation Army fame, and Andrew Mearns, a Congregational Minister. Charles Booth's work, on the other hand, was of a much more scientific character, and his enquiry culminated in the seventeen volumes of *Life and Labour of the People in London*, the first volume appearing in 1889, based on statistics he had started collecting in 1886.

Both his approach and his contribution were distinctive. Speculations on the causes of poverty had so far largely rested on individual shortcomings or moral delinquencies, notably drunkenness, but Booth demonstrated that social structure, social welfare and individual behaviour were closely interconnected. Poverty was the central object of Booth's enquiry and one of his solutions was the provision of old age pensions. We need not be concerned here in carefully tracing the establishment of Labour Exchanges and unemployment and health measures, but we should note the wealth of objective data that was provided at this time: ammunition in plenty for those who sought through protest literature to exercise pressure on public opinion about towns and the quality of town life.

Booth's first results were published in 1889 and were confined to East London. This was a volume with charts, maps and statistics giving harrowing descriptions of families, homes and streets, and conditions of work. The central theme was poverty. He found that from a population of 900,000, 35 per cent, or 314,000, were poor, and that almost one-third of these suffered from acute distress. His definition of 'the poor' was those with regular family earnings of 18 to 21 shillings a week, while 'the very poor' earned less. The principal factors were lack of work, low pay, family size and ill-health. After 1889, Booth set out to complete his survey of poverty in London and his second volume covered Central, South, and outlying London, areas with an overall population of three millions. Once again, he found that approximately one-third of the people (30.7 per cent) lived on or below his poverty line. Later volumes were concerned with industry and religion.

Booth was a careful observer, and his descriptions were full of detail. In his volume on East London, an impressive record is given in his portrayal of overcrowding: 'In the inner ring nearly all available space is used for building, and almost every house is filled up with families. It is easy to trace the process. One can see what were the original buildings; in many cases they are still standing, and between them, on the large gardens of a past state of things, has been built the small cottage property of today. Houses of three rooms, houses of two rooms, houses of one room — houses set back against a wall or back-to-back fronting it may be on to a narrow footway, with posts at each end and a gutter down the middle. Small courts contrived to utilize some space in the rear, and approached by archway under the building which fronts the street. Of such sort are the poorest class of houses' (10).

Seebohm Rowntree, a wealthy chocolate manufacturer from York, was also concerned with poverty, and his book *Poverty, a Study of Town Life* appeared in 1901. As a Quaker and an industrial philanthropist, his outlook and interests led him to be concerned with the outstanding social problems of the day. One of the most obvious was poverty; no less perplexing to society at the turn of the century than it had been to Booth a decade earlier. From one point of view the keynote of the age was prosperity and individual enrichment; the paradox was that impoverishment remained and grew relatively more severe.

Whereas Booth had pointed to the miseries of London, the greatest city in the world, where, after all, its squalor had been chronicled before and was known about, Rowntree's investigation was at York, a small, provincial, cathedral city with none of the problems of unmanageable size or of a history of accommodating outcasts, a particular problem in London. His findings were consequently perhaps even more important. He began his investigations in the spring of 1899 and was able to show that in York over 15 per cent of the working class population, and nearly 10 per cent of the total population, were living in what he called 'primary poverty', and that a further 18 per cent of the population were in 'secondary poverty'. Using the same standard of poverty as adopted by Booth, Rowntree showed that 27.8 per cent of the York population was living in poverty (compared with 30.7 per cent for London). The closeness of the figures is striking, especially when we recall that Booth's data was collected in a period of average trade prosperity, and Rowntree's at a time when trade was buoyant.

During the last twenty years of the 19th century, there had been a quickening interest in social problems. Social and economic questions were seen bound up increasingly with moral issues. In this respect the influence of John Ruskin was considerable. His early writings had won him support of intellectuals, and, while his later works on political and social systems shocked many, he had lasting fame and became a prophet of a new social consciousness. His writings on economics were a spur to action and Ruskin Societies sprang up all over the country.

Ruskin's early consideration of architecture as a reflection of social conditions was contained in *The Seven Lamps of Architecture*, published in 1849. Subsequently, his views on the place of labour in a social and economic system were given in a chapter of the second volume of *The Stones of Venice*. In 1854, the year following this publication, the relevant section was printed separately by the founders of the first Working Men's College as their introductory pamphlet, and Ruskin became a lecturer at the College. Later, this economic thought, dangerously alien to the orthodox political economy of mid-Victorian Britain was contained in a little book *Unto this Last* (1860). Ruskin's writings on social problems then became channelled in a series of letters 'To the Workmen and Labourers of Great Britain' to which he gave the name *Fors Clavigera*, written monthly between 1871 and 1878 and then irregularly from 1880 to 1884. They were savage attacks on *laissez-faire* economics and a capitalist social system which condemned a large proportion of the population to poverty and an environment that was squalid and ugly. Moreover, he had his own plans for social regeneration and founded an organization called the Guild of St George of which he was Master.

Intellectual and practical contributions such as these considerably affected attitudes towards social questions. Awareness and interest was also stimulated by such matters as the industrial depression of the mid-1880s, the immigration of Eastern European Jews, the publication of the *Report of the Royal Commission on the Housing of the Working Classes* (1884–5), and the *Report of the Committee of the House of Lords on Sweating* (1890) which looked into the problems of ill-organized workers in trades such as tailoring. In 1883, Andrew Mearns, a Congregational clergyman in East London, published a startling pamphlet, *The Bitter Cry of Outcast London,* a portrait of destitution, squalor and vice.

After half a century of continuous protest about urban living conditions, slum housing suddenly became an important political and social question. Both Lord Salisbury and Joseph Chamberlain, two major political figures, took a lively interest in working class housing. Mearns' pamphlet was a religious message: 'Whilst we have been building our churches and solacing ourselves with our religion and dreaming that the millennium was coming, the poor have been growing poorer, the wretched more miserable, and the immoral more corrupt; the gulf has been daily widening which separates the lowest classes of the community from our churches and chapels, and from all decency and civilization.' But it was also a plea for housing reform. Mearns wrote: 'Few who will read these pages have any conception of what these pestilential human rookeries are, where tens of thousands are crowded together amidst horrors which call to mind what we have heard of the middle passage of the slave ship. To get into them you have to penetrate courts reeking with poisonous and malodorous gases arising from accumulations of sewage and refuse scattered in all directions and often flowing beneath your feet; courts, many of them which the sun never penetrates, which are never visited by a breath of fresh air, and which rarely know the virtues of a drop of cleansing water. You have to ascend rotten staircases, which threaten to give way beneath every step, and which, in some places, have already broken down, leaving gaps that imperil the limbs and lives of the unwary. You have to grope your way along dark and filthy passages swarming with vermin. Then, if you are not driven back by the intolerable stench, you may gain admittance to the dens in which these thousands of beings who belong, as much as you, to the race for whom Christ died, herd together' (11).

In 1885, the *Pall Mall Gazette* serialized the results of a survey of

working class districts taken by the Social Democratic Foundation, which found that one in four Londoners lived in abject poverty. Later, General William Booth described the lot of the homeless, the workless, criminals, drunks and prostitutes of contemporary Britain in *In Darkest England and the Way Out* (1890). His analogy with Stanley and Darkest Africa was pertinent: 'Read the House of Lords' Report on the Sweating System, and ask if any African slave system, making due allowance for the superior civilization, and therefore sensitiveness of the victims, reveals more misery'. Booth considered that the paupers, the homeless, the starving, the criminals and the lunatics, totalled three million people, a tenth of the population of the country: 'a population sodden with drink, steeped in vice, eaten up by every social and physical malady, these are the denizens of Darkest England', he declared (12). His book sold 200,000 copies within a year of publication.

In this climate there was increasing talk of social Christianity and agitation for a more equable distribution of wealth. Opportunities

This photograph of Dufton's Yard, Leeds, taken in 1901 prior to the Yard's demolition, is a vivid record of the squalor and poor housing conditions at the turn of the century. Although lit and crudely paved, open space is minimal, opportunities for privacy non-existent, and surface drainage from the court is collected in a shallow central trough.

abounded for the visionary to postulate ideal social structures in ideal urban settings. In a chronological sense we are now very near to the influential writing of Ebenezer Howard, whose activities concerning Garden Cities were to support a powerful protagonist view on the size of towns and the distribution of population. There were others, too, who were to contribute to a developing view about consciously shaping city size and form, for example the architect Lethaby who wanted to divide off London from non-London by a belt of 'fruitful garden ground' embracing Richmond Park, Putney and Wimbledon (13). Views such as these were influenced, if not directly shaped, by the conventionally progressive social viewpoints of the day.

Howard was certainly influenced by Henry George, an American social thinker, whose publications included *Progress and Poverty* and *Social Problems.* It is particularly interesting to refer to the flavour of such contemporary writings. George's view that 'men are compelled to an unnatural competition for the privilege of mere animal existence, that in manufacturing towns and city slums reduces humanity to a depth of misery and debasement in which beings created in the image of God sink below the level of the brutes' (14) was a view shared by many other observers and in itself helped to shape a view about urban life. But more specifically George drew attention to the underlying issues of inequality in the distribution of wealth and the nature of social adjustment. He observed: 'As the earth must be the foundation of every material structure, so institutions which regulate the use of land constitute the foundation of every social organization, and must affect the whole character and development of that organization'. George deplored the concentration of population into big cities and railed against unnatural distribution of wealth and excessive land values in town centres.

George did much to stimulate and articulate an anti-urban outlook: the evil of the big city with its population divorced from nature, its overcrowding, disease and crime, and the sad decline of rural areas. Howard was to echo much of this philosophy in his arguments for Garden Cities. But to reinforce the message there was needed the dramatic, popular visionary and the political agitator; they were both present.

William Morris is a good example of the visionary (15). He is remembered for his association with Ruskin in founding the Arts and Crafts movement and his establishment of the Society for the Protection of Ancient Buildings. But perhaps his biggest influence was as an idealist, espousing the growing socialist movement, and tireless in his denunciation of squalor and shoddiness and the poverty of contemporary civilization. He was a dreamer, but a powerful one, and his vision of the just society and a better world caught a popular imagination. His horror of the ugly city was expressed early in *The Earthly Paradise* (1868–70). From the Prologue:

> Forget six counties overhung with smoke,
> Forget the snorting steam and piston stroke,
> Forget the spreading of the hideous town;
> Think rather of the pack-horse on the down,
> And dream of London, small, and white and clean,
> The clean Thames bordered by its gardens green.

A dream, perhaps, but at the same time, Morris was concerned to achieve the things that might be. In *How We Live and How We Might Live*(1888), he showed the possibilities of the socialist society in contrast to the unjust capitalist society of his day. He found it 'difficult to believe that a rich community such as ours, having such command over external Nature, could have submitted to live such a mean shabby, dirty life as we do'. He blamed the pervading influence of profit. 'It is profit which draws men into enormous unmanageable aggregations called towns, for instance; profit which crowds them up when they are there into quarters without gardens or open spaces; profit which won't take the most ordinary precautions against wrapping a whole district in a cloud of sulphurous smoke; which turns beautiful rivers into filthy sewers; which condemns all but the rich to live in houses idiotically cramped and confined at the best, and at the worst, in houses for whose wretchedness there is no name'.

This was the verdict of a man who had a 'cause', and his message was popularized in *News from Nowhere*, first published in *The Commonwealth*, the organ of the Socialist League, in instalments during 1890. The theme was similar to another popular book of the day, *Looking Backwards*, where Edward Bellamy had his central character fall asleep in Boston to awake in 2000 A D to discover a much improved city. In Morris' case it is the dream of a person in a shabby Thames-side London suburb, and the narrative provides us with imaginary descriptions of a cleansed River Thames, an improved Hammersmith, Piccadilly and Trafalgar Square, a new East London where no slums exist, the abolition of manufacturing towns in the provinces and the revitalized villages of the countryside, rescued from decay. This indeed was a prospect of the future which a town planning movement was to incorporate. 'Yes surely!', concluded Morris, 'And if others can see it as I have seen it, then it may be called a vision rather than a dream'. The dream was radical; it concerned the social problems of the day, and incorporated a sensitivity for art and beauty. It had comprehensive implications for those whose concern was the nature of towns and town life.

Popular radicalism and the search for things that might be was advancing. A number of factors contributed to this. We have noted that the middle classes were confronted by the uncomfortable facts of working class life. A series of hideous murders by Jack the Ripper in East London stirred the imagination and, in view of the background of squalid living conditions, perhaps increased the recognition of the need for public intervention in housing matters in the poorer districts (16). There was also the influence of Evangelical Christianity, home missionary activities by Methodists and the activities of General Booth and the Salvation Army. The University Settlement movement, which we have mentioned in connection with Octavia Hill, had been launched with the establishment of Toynbee Hall in 1884. In many ways the old order was changing. There was a rapid growth of Public Libraries in the 1890s and there were the beginnings of the popular press with Harmsworth's halfpenny *Daily Mail,* both consequences of the spread of literacy through elementary education. First steps were being taken towards the emancipation of women. Old established social institutions were in flux.

The search for social progress, which exposed existing tensions and inequalities, was the forcing ground for increasingly radical movements. As Sir William Harcourt, Gladstone's Chancellor of the Exchequer declared, 'we are all socialists now'. Robert Blatchford and *The Clarion* provided the most vigorous and enterprising socialist propaganda (17). His most famous contribution was *Merrie England,* first published in 1893 as a series of open letters to an imaginary 'John Smith of Oldham': 'Go out into the streets of any big English town, and use your eyes, John. What do you find? You find some rich and idle, wasting unearned wealth to their own shame and injury and the shame and injury of others. You find hard-working people packed away in vile, unhealthy streets. You find little children famished, dirty and half naked outside the luxurious clubs, shops, hotels and theatres. You find men and women overworked and underpaid. You find want and disease cheek by jowl with religion and culture and wealth. You find the usurer, the gambler, the fop, the finnikin fine lady, and you find the starveling, the slave, the drunkard and the harlot. Is it nothing to you, John Smith?'

Merrie England was later published as a shilling book and eventually sold two million copies. Conscience was stirred, popular moods aroused and the search for improvements or solutions intensified. It is in this context that a town planning view of urban social problems emerged.

MODEL TOWNS AND SETTLEMENTS

The social reformer and visionary was frequently a practical experimentalist, and the 19th century was marked by a series of attempts, on an ever widening scale, to set up ideal communities and types of model villages and towns. We need not be too concerned with the search for new social relationships, but the point we should note is the attempts to secure new physical forms which would serve as the basis for happier communities. By the end of the century the number of these experiments clearly affected the ideas of those who postulated new urban forms, challenged by the increasing growth of London and the larger cities, and their social problems.

We can mention quite briefly the examples which occurred in the first half of the century (18). The community experiment at New Lanark during the first two decades by Robert Owen attracted considerable attention. New Lanark was a cotton manufacturing village built at the Falls of Clyde in 1784, taken over by Owen in 1799 and subsequently governed as a community on paternalist lines when his measures for social reform were advanced. His ideas for the building of a township were described in his *Report to the County of Lanark* (1820) when, in an attempt to meet the problems of unemployment, he conceived the creation of what he termed 'agricultural and manufacturing villages of unity and mutual co-operation', housing populations of between 1000 and 1500 persons.

The Owenite tradition continued with many groups setting up colonies or communities in new settlements. Owen himself founded further colonies, and there were a number of others run on co-operative lines. An ambitious scheme which never materialized was that of an Anglican Clergyman, John Minter Morgan, for a Christian Commonwealth which was based on self-supporting villages in the centre of 400 hectares of land. The Chartist movement had its own community experiment based on colonies of small holdings, but very few members of O'Connor's National Land Company succeeded in getting allotments. These experiments were not just national phenomena; America was also an important area for similar attempts.

The real concern of this chapter begins in mid-century, because of much more immediate importance were the proposals for a Model Town Association made by James Silk Buckingham in a book, *National Evils and Practical Remedies*, published in 1849. This was a long, rambling publication of more than 500 pages, containing seven parts. The first dealt with 'existing evils of society' and contained the author's views on ignorance, intemperance, national prejudice (between the English and French), 'restrictions on the free interchange of commodities', war, competition versus co-operation, and the condition of the poorer classes. The remaining sections allowed Buckingham to express his views on solutions, such as financial reform, emigration and colonization, electoral reform and the regeneration of

Ireland. One of these sections contained his proposals for the Model Town, which he called Victoria and associated Community. It is significant to see this particular proposal in its wide, sweeping context. The nature of an ideal town was part of social regeneration, and this moral theme held the imagination of the Victorian urban reformer.

He proposed his Association to build a New Town 'to combine within itself every advantage of beauty, security, healthfulness and convenience, that the latest discoveries in architecture and science can confer upon it'. Victoria was, in fact, a carefully detailed plan for 10,000 people, the design built up in a series of concentric squares, the focal point being a central tower for electric light, with clock and gallery, 92 metres high. The area, about 1½ kilometres square, was divided by eight main radial avenues, named Justice, Unity, Peace, Concord, Fortitude, Charity, Hope and Faith. Manufacturing trades were to be established near the outer edge of the town and inner areas reserved for houses and public offices; working class houses were on the outside. All dwellings were to have a flush toilet; there were to be houses of many different sizes, and each was to accommodate the appropriate size of household. Public baths were to be provided 'at convenient distances in each quarter of the Town'. All more unsavoury buildings, such as abattoirs were to be located away from residences and workshops. To answer pollution, 'the most perfect apparatus was to be applied for consuming smoke'. Beyond the town would be 4000 hectares of farmland where there would also be a public promenade or park. All land was to be owned by the company, and buildings occupied on rent.

This was the first time a town plan had been sketched in such detail. As a design it was rigid, romantic and idealistic. But in containing 'every improvement and convenience' it pointed to the limitations of existing towns and incorporated all the main objectives of the health and environmental reformers. In Buckingham's words, the Plan 'unites the greatest degree of order, symmetry, space and healthfulness, in the largest supply of air and light, and in the most perfect system of drainage, with the comfort and convenience of all classes; the due proportion of accommodation to the probable numbers and circumstances of various ranks; ready accessibility to all parts of the town, under continuous shelter from sun and rain when necessary; with the disposition of the public buildings in such localities as to make them easy of approach from all quarters, and surrounded with space for numerous avenues of entrance and exit. And, in addition to all these, a large inter-mixture of grass lawn, garden ground, and flowers, and an abundant supply of water — the whole to be united with as much elegance and economy as may be found practicable'.

Here, then, was a model to aim at, and it is surprising to note how many of the features were to be repeated in other later proposals, constantly providing an ideal against which the deficiencies of the existing towns were set. Moreover, Victoria was to be a social utopia, a frequent objective of the Victorian urban reformer, with proposals for employment, education, communal eating, medical assistance, justice, temperance and religious observance. The environmental determinism was crude, but sustained the beliefs of the reformer. Buckingham declared that his Model Town 'would banish nearly all the evils of disease, vice, crime, poverty, misery, and hostile and antagonistic feelings from amongst its members; and produce a larger amount of happiness than is possible to be obtained by the great mass of mankind' (19).

Closely parallel to Victoria was a proposal for a Model Town on a Pacific Island by Robert Pemberton in a book called *The Happy Colony* (1854). This was to be called Queen Victoria Town and was designed not on concentric squares but on circular lines. There was to be an inner ring of 20 hectares with four colleges with conservatories, workshops, swimming baths and riding schools. In the outer circle were the factories, public hospitals and gardens, beyond which was a park. Pemberton died before his ideas could be translated into practice. But a few years later they were successfully realized in a colony in Canterbury, New Zealand.

A more prosaic model was sketch by Benjamin Ward Richardson for an ideal city perfectly arranged from the point of view of health, touching aspects such as cemeteries, sewage, house design, and factories. Appropriately, his publication was dedicated to Edwin Chadwick. The name of his town was Hygiea and was designed to meet the widespread disease and high mortality rates of his day. The city was to house 100,000 people in 20,000 houses on 1600 hectares of land, a considerable density reduction on existing towns of his day. Three wide main streets were to run from east to west, and beneath each he planned a railway for heavy traffic. All minor streets were to be wide and airy.

Emphasis was on provision for health: 'in our model city certain forms of disease would find no possible home, or, at the worst, a home so transient as not to affect the mortality in any serious degree' (20). There were to be 20 model hospitals; factories were to be at short distances from the town; there were to be no places 'for the public sale of spirituous liquors'; no rooms were to be permitted underground; the city was to be smoke free, and the daily accumulation of street dirt would be washed away through side openings into subways.

While such models as these were being prepared, existing towns were being improved by the additon of model settlements, and increasingly by the creation of model townships in their own right. This was to be a substantial contribution to the stream of ideas and practice which helped to shape the development of urban Britain (21).

An early example of a philanthropist's village was in Northern Ireland where in 1846 John Grubb Richardson established a settlement round a mill at Bessbrook, near Newry. Houses were planned round open greens, and there was a community centre. Additionally, there was an early cluster of model villages in the Halifax area of the West Riding, again built by benefactors who were factory owners. For instance, the Crossley family developed the West Hill Park area of Halifax and Edward Ackroyd built at nearby Copley and Ackroydon.

Better known is the development of Sir Titus Salt, the Bradford wool merchant, at his model town of Saltaire, created in the 1850s when he moved his mill to an outlying locality. Eight hundred and fifty houses, mainly of the two bedroomed cottage type, were built for his textile workers, together with forty-five alms houses. The philanthropy extended to public and social buildings including churches, baths, a public wash house, a village institute, shops, a park and a hospital. The mill, then among the largest in the world, was opened in 1853, and the twenty-two streets, laid out on a rigid grid system, were almost complete by 1863. The houses were fully built by 1870 when the mill employed nearly 4000 people.

At about the same time, a model village on the Wirral was begun by James and George Wilson of Price's Patent Candle Company at Bromborough Pool (22). Again the impetus was the construction in 1853 of a new manufacturing concern and model housing development followed. Expansion of existing plant was found to be necessary, and this was not possible or desirable in Battersea where the original factory was located. The Merseyside area was required, and a site for factory and village was found at Bromborough. Building went on sporadically until 1900, with the provision of a school, hospital and church.

The second half of the century and the early decades of the 20th provided many examples of this relationship between concern for working conditions and improved housing and environment, when the opportunity was taken to produce small scale improvements in urban life in advance of contemporary conditions elsewhere. They served as a spur to improvement on a broader front. Instances are widespread both in this country, on the Continent and in America. Company cottages, built by the Strutt family at Belper near Derby, dated from as early as 1792. Much later, Vickerstown on the Isle of Walney, Barrow, was built for employees of a shipbuilding firm. At Street, near Glastonbury, there were cottages for Clark's boot factory. In France, Italy, Austria, Germany and Holland, there were workers' colonies, and in America too, where the company town of Pullman (1880—84) with its many social facilities was perhaps the best known. The founding in 1883 of the Society for Promoting Industrial Villages, with the support of a number of distinguished Victorians, reflected the national interest in improvements on these lines.

In the last two decades of the century two experiments in Britain proved to be more than industrialists' housing schemes, but extensive enough to become model towns. These were Bournville and Port Sunlight, and their success greatly stimulated the ideas of those later concerned with Garden Cities and improved layout and design in garden suburbs.

In south west Birmingham in 1880 the Cadbury Brothers had transferred their factory from the city centre to a green field site on the outskirts and built a number of workers' houses close to the works (23). The estate proper began in 1893 when George Cadbury bought 49 hectares of land next to the factory and began building a year later. Great attention was paid to house design and the provision of open space and sunlight and environmental conditions as a whole. Suitably sized gardens, tree lined roads, and parks and recreation grounds made for workers' living conditions quite different from anything that the rest of Birmingham could show. As a social philanthropist Cadbury completed the estate with a village institute and a hall for the Adult School movement. The chocolate trade-name, Bournville, was applied to the estate.

By 1900, 313 houses had been built and the estate covered 134 hectares. The houses were not reserved for Cadbury Brothers' employees: the Bournville Estate was always independent of the firm and, on average, only about 40 per cent of the householders were (and subsequently have been) connected with the factory. At the turn of the century, George Cadbury founded the Bournville Village Trust, through which he sought to ensure that his purposes and ideas would be given permanent form. Since then, the estate has expanded and development has gone on to the present day in various schemes, largely through the schemes of a number of housing societies.

Port Sunlight, near Liverpool, was a rival model township, with the same emphasis on improved housing, enhanced setting and provision of social facilities. It was begun in 1888 as part of an expansion scheme of an already established business. The keynotes were good housing and generous amenities: by 1904, two schools, social clubs, a church, technical institute, theatre and swimming baths had all been provided.

The century ended with its focus on social enquiry and the plight of the under privileged and badly housed in the big cities. The success of a handful of benefactors in providing better conditions for their workers was well known, but the problem, particularly of London, seemed to be getting worse and more radical solutions were necessary. The century ended in a welter of agitation when a popular remedy was to hive off communities or colonies from London. This was General Booth's solution. For example, he proposed two types of communities for the unemployed in city colonies, farm colonies and the overseas colony, 'self helping and self sustaining communities, each being a kind of co-operative society, or patriarchal family, governed and disciplined on the principles which have already proved so effective in the Salvation Army' (24). A Farm Colony was actually bought in South Essex in 1891 and 7000 colonists installed.

There was a rash of colony experiments largely of a co-operative and politically radical nature in many parts of the country and elsewhere. A book called *Freeland*, published in 1890, was a proposal by Theodore Hertzka, an Austrian economist, for a colony based on voluntary economic association and full democratic participation. Subsequently, the International Freeland Society, founded in Austria and Germany, began a colony in East Africa.

The anarchist movement in the 1880s and 1890s was concerned

The Red Lion Street area, Nottingham, 1919. The high residential density, congested buildings and the disorder of conflicting land uses were general features of late 19th-and early 20th-century cities. These characteristics are well illustrated in this view of Red Lion Street, an inner area of Nottingham. The sheer intensity of land use and the absence of open space is striking.

internationally with the revolt against industrial society and searched for a new moral and social order. Much of their thinking was contrary to any idea of large scale industry and of mass production and consumption, and they naturally turned to a society based on small units. A powerful exponent was Peter Kropotkin who published his *Fields, Factories and Workshops* in 1898. He recommended the formation of small colonies for the intimate development of factory workshops and agriculture.

And so, at the end of the 19th century, there was a particular situation marked by a combination of factors: increasing disquiet at the size and unmanageable spread of London, deep concern at under-privilege and endemic poverty, and despair at the housing situation, particularly for the needy. This was matched by examples of improved conditions where development took place designed for amenity and the prized conditions of air and sunlight. At the same time the desire to escape the big city by founding colonies was an entrenched outlook. From many points of view the time was clearly ripe for an integrating plan, building on previously conceived models. We can now turn to the influence of Ebenezer Howard and the achievements of the Garden City movement in the context of rapidly developing events at the turn of the century.

References

(1) Cherry, Gordon E., *Influences on the Development of Town Planning in Britain,* Journal of Contemporary History, Vol. 4, No.3, 1969.
(2) Pollard, Sydney, *A History of Labour in Sheffield,* Liverpool University Press, 1959.
(3) Ashworth, William, *The Genesis of Modern British Town Planning,* Routledge, 1954.
(4) *Report of the Royal Commission on the Distribution of the Industrial Population,* Cmd. 6153, HMSO, 1940.
(5) Cherry, Gordon E., *Town Planning in its Social Context,* Leonard Hill Books, 1970.
(6) Hole, James, *The Homes of the Working Classes with Suggestions for their Improvement,* Longmans, 1866.
(7) *Op cit* Hole, James.
(8) Bell, E. Moberley, *Octavia Hill,* Constable, 1946.
(9) Bradley, John L. (Ed), *Selections from 'London Labour and the London Poor',* Henry Mayhew, Oxford University Press, 1965.
(10) Pfautz, Harold W., *Charles Booth on the City,* University of Chicago Press, 1967.
(11) Mearns, Andrew, *The Bitter Cry of Outcast London. An Inquiry into the Condition of the Abject Poor,* London, 1883.
(12) Booth, General W., *In Darkest England and the Way Out,* London, 1890.
(13) Lethaby, W.R., *Of Beautiful Cities,* Arts and Crafts Exhibition Society, London, 1897.
(14) George, W.L., *Engines of Social Progress,* Adam and Charles Black, 1907.
(15) Briggs, Asa (Ed), *William Morris: Selected Writings and Designs,* Penguin Books, 1968.
(16) Curl, James Stevens, *European Cities and Society,* Leonard Hill Books, 1970.
(17) Rodgers, W.R. and Donaghue, Bernard, *The People into Parliament,* Thames and Hudson, 1966.
(18) *Op cit.,* Cherry, Gordon E., *Town Planning in its Social Context.*
(19) Buckingham, James Silk, *National Evils and Practical Remedies,* London, 1849.
(20) Richardson, Benjamin Ward, *Hygiea, a City of Health,* Macmillan, 1876.
(21) *See* Bell, Colin and Rose, *City Fathers: the early history of town planning in Britain,* The Cresset Press, 1969.
(22) Watson, Alan, *Price's Village,* Price's (Bromborough) Ltd, 1966.
(23) *The Bournville Village Trust, 1900—1955,* The Bournville Village Trust.
(24) *Op cit.,* Booth, General W.

6 The turn of the Century

In history it is always tempting to tag convenient labels to particular dates or ascribe significance to certain temporal watersheds in order to suggest a chronological framework. The temptation extends to urban history. But the complex interrelationship of underlying factors — physical, social, economic and political — suggests that we should avoid selecting magic dates for any special emphasis. Nevertheless the year 1900 and immediate years following the turn of the century is a convenient time at which to pause and review a number of features. In the last decade of the 19th and particularly in the first decade of the 20th century, there were a number of developments and broad movements of ideas and attitudes that not only distinguish these years from previous periods but also provide a base on which to examine subsequent events. It is also convenient because the turn of the century permits an interesting retrospect of change in the 19th century and a prospect for urban developments over the years ahead.

Considerable changes had been effected in the second half of the 19th century, so much so that in the opening years of the 20th it is possible for the modern observer to recognize most of the fundamental characteristics of urban life today. The harsh description which Engels gave in 1845 of housing and employment conditions belonged to a distinctly different phase of history. Before the outbreak of the First World War there were schemes for old age pensions, health and unemployment insurance and minimum wages; free and compulsory education had produced a situation where full-time and everyday attendance at school was normal, and the public health movement was at last producing rapidly falling death rates, with medicine and sanitation based on the work of Pasteur and Lister.

Housing conditions had improved substantially, particularly for the middle class. The late Victorian and Edwardian residential street today forms a solid, if outmoded, core of towns and cities. For the working classes, there had been the beginnings of intervention in slum clearance, and reformers and industrial benefactors had shown what could be achieved. City centres and their patterns of commercial life had taken on very recognizable characteristics. The branches of the great chain stores were almost fully grown; the major Department stores gave to the bigger towns elegance and comfort; and the bazaars of Marks &

Spencers and Woolworths were foretastes of a new shopping era. Public transport was well organized with choices between bus and tram and, in London, there was the Electric Underground too; numbers of private cars were soon to rise dramatically. Parks, libraries and swimming baths were provided and maintained out of the rates, and formed important features in an urban recreation pattern. New uses of leisure were emerging, none more striking than the cinema.

A distinctive urban culture could now be recognized characterizing town life over the whole country. For entertainment, the music hall had developed from saloon theatres popular in London with the lower classes from the 1830s. After the 1870s most towns had a Palace of Variety, a Palladium, Empire, Hippodrome or Pavilion. The first Working Men's Clubs had been founded in 1862, and by the 1880s they existed in all sizeable towns; they were of political and social importance with reading rooms, debating halls and provisions for

A design for the Chester Street Schools, Manchester. The principle of universal elementary education was established in 1870, although it was not until 1880 that the school Boards were obliged to make attendance compulsory, and not until 1891 that elementary education became virtually free. The school shown in this drawing and built at Ardwick, Manchester, was one of the first to be erected by the Manchester School Board. From this time on, schools, generally monumental buildings with applied Gothic ornament, became a new feature in the Vitorian townscape.

billiards and chess. Choral singing had its adherents in a number of towns; in South Wales singing was focused on the chapel choir. The brass band movement had begun in the 1840s and remained important, especially in the North. After the 1870s the seaside holiday became popular and was exploited by the railway companies. Mass spectator sports had appeared, with both cricket and football drawing large crowds. For popular daily reading there was the Daily Express, the Daily Mail, and the Daily Mirror.

Much of the rawness of the early 19th century urban life, therefore, had gone. This is not to say that the wretchedness of living conditions had been overcome for all — far from it — but the rich potential of community derived from people living together in cities was being realized. There were clearly enormous advances still to be made, but increasingly there was the likelihood of this being achieved. The Victorian belief in 'progress' had been a powerful force and, as we have seen, it was this that stimulated the visionary who contemplated the things which might be, and encouraged the reformer, particularly the political agitator, who demanded better conditions for those for whom progress was too slow.

Roundhay Park, Leeds, 1890. About six kilometres north east of the city centre, this Park has long been a popular open air venue for recreation. In appearance it is largely unchanged today, but communal enjoyment, including listening to the band, belongs to the past. The photograph evokes the sense of social occasion: an opportunity for relaxation, social concourse and a display of respectability and finery.

By 1901 Britain was quite decidedly an urban country. Twenty-five million people lived in towns, including 4½ millions in London; only 7½ millions lived elsewhere, outside the urban areas. Britain was still a 'young' country, with 42.5 per cent of the population between the ages of one and 19; but this was the period in which a change began to occur. In the Edwardian decade the birthrate fell and in 1911 the annual percentage increase of the population, compared with the previous decade, fell below 11 per cent for the first time for a century (1).

The concentration of population in the country as a whole had acquired certain urban fixes: these were London, south-east Lancashire, centred on Manchester and its ring of towns, Merseyside, Clydeside and central Scotland, Tyneside, West Yorkshire, the West Midlands, centres in the East Midlands and more isolated foci elsewhere. Outside London, the coalfields broadly determined the distribution of urban population, but coal output was soon to reach its maximum and new sources of power, notably electricity, were to facilitate a wider spread of industrial development in alternative locations, a feature stimulated by new forms of transport. The old coalfield towns, based on industries which were increasingly vulnerable to foreign competition (textiles, shipbuilding etc.), entered on a period of relative decline and found it difficult to share in the expansion of new consumer goods industries and service employment. Coal was

The Jolly Butchers' Inn, Bradford, 1902. A turn of the century snapshot. Advertisements for Rugby and Association football suggest the place of these two sports in the urban culture of the day. The mass advertisement for Bovril invades even licensed premises. A new King is on the throne and recruits are wanted for His Majesty's Army.

still an essential foundation of the national economy, but the rise of new industries, such as the electrical and chemical trades, light engineering and vehicle construction, served to alter the pattern of population distribution. The London region in particular took on a new emphasis.

The gap between the wealthy and the poor was still great. In 1901 only 400,000 out of a population of 32.5 millions earned more than £400 per year. Income tax began with incomes of £160 per year, but less than one million people were liable. High percentages of workers in major industries earned £1.25 per week or less; on the other hand, wages of more than £2.25 were not common (2). The first Workmen's Compensation Act had been passed in 1897, but it was not until 1906 that the legal obligation to compensate a workman who suffered injury was extended to include virtually all employers. Low wages, uncertainty of employment and unemployment itself provided the backcloth of an urban way of life which was to change markedly with social legislation. The Liberal Government of Sir Henry Campbell-Bannerman and his successor H.H. Asquith was particularly prominent with reforms, including free school meals, a free school medical service, non-contributory old age pensions, the establishment of Labour Exchanges, a National Insurance Scheme and a Shops Act. It is significant that the first Planning Act dates from this time.

This was indicative of a new determination to intervene in general matters of social policy, of which planning and housing were part; but at the beginning of the 20th century there was still considerable resistance to central power. Housing Acts, for example, permitted, not compelled, local Authorities to build houses for the poor, and there was no question of financial assistance to lessen the burden on local rates.

It was a matter for private enterprise to provide housing, and in 1913 the shortage of houses was officially estimated at between 100,000 and 120,000. No wonder that available statistics make disquieting reading. In 1911, 8.6 per cent of the population of England and Wales was living more than two to a room, and much higher figures were recorded for certain towns. The London average, for example, was 16.7 per cent and in the East End at Shoreditch, the figure was 36 per cent. In Birmingham it was 10 per cent and for a town which was then above the half-million mark, we might note that there were still 40,000 back-to-back houses and areas where 30 persons had one tap as their sole water supply (3). In Scotland, overcrowding in the towns and cities was substantially worse. The poverty and urban squalor which Charles Booth had painstakingly recorded was slow to improve and was the ready target for the commentators of the day, whether it was Bishop Earl from Birmingham or Jack London the American journalist who visited the Capital in 1902.

Ruston's Place, Nottingham, 1919.
After the First World War, the housing
situation had become acute, with
shortages and a deteriorating housing
stock. The poorly maintained brickwork in this photograph suggests the
unfit conditions while the communal
water tap adjoining the central
shallow drainage trough indicates the
lack of individual facilities. But
through the gloom the close communal life common in these courts
can be sensed.

But it is still fair to say that there was a widening lower middle class
for whom stubstantially improved living conditions were available.
Solidly built terrace houses could be obtained for a rent of 62½p a
week, at least in the London area. Robert Cecil described typical living
conditions in this type of house: 'There would be five or six rooms and
a scullery and, if the family was small, or one of the daughters had
married or left home, there would probably be room for a lodger
contributing 10s a week to the exchequer; he would share the family
supper and also the mid-day meal on Sundays. The front room, which
might contain a pianola, would only be used on special occasions.
There would be no bathroom, but in the kitchen a galvanized iron bath
would serve both for laundering and for the regular bath-nights of the
members of the family. A mangle would probably be the only
labour-saving device in the kitchen. If father had chosen well, the house
would have a small garden at the back and here he would grow such

vegetables as could survive the soot of London's millions of coalfires and the constant drip of mother's washing on the line. The kitchen stove would burn coal, bought at 19s. 6d. a ton; the lighting would probably come from a gas-bracket or oil-lamp. Although all the houses would look much the same, there would be life in the streets; the cries of vendors would compete with the barrel organ . . . . . ' (4).

The middle and upper middle class suburbs constituted an equally distinctive part of the urban scene, and it was here that the developing tastes of the housewife, which both stimulated and reflected many aspects of change, were most to be seen. Lord Northcliffe launched his Daily Mail Ideal Home Exhibition in 1908, and although household gadgetry developed slowly, the days of domestic service were clearly numbered. Electric fires, kettles and irons were coming into use. There were gas-heated washing machines and by 1908 the vacuum cleaner was past the experimental stage. A widening middle class acquired new tastes which the consumer goods industries were to meet. Cooking was now done on gas stoves, and the first refrigerators were to be seen. Houses were now lit by electricity and some had telephones. The gramophone was introduced to vie with the piano in providing musical entertainment.

CIVIC DESIGN

As an occasion for stocktaking, the period at the turn of the century was particularly important for those who had a concern for the appearance of towns. The architect came to have a renewed interest in form and civic design, a concern which was to be expressed both in this country and on the Continent and in America. In 1889 a Viennese architect Camillo Sitte, published *The Art of Building Cities* which was to have a very big impact on town building. In America, the 'City Beautiful' movement affected planning ideas in most of the major cities, and in this country, British architects were prominent in attempts to set new design standards in urban life.

Sitte's particular contribution stemmed from his survey of the arrangement of public squares in Italy and Northern Europe. He praised the squares of the Middle Ages and Renaissance; he noted that they formed an entity with the buildings which enclosed them, contrasting the openness of modern plazas. Sitte regarded city building as an art form and pointed to the need for the talent of the artist: 'The thing that is truly astonishing', he said, 'is the complete oblivion into which the principles of town building art have fallen in our own times'. He deplored the loss of the enclosed character of street areas and the absence of any proper relationship between built-up area and open space. The standardization of street patterns, reducing 'the street system to a mere traffic utility, never serving the purposes of art', was, for Sitte, one of the more sad characteristics of the 19th century city (5).

Sitte wrote from a central European standpoint, but he reflected a new universal concern. In England the need to restore art and beauty to the normal lives of urban dwellers had been a rallying point for some time. William Morris in launching the Arts and Crafts movement drew attention to this, and in his novel *News from Nowhere* new architectural forms were ambitiously described in his envisioned future London (see page 99). But to secure new forms of domestic architecture and town building, it needed practical innovation to translate the romantic Utopianism of Morris. A new generation of English architects was to help in this: Norman Shaw (1831–1912), Philip Webb (1831–1931), C.F.A. Voysey (1857–1941), Baillie Scott (1865–1945), and Edwin Lutyens (1869–1944). When Webb built the Red House for William Morris in 1859 the change in practice and style had begun; this famous house indicated a genuine revival of the English vernacular and of craftsmanship in building.

Equally important were the architects' views on applying art to urban form. At the end of the century Lethaby, for example, took up Morris' concern for town life and commented adversely on the London of his day. His precept was disarmingly simple. 'Unless there is a ground of beauty, vain it is to expect the fruit of beauty' he declared in his lecture to the Arts and Crafts Exhibition Society in 1896 (6). Lethaby was aghast at the visual prospect of the London of his day: 'a half-hundred square miles, once wood and cornland, roofed over, where we grow sickly like grass under a stone, intersected by interminable avenues all asphalt, lamp posts, pipes and wires'. He urged improvements at all levels. He wanted to begin by sweeping streets better, by whitewashing houses and by taking care over railways and lamp posts. He suggested the creation of a wide pedestrian way in London from Waterloo Bridge to the British Museum, an embankment on the South Bank and an improvement of central railway stations. He also urged a containment of London by a belt of 'fruitful garden ground' embracing Richmond Park, Putney and Wimbledon.

This search for more conscious creativity in town building developed rapidly and one of the first town planning text books at the turn of the century was significant in its title: *Town Planning in Practice: an introduction to the art of designing cities and suburbs.* The author, Raymond Unwin, was careful to point out that civic art was not a case of 'filling our streets with marble fountains, dotting our squares with groups of statuary, twining our lampposts with wriggling acanthus leaves or dolphins' tails, and our buildings with meaningless bunches of fruit and flowers tied up with impossible stone ribbons'. For him, town planning needed the infusion of the spirit of the artist in its widest sense. It was a matter for whole communities seeking 'to express their needs, their life and the aspirations in the outward form of their towns, seeking, as it were, freedom to become the artists of their own cities, portraying on a gigantic canvas the expression of their life' (7).

Unwin was able to develop these ideas in practice. Born near Rotherham in 1863, he joined Barry Parker in an architectural partnership at Buxton in 1896. He began the development of New Earswick, the Rowntree village near York, in 1901, and two years later designed the first Garden City, Letchworth. From 1905 onwards, he was responsible for plans for Hampstead Garden Suburb. From 1911–14 he was the first lecturer in Town Planning at Birmingham University, a post resulting from a grant from the Cadbury family. He continued to exercise an enormous influence on both town design and the course of the town planning movement up to his death in 1940 (8).

The immediate importance of Unwin and Parker was that they were willing to limit their architectural practice to the smaller cottage and omit the design of large buildings, but this was more than compensated for by their interest in town design as a whole. Their functional approach to housing layouts yielded solutions which set standards for many years. Regularized, though sanitary, bye-law development was not enough and an attack was launched on accepted design precepts which produced backyards and alleys. Streets had become more important, and therefore they should be carefully designed and not allowed to remain inflexibly regular in layout.

His design principles had an attractive financial base, as he explained in his paper written in 1912, *Nothing Gained by Overcrowding!* (9). He compared a 4 hectare (10 acre) layout taking 'the conditions as they exist in many large towns where bye-laws of the usual type are in force, and where provision is made for a back road to give access to the cottage yards' with a layout 'developed in accordance with the Garden City principles'. In the first case, with houses of 5 metres frontage, a total of 340 houses could be placed on the 4 hectares, built in parallel terraces. In the second case, with houses of similar size and frontage, but built in groups of two, four or six with spaces between for direct access to gardens, 152 houses could be accommodated. A reduction in density from 84 to 37 to the hectare (34 to 15 to the acre) was more than recompensed by substantially larger house plots and a smaller proportion (and therefore cost) of land taken up by roads.

A particular facet of the drive to secure an improvement in the appearance of cities was concerned with advertising, and in the years surrounding the end of the century, hostility against street advertising was a popular lobby. Considerable changes had, in fact, taken place during the second half of the 19th century and billsticking and fly-posting gave way to the taking of rented and protected stations. As an instance of the rising importance of the advertising trade, the first annual meeting of the United Kingdom Billposters' Association was held in 1862 at Longsight, Manchester.

Popular discontent with street advertisements was heightened when a fierce gale in November 1891 blew down hoardings in many places, notably in Hyde Park, injuring a number of people. Dangerous structures could be repaired, but the vulgarity of some advertisements (seen in the context of the day) was a matter for more lasting concern. Posters which offended against prudery caused the greatest stir, for example the poster which depicted a woman acrobat in flesh coloured tights. A poster of a ballet dancer was objected to because the girl's skirts were considered too short, and at Cork 'the Bovril bull was condemned as likely to corrupt the morals of the young people of that city, who were presumed to be properly unable to tell a bull from a cow' (10).

In these circumstances it was not surprising to see the founding of the National Society for Checking the Abuse of Public Advertising (SCAPA), in February 1893, with the objective of preventing the disfigurement of both countryside and towns. Its aims reflected the imagination and concern of those who cared for environmental quality: 'to protect the picturesque simplicity of rural and river scenery, and to promote a due regard to dignity and propriety of aspect in towns, with special reference to the abuses of spectacular advertising; and to assert generally the national importance of maintaining the elements of interest and beauty in out-of-doors life'.

Apart from the Manchester Act of 1844 and the Indecent Advertisement Act of 1889, there was no public Act containing a provision expressly directed against, or regulating, hoardings or posters. In November 1893, a Bill was introduced in the Commons to prohibit advertisements in public places in rural areas, but failed to obtain a second reading. Early in the next year a Bill was introduced to enable County Councils to make bye-laws regulating or prohibiting advertisements in the countryside or seashore. Attempts to obtain legal control of out-door advertisements continued with a London County Council Bill which provided conditions for obtaining a licence to erect hoardings. In the meantime, many legal authorities obtained powers in local Acts designed to limit hoardings which exceeded a certain height.

Powerful interests in the advertising trade managed to fight off the legislation that was threatening them, but public concern was again aroused when, in 1900, two enormous boards advertising a Chicago cereal food were erected on the cliffs at Dover. The first important legislation, forerunner of far more extensive Acts in later years, came in 1907 with the Advertisements Regulation Act. It had been promoted and presented during each of the three previous sessions of Parliament, but was at last passed. It empowered local Authorities to make bye-laws controlling hoardings over 3.7 metres in height, and for regulating 'the exhibition of advertisements in such places and in such manners, or by such means, as to affect injuriously the amenities of a public park or pleasure promenade, or to disfigure the natural beauty of a landscape'. Public pressure had been harnessed to political power and the battle for some measure of community control over the appearance of our towns and cities had moved into another arena.

SOCIAL CONSIDERATIONS

While the design lobby was strengthening, the 'social' concern for the quality of urban life which, as we have seen, had been expressed for some years, showed no signs of diminishing. A determinist view which saw a correlation between poverty of environment and certain behavioural characteristics of the population, allowed the designer to interpret the results of social enquiry and reflect the force of social agitation. The common approach was to question continued growth in the size of towns (particularly London), and therefore most urban solutions centred on reducing town size or creating opportunities for new settlements beyond them.

The idea of colonies was still attractive; recall the popular appeal of General William Booth's schemes. A task assigned to the novelist H. Rider Haggard in 1905, is interesting in this context (11). The Colonial Office nominated him a Commissioner to go to the United States and 'inspect and report upon the conditions and character of the agricultural and industrial settlements which have been established there by the Salvation Army, with a view to the transmigration of suitable persons from the great cities of the U S to the land and the formation of agricultural communities'. It appeared to the Secretary of State that 'if these experiments are found to be successful, some analogous system might, with great advantage, be applied in transferring the urban populations of the United Kingdom to different parts of the British Empire'.

Haggard duly inspected settlements in California and Colorado named Fort Romie and Fort Amity. He found the settlers 'healthy, happy, hopeful and, almost without exception, doing well'. In his report he urged acceptance of the idea: 'To combine a judicious use of the Public Credit with that of what I have called the "waste forces of Benevolence", and by means of these two levers to lift some of the mass of human misery which demonstrates itself in the great cities of civilization to a level of plenty and contentment'. But Haggard's assignment already appeared dated. The Garden City movement had been launched and Garden Suburb schemes were being contemplated. Furthermore, the beginnings of legislation, designed to intervene in general matters of land use or the detailed way in which land was developed, were not far off. At the same time, it is fair to reflect that some return to the land through agricultural associations, but more especially through the action of emigration societies, was certainly important in shifting superfluous population from the towns. A measure of the scale of emigration was that in 1913 nearly a quarter of a million people left this country.

But improved municipal hygiene and housing was still reckoned to be crucial by the social reformers of the day. The pressing problems inherited from the Victorian city could not be ignored. W.L. George, for example, writing in 1907 about what he called 'engines of social progress', recognized housing as the most important of all social questions: 'Societies that provide good houses for people within reach of their occupation, or who improve dwellings already erected, are doing apostolic work; the improvement of rural housing, the foundation of new cities under model conditions, are on the same plane' (12).

Britain was by no means alone in this pre-occupation. Much the same concern was typical of other countries. In France, for example, a single institution in Paris became the focal point of studies in hygiene, social reform and urbanism. This was the Musée Social, founded in 1894, dedicated to improving the physical and social conditions of the working classes. In 1908, a new section was formed within the Musée under the direction of Eugène Hénard who was to become internationally known amongst planners. This was the 'section d'hygiène urbaine et rurale', the aim of which was to translate desirable public health and social reform principles into concrete urban legislation and plans (13).

In America, too, there was a new urgency about urban affairs. Illustrations of city life, such as in *How the Other Half Lives* (1890) by Jacob Riis, paralleled similar English examples. The Settlement House movement was taken from East London to Chicago by Jane Addams who opened Hull House in Halstead Street in 1889. In other words, there was a universal recognition of the need for well-being in community life in large towns and cities secured through adequate housing and an eradication of poverty and under-privilege.

GARDEN CITIES AND GARDEN SUBURBS

The most influential figure to shape the course of urban history at this time was Ebenezer Howard, who achieved fame, first with the publication in 1898 of his book *Tomorrow: A Peaceful Path to Real Reform*, revised in 1902 with slight changes as *Garden Cities of Tomorrow*, and then with the founding of Letchworth as the first Garden City in 1903. His influence was remarkable. Although one must

acknowledge that his ideas were propounded at a particularly favour-
able time, his own immensely practical drive was the force behind
the first experiment which attracted others to his views.

Howard was a Londoner, born in 1850, the son of a small
shopkeeper (14). He became a clerk at the age of 15. Later he went to
America for a short time, but returned to England to join Gurneys, the
official Parliamentary reporters. He was exposed to earnest circles of
non-conformist churchmen and reformers who were concerned with
the questions of land, land values and the growth of towns. He read
widely and was influenced particularly by the economist Alfred
Marshall, by Henry George, social thinker and author of *Progress and
Poverty* and *Social Problems*, and by the vision of the future in Edward
Bellamy's *Looking Backwards*. His views were no doubt shaped by the
popular radicalism of the day. As we have seen, agricultural colonies
and a back-to-the-land movement had become common responses to
urban problems, and the origins of his Garden City proposals can easily
be traced. Take, for example, the idea of Rev. H. Solly, writing in 1884
in his *Re-housing of the Industrial Classes*: '... the remedy
unquestionably seems to be to turn back the tide from the town to the
country by finding these folk employment, profitable to themselves
and the community, where they can be decently housed and fairly well
remunerated' (15). This standpoint was espoused by the Nationalization of Labour Society and the Land Nationalization Society, and in
1893 Howard addressed these two bodies, bringing to them a proposal
for a 'Co-operative Commonwealth'.

The familiarity of Howard's proposals can be seen in other
directions. A.F. Weber, an American, whose book, *The Growth of
Cities* (1899), indicated such a firm grasp of the course of urban
change, saw the removal of the evils of city life in the rise of the
suburbs. He argued that if society wanted to minimize the evils of
concentration of population, it must abandon the hope of accom-
plishing great things by such palliatives as model tenements, building
laws and inspection of buildings and seek wider goals. He suggested a
modified concentration of population which offered the advantages
of both city and country life, and quoted the prediction of Charles
Kingsley (*Miscellanies: Great Cities*): 'a complete integration of city
and country, a complete fusion of their different modes of life and a
combination of the advantages of both' (16). Weber did not
acknowledge Howard's work, so perhaps we should conclude that
both were drawing on very similar writings.

Howard's book contained a number of important proposals. The
physical spread of cities was to be limited. Satellite towns of 30,000
people, self-supporting by their own industry, should be built at
distances from the parent city. Between the two there should be a

permanent belt of open land used for agriculture. The ownership of the satellite town was to be in the hands of the municipality and the unearned increment from the growth of the town was to be reserved for the community as a whole. Within this framework, he outlined a scheme for a Garden City to be built near the centre of a 2,400 hectare (6,000 acre) area. The city would cover one-sixth of this; it would be of circular form with a radius of just over a kilometre. Six radial boulevards, 39 metres wide, would divide the town into six equal parts, or wards. Just over 2 hectares (five and a half acres) in the centre were to be a garden area containing the larger public buildings, and this itself would be encircled by a 58 hectare (145 acre) public park and a wide glass arcade called the Crystal Palace. An additional park was provided in a concentric 130 metre wide belt and the concentric pattern was to be emphasized by the location of factories on the outer ring of the town.

All this might appear as crude and idealistic as Buckingham's square-shaped *Victoria*. The difference was in the context of the period in which it was written. Howard's was a time when people had a far greater grasp of the comprehensiveness of the problem being faced than the earlier Victorians. His objective was 'to raise the standard of health and comfort of all true workers of whatever grade — the means by which these objects are to be achieved being a healthy, national and economic combination of town and country life, and this on land owned by the municipality'. His main concern was the plight of overcrowded cities and depleted country districts, and concluded that there were just not two alternatives — town life and country life — but a third alternative — town life in a country setting 'in which all the advantages of the most energetic and active town life, with all the beauty and delight of the country may be secured in perfect combination' (17). This simple view, the mainspring of the Garden City areas, has sustained an attitude in town design for the rest of this century. Indeed, Howard made a world-wide contribution in that he endowed foreign languages with a new urban term: garden city, *cité-jardin, gartenstadt, ciudad-jardin*.

Howard was careful to indicate on his sketches, which suggested the circular nature of the proposed development, remarks such as: 'Diagram only. Map cannot be drawn until site selected'. In fact, there was no attempt to impose any geometric pattern, and when the first experiment at Letchworh was undertaken, the designers' creativity was shaped by the physical conditions of the site. A company called the Garden City Pioneer Company was formed in July 1902 to take preliminary steps for establishing the first garden city. Within a year it had entered into contracts for the purchase of properties, and in September 1903, the First Garden City Limited was formed to complete the contracts and to establish the town. A site at Letchworth, totalling 1529 hectares (3,822 acres), was obtained by private treaty from fifteen different owners, the cost averaging £101 per hectare (18).

This might have been considered dramatic progress in itself, but a further important step was still to come. So far in Britain there had been little interest in the preparation of town plans as the basis for development over a lengthy period. This was contrary to continental experience, as T.C. Horsfall had shown in his book on German town planning that appeared at the time. But Letchworth was the opportunity in this country for drawing up a plan for a complete town, the first attempt on a large scale to express the emergent town planning practice and ideas. Sketch plans were prepared by Parker and Unwin, and Ricardo and Lethaby. Parker and Unwin's scheme was selected and they were commissioned to prepare the plan.

Some measure of the speedy progress can be gleaned from a report only a few years later of the chairman of the company, Mr Aneurin Williams, at the Garden City Association Conference in London in 1907. The unique experiment of planning a whole town was described: 'There they had taken what was agricultural land, with only 400 inhabitants, and had laid it out and created a town which had now about 5,000 people, and was very rapidly growing. The principles of town planning had been there adapted in their fulness. Their design contemplated eventually a town of 32,000 people, on about 1,300 acres, including roads and open spaces, and with an agricultural belt of, say, 2,500 acres around it. All the essentials of that town, from the factory sites to the plots for cottages and villas, had been planned from the beginning ... They had, however, already proved the very great advantages which result to all classes from working on such a deliberate plan — determining the size and contour of the town before a brick was laid; providing streets, gas and water according not to present needs but to those of the town when complete; allocating sufficient garden space to the poorest houses, as well as to the best houses on the estate; reserving open spaces, parks and recreation grounds; reserving sites for public buildings, such as schools in neighbourhoods which were certain to require them; assigning a distinct position to factories so that they should have communication with the railway, and should not be mixed up unnecessarily with the residential part of the town; while around all this a belt of open land had been reserved, so that the inhabitants would always be within reach of the real country' (19).

The Letchworth experiment encouraged the paternalist interest in providing more attractive houses in pleasanter surroundings and it stimulated the architect to improve residential layouts. In this respect, Unwin took a lead which others were to follow for many years. The Garden City ideal, and what was actually achieved at Letchworth, had widespread repercussions before the advent of the First World War.

With Bournville, Port Sunlight and Earswick also receiving a good deal of publicity at this time, the model village was very much in vogue. In South Yorkshire, another example was provided by the colliery village. Woodlands, north of Doncaster, was established by the Brodsworth Main Colliery Company which sank a new pit in 1906. A large area of land was acquired near the collieries and laid out with pleasant, tree-lined streets with plenty of open space and recreation grounds. Houses built in pairs or small groups had gardens; all had three bedrooms, a bath and hot and cold water. This was an almost revolutionary improvement on housing conditions prevalent in the older part of the coalfield (20).

Hull Garden Suburb, opened in 1908, was a rather different example. Nominally it was an independent village owned by the Hull Garden Village Company, but it was in large measure the preserve of Reckitts, an adjoining manufacturing firm. On part of the estate of 56 hectares (140 acres), houses were reserved and let to employees (21).

In London, Hampstead Garden Suburb became well-known as a further example of what sort of urban improvements could be achieved. Eton College had owned a 128 hectare (320 acre) estate in the parish of Hendon, immediately to the north of Hampstead Heath, and the extension of the Hampstead Tube made the land ripe for development. Through the intervention of Mrs Barnett, wife of Canon Barnett who was engaged in many social issues, the land was acquired for the Hampstead Garden Suburb Trust. Thirty two hectares (80 acres) were preserved as open space and added to the Heath; 96 hectares (240 acres) were laid out as garden suburb to the design of Raymond Unwin.

The Hampstead development was unrivalled as a piece of informal suburban architecture. But there were many other schemes, particularly by co-partnership housing societies throughout the country, all of which drew attention to the possibilities inherent in preparing layout plans for residential development and adopting the new suburban architecture. The scheme in Birmingham by Harborne Tenants Ltd was an example. Here the density was brought down to 25 houses per hectare (ten houses per acre), and 4 hectares (10 acres) out of 53 were reserved as open spaces, playgrounds and allotments. Before development began, a survey of natural features plotted the position of all trees in order that those which could be accommodated with advantage in the layout could be retained (22).

THE PLANNING MOVEMENT

The layout of garden cities and garden suburbs inevitably laid emphasis on scheme preparation, and this was also an essential element of the first planning legislation, the Housing, Town Planning etc Act, 1909.

The Act, permissive and not mandatory, related to land in course of development or likely to be used for building and gave to the Local Government Board a general power to make local Acts of Parliament. These were Schemes' dealing with streets, roads, buildings, sewerage, lighting, water supply, ancillary works and the extinction and variation of private easements. The provisions were far from extensive and the procedure cumbersome; very few schemes were approved before the war. But as an example of Government intervention, the power of interference with private rights by a Government Department was unprecedented.

John Burns, the Minister concerned, as a member of the reforming Liberal Government, was clearly influenced by the pressure groups of his day. His opening address to the Royal Institute of British Architects' Town Planning Conference in London in October 1910, a gathering which brought together most of the planning practitioners of the time, reflected what they wanted to achieve. He was aware of the problems of our great towns: 'it seems incredible, but in thirty years 550,000 houses have been built in Greater London; 8,500 new streets have been formed; only twenty-three squares have been created . . . . This shows the extent of possible future harm resulting from that unorganized expansion which may not be true development'. But he knew what needed to be done: 'What is our modest object? Comfort in the house; health in the home; dignity in our streets; space in our roads; and a lessening of the noises, the smoke, the smells, the advertisements, the nuisances that accompany a city that is without a plan because its rulers are governors without ideas and its citizens without hopeful outlook and imagination'. A later remark summarized his hopes: 'Make your plan, if you do plan, bold enough, fair enough, and in a neighbourly way gather all the straggling suburbs into a noble and dignified scheme of expansion' (23).

The principal ideas of an emergent town planning movement were being formulated and the principles of intervention in the course of urban development laid down. Patrick Geddes (24) and Raymond Unwin (25), in particular, stressed the need for preparatory surveys. The technique of plan preparation was developed, based on the segregation of different land uses; objectives were clarified, particularly the provision of social facilities. Indefinite expansion of urban areas was to be checked at all costs. The creation of supplementary centres on the outskirts with defined belts of park, woodland or open country was a common solution. Everywhere there was the search for planned unity: 'no city can be possessed of great civic dignity unless in places it conforms to a symmetrical binding together of parts, and unless it subordinates its units to the dictates of a scheme', wrote S.D. Adshead, a foremost architect and planner, for the same Conference which Burns had addressed (26). And, finally, there was the demand for more beautiful cities, the application of civic art to town building. A rallying point as far as residential development was concerned was lower densities in order to secure the new prizes of light, air and space — Unwin's *Nothing Gained by Overcrowding* proved the point.

The biggest driving force remained the over-riding characteristic of the large towns: a drab environment and poor housing. This enabled J.S. Nettlefold, Chairman of the Birmingham Town Planning Committee and a prominent 'lay' planner to write in 1914: 'The main objective of town planning in this country is to enable all classes of the community to live and work in decent surroundings so that they may be fit for their work and able to enjoy life in a rational manner. The first necessity is an abundant supply of good, cheap houses with a sufficiency of open ground attached to each, and a free circulation of light and air'. The twin solutions of dispersal of population and low density were for adoption. 'In order to provide all classes of the community with the amenities they need, and have a right to, it is necessary to empty the slums into the country, and it must be real country, not a fresh slum. This implies that in the development of new districts plenty of room must be left for allotments, playgrounds and playing fields and in districts a little further out, small holdings should be provided from which it follows that there must not be too many houses per acre' (27).

TRANSPORT

While the planner was making his plea for the disperal of population, important and far reaching technological inventions were permitting suburban development at increasing distances. Electric traction encouraged the underground railway and its extension, as we have seen. Additionally, the development of the petrol engine brought in a new phenomenon. As far as public transport was concerned, the change over from horse-drawn buses to motor-buses was rapid. In 1903 only 13 licences for mechanical stage carriages were issued by the Commissioners of Police for the Metropolis out of a total of 3636 carriage licences. In 1909 there were 1180 out of 2951. In 1913 there were 3522 out of 3664. Within ten years the revolution was virtually complete (28).

From the point of view of private transport, the motor era has had consequences that have torn through patterns of social habit and the physical fabric of the urban environment like shock waves (29). Over something like 30 years, the car has been the centre of a veritable industrial revolution, transforming the hand production of a wheeled gadget of the late 19th century into the mass production of a necessary component of 20th century living.

Carl Benz had built a three-wheeled car in 1885 and Gottlieb Daimler a four-wheeler in 1886. Within the next ten years others such as Panhard, Peugot, Dunlop, Ford, Renault and Michelin, were all actively associated with a developing industry. In Britain the new legislation of 1896, the Locomotives on Highways Act, which allowed a speed limit of 14 m.p.h., encouraged manufacturers who had pioneered the bicycle to turn to the motor car. Speed restriction had previously served to dampen engineering initiative. The Humber Company expanded in Coventry; the first Sunbeam was built in a Wolverhampton cycle shed in 1899; the first Riley in 1898 by one of the co-owners of the Riley Cycle Company, and William Morris (later Lord Nuffield) leart his skills at a cycle bench.

The first decade of the century produced figures who are now legendary — Herbert Austin, Henry Royce and W.O. Bentley for example — and was the period of the first major experiments in mass production. The Standard Motor Company was set up in Coventry in 1903. The first Vauxhall car was produced in the same year; the first Singer in 1904, and the first Hillman in 1907. The Morris Oxford, a two-seater priced at £165, was marketed in 1913. By that year a total of 198 makes of cars had been put on the market, although less than half of them were still in production. Before the outbreak of the First World War, the total annual output had risen to 25,000 cars — a miniscule number compared with America however, where the total had risen to 462,000 by 1914.

Even before the war the rapidly changing transport situation in London was demanding co-ordinated investigation. In 1913, an Arterial Roads Conference was called in London by the President of the Local Government Board for 115 local Authorities within the London Region. A plan of arterial roads was subsequently prepared, and this might be considered the first regional highway plan in Britain.

But the greatest attention was devoted to road surfaces (30). Both cyclists and motorists campaigned to make travelling easier and less uncomfortable. The Cyclist's Touring Club, founded in 1878, provided funds to form the Roads Improvement Association in 1886, and there was a subsequent growth of pressure groups calling attention to grievances. Dust was the major problem and itself a source of considerable nuisance. The Development and Road Improvements Fund Act of 1909 established the Road Board, the first national authority for roads in England and Wales, with powers to make grants and loans to local Authorities for the improvement of roads. A petrol tax of just over 3d a gallon and a motor licence duty, provided the financial resources. The Road Board appointed an advisory engineering committee, the secretary of which was Rees Jeffreys, and the National Physical Laboratory at Teddington agreed to operate a road laboratory. Tar spraying became generalized and a standard specification for road stones was adopted.

And so the turn of the century marks a period in transport characterized by rapid change. A new technological and social force was being created which, in many ways, marked a turning point in contemporary urban history. The urban questions we have discussed in this chapter were to be radically affected. The very appearance of towns was to be changed and their spatial structure transformed. The plea for decentralization on social grounds to overcome overcrowding was in part achieved through a new transport medium. The planning movement widened its concern as the process of intervention in the conduct of urban affairs became more complex. In the next chapters we shall see what success attended the search for the machinery of intervention.

References

(1) Cecil, Robert, *Life in Edwardian England,* Batsford, 1969.
(2) *Op cit.,* Cecil, Robert.
(3) *Op cit.,* Cecil, Robert.
(4) *Op cit.,* Cecil, Robert.
(5) Sitte, Camillo, *The Art of Building Cities,* Vienna 1889. Trans. Charles T. Stewart, Reinhold Publishing Corp. New York, 1945.
(6) Lethaby, W.R., *Of Beautiful Cities,* Arts and Crafts Exhibition Society, London, 1897.
(7) Unwin, Raymond, *Town Planning in Practice,* Ernest Benn, 1909.
(8) Creese, Walter L. (Ed.), *The Legacy of Raymond Unwin,* The M.I.T. Press, 1967.
(9) Unwin, Raymond, *Nothing Gained by Overcrowding!,* 1912, *see* Creese W.L., *op. cit.*
(10) Sheldon, Cyril, *A History of Poster Advertising,* Chapman and Hall, 1937.
(11) Haggard, H.Rider, *The Poor and the Land,* Longmans, Green, 1905.
(12) George, W.L., *Engines of Social Progress,* Adam and Charles Black, 1907.
(13) Wolf, Peter M., *Eugène Hénard and the Beginning of Urbanism in Paris, 1900—1914,* International Federation for Housing and Planning, 1968.
(14) Howard, E., *Garden Cities of Tomorrow,* (Ed.) with preface by F.J. Osborn, Faber, 1946.
(15) Solly, H., *Rehousing of the Industrial Classes,* London, 1884.
(16) Weber, Adna Ferrin, *The Growth of Cities in the Nineteenth Century,* 1899. Cornell University Press, reprint, 1963.
(17) *Op cit.,* Howard, E.
(18) Purdom, C.B., *The Building of Satellite Towns,* Dent, 1925.
(19) *Town Planning in Theory and Practice,* Report of Conference, Garden City Association, London, 1907.
(20) Jevons, H. Stanley, *The British Coal Trade,* 1915. Reprint, David and Charles, 1969.
(21) Ashworth, William, *The Genesis of Modern British Town Planning,* Routledge, 1954.
(22) *Op cit., Town Planning in Theory and Practice.*
(23) Burns, John, *Opening Address,* Transactions of the Town Planning Conference, The Royal Institute of British Architects, London, 1910.
(24) Geddes, P., *Cities in Evolution,* London, 1915.
(25) Unwin, Raymond, *Town Planning in Practice,* Ernest Benn, 1909.
(26) Adshead, S.D., *City Improvement,* Transactions of the Town Planning Conference, The Royal Institute of British Architects, London, 1910.
(27) Nettlefold, J.S., *Practical Town Planning,* St Catherine's Press, 1914.
(28) Sherrington, C.E.R., *100 Years of Inland Transport 1830—1933,* Reprint, Frank Cass, 1969.
(29) Cherry, Gordon E., *Town Planning and the Motor Car in Twentieth Century Britain,* High Speed Ground Transportation Journal, Vol. IV. No. 1, January 1970.
(30) Armytage, W.H.G., *A Social History of Engineering,* Faber, 1961.

7 The inter-War years

On 28 June 1914, Archduke Ferdinand of Austria was assassinated in the Bosnian capital of Sarajevo. Five weeks later Britain declared war on Germany and for four years the western world was thrown into bloody confusion. Britain emerged with every intention of setting a new house in order: the Edwardian pattern of change had been broken and was to be followed as far as urban development was concerned by some radically new departures. 'War', remarked Trotsky, 'is the locomotive of history', and the 1920s and 1930s certainly were to provide ample evidence of war as an agent of change.

'What is our task?', asked David Lloyd George in a speech at Wolverhampton in 1918 in the same month as the Armistice, 'To make Britain a fit country for heroes to live in'. There were others also fighting for this aim. The Labour Party had drawn up its post-War policy and, in a document entitled *Labour and the New Social Order*, urged the building of a 'new social order based, not on internecine conflict, unequality of riches and dominion over subject classes . . . . but on the deliberately planned co-operation in production and distribution . . . . the widest possible participation in power, both economic and political, and the general consciousness of concert which characterizes a true democracy' (1).

Both these aims, the simple and the comprehensive, affected the development of towns and cities, because they required policies for housing and employment. But new national forces were at work. The emergent use of the motor car, the growth of towns through rapid suburban spread, and the redistribution of work opportunities called for even wider powers of intervention. This then was the period when administratively the country grappled with the ideas concerning the need for planning and with devising the machinery of government. It was a critical time and there was a growing debate about the appearance of our cities, their form and shape. It was a time too when ideas about community planning were being considered: then as now, planning was for people.

HOUSING

During the War, a reconstruction committee under the chairmanship of Sir Tudor Walters had considered the type of houses to be built in the future for the working classes. The Tudor Walters Report in 1918 (*Report of Committee on Building Construction in connection with the Provision of Dwellings for the Working Classes in England and Wales, and Scotland*), proposed an entirely new standard of working class housing; and the adoption of the Report laid down the pattern for Council housing in local Authorities throughout the country. The inter-War Council estate became a highly distinctive element in any urban landscape: low density with blocks of houses arranged along streets following geometric layouts; dwellings set back behind front gardens; building lines splayed at all road junctions and, noticeably, at roundabouts; incidental green spaces to complement garden space; and with a deadening similarity of house styles and materials over vast areas, monotony was reinforced by occupancy largely from one social class.

The Tudor Walters ideal was houses built at not more than 30 to the hectare (12 to the acre) each standing in its own garden, in a well developed estate. A large living room with a sunny aspect was laid down as essential and every house was to be fitted with a bath in a separate room, a wc approached under cover, a larder of reasonable size and a coal store. The protagonists of half a century or more had won. The ideals of the designers of Bournville, Port Sunlight and a host of garden suburb schemes had gained public acceptance.

Equally important was housing legislation which tackled the serious housing shortage immediately after the War. There was an estimated deficiency of 600,000 dwellings. It was very doubtful whether the private sector could make up this shortage, particularly at rents which people could be expected to pay. Dr Addison's Housing and Town Planning Act of 1919 attempted to meet this situation by calling upon local Authorities to prepare immediate surveys of their housing needs, draw up plans for dealing with them and to submit these plans to the Ministry of Health for approval. Losses incurred in executing these plans would be borne by the Exchequer. Other measures considerably extended State intervention in providing working class housing at reasonable rents. John Wheatley's Housing Act of 1924 continued Government support, and in nine years over half a million local Authority houses had been built.

The inter-War period, therefore, saw local Authority estates built in virtually every sizeable town in the country. In some cities the estates were extremely large, the size of demand being reflected in the size of city concerned, the degree of need and the extent of slum clearance programmes. The largest, perhaps, was the Becontree Estate, a so-called cottage estate built in Essex by the London County Council between Barking and Hornchurch, south east of Ilford. The development extended over a long period from 1921 to 1934, but with the most rapid growth in 1928 and 1929 (2). Virtually a new settlement of over

Wollaton Park Estate, Nottingham, is a vivid example of the geometrical layout that typified inter-War Council housing estates. Notice the extremely low density that was achieved with wastage in odd angles and adjoining roundabouts, which, in traffic flow terms, were largely ineffectual anyway. Also, notice the provision of playing fields on the periphery of the estate and the extensive area given over to allotments. Original tree cover is retained in highly artificial circles. The dual carriageway road is a gesture to advanced inter-War highway design.

100,000 persons was built and it served both as a model for other towns to copy and, for those who decried this sort of mass uniformity with all the social problems involved, an illustration of their argument for adopting other methods.

Becontree was planned as a town, but continuity in the building programme was strongly influenced by financial and other considerations in successive Housing Acts, and modified from time to time by varying estimates of the Council of the pressure of demand for houses in London. The London County Council provided the essential services (gas, water, electricity and sewage disposal). It also planned sites in its total layout for development by public and voluntary social services. This may seem commonplace and obvious enough in our day, but was an extremely important step forward in the 1920s. In fact, the tentative nature of planned provision was revealed by short-comings in full integration of various aspects of development. For example the L C C did not stop building houses in an area even if it was evident that there would be no immediate school accommodation for the children of the new tenants. There was also a problem concerning local employment. New industry did not move to the district at the same time as the incoming people, and, in fact, there was virtually no industrial development until the Estate had been in existence for something like ten years.

The large local Authority estate had many variations. Becontree was a dormitory town on the outskirts of the capital. In the provinces most estates were additions on the outskirts of a growing town, now wrapped, fossil-like, in later public or private suburban expansion of different style. In Manchester the objective of developing a satellite garden town was taken up. This was at Wythenshawe, 'which would have industries of its own and be partly self-contained, but which would nevertheless be a part of Manchester and provide accommodation for Manchester workers' (3). The land was bought by the Corporation in 1926. After much opposition an extension of borough boundaries was obtained giving Manchester another 2,200 hectares (5,500) acres in 1930. Liverpool's development at Speke was of comparable order.

By September 1939 there was a total of 12.7 million dwellings in this country, and 10 per cent of these had been built by local Authorities in the preceding 20 years. This was the measure of their contribution in the inter-War period. A new element in tenure options had emerged. Improved housing for the working class was a reality and the shape and structure of cities had been considerably affected.

But private ownership had also increased between the wars and nearly one-third of all dwellings in 1939 were owner occupied. The 1920s and 1930s saw a substantial suburban expansion in the private

Opposite, above: Eastern Avenue, Redbridge, London, 1928; *below:* Private housing in Redbridge, 1925-28. These photographs show the sprawling private housing that was being built in the late 1920s along the Eastern Avenue out of London. Substantial middle-class properties with their fashionable designs to suit the mass market, fronted the Avenue; estate development proceeded at depth behind. The new layout principles can readily be seen: semi-detached houses or short terraces front estate roads; short front gardens but longer ones at the rear provide good space standards. There was as yet relatively small provision for the private car. Shops sprang up at strategic road intersections; for example, at the roundabout which was built at Gants Hill. Provision for playing fields seems to be available, but this land would always be at risk because of encroaching building.

sector. The inter-War estate of semi-detached houses, typified by the ribboned frontage to radial and other main roads in the larger towns, is a characteristic feature. From the point of view of appearance there is rather more visual variety than in the local Authority estate, because of more frequent variations in house elevations and differences in style stemming from many small scale building operations with different architects. The estate road was dominant and the 'semi' ubiquitous. The search for space was reflected in sizeable gardens, but incidental open space in the estate layout itself was infrequent.

This new block of property owners was distinctive and constituted a new factor in British social life. Mark Abrams (4) has equated this tenure group in its economic interests and fears, and in its political values and ambitions, with a European peasantry, blurring the classical social dichotomy of proletariat and capitalist because of an attachment to a substantial investment. The growth of Building Societies was of course strongly associated with this development in private house building. In 1924 the total outstanding amount on mortages came to £120 million; in 1935 it was £530 million and in 1940 £678 million. The last figure represented advances to one and a half million borrowers, or an average debt of £450 attached to the domestic economies of one British family in eight.

Over four million new dwellings were built in Britain during the two wars, a major consequence of which was that a substantial improvement in overall housing conditions took place and the quality of life in towns improved sharply (5). But there was of course a backlog of unfit housing particularly in the larger and older towns and cities, and the problems of overcrowding and squalid accommodation remained. In 1921, 14 per cent of the population of Great Britain was living with more than two people to a room. Over most of the country aggregated figures for counties were less than 10 per cent, and the blackspots were Northumberland and Durham (30 per cent) and Scotland (43 per cent). But even in English towns high proportions were recorded: St Helens, Carlisle, Dewsbury, Darlington, West Bromwich, Plymouth, West Ham, London C C, Middlesbrough and Barnsley all had between 15 and 21 per cent.

But improvements did take place. Between 1921 and 1931 the population of the country increased by 5 per cent, but the number of dwellings increased by 17 per cent. Even so a national overcrowding survey in 1936, called for by the Housing Act of 1935, showed certain towns still in very poor light. Sunderland, for example, had 20.6 per cent of its working class families considered to be overcrowded, and elsewhere in the North East high proportions were recorded: Gateshead (15.2 per cent), South Shields (13.1 per cent), and Newcastle upon Tyne (10.7 per cent). But London's East End (Bethnal Green,

Poplar, Shoreditch and Stepney) had 14.4 per cent, and West Ham 8.4 per cent. In the North West, St Helens (8.8 per cent), Wigan (8.1 per cent) and Liverpool (7.4 per cent) were the highest, and in the Midlands, West Bromwich with 7.0 per cent. In Scotland the picture was very much worse, with 25 per cent of families overcrowded.

The second major housing evil also remained. A limited slum clearance programme meant that a very large number of old and unfit dwellings were still habited, where sanitary conditions were primitive and amenities rare. In the later 1930s perhaps one third of working class dwellings in London were due for demolition. Before the outbreak of the Second World War, Manchester had 68,000 dwellings (one-third of the total in the city) unfit for human habitation. In Birmingham a survey suggested that 20 per cent should be condemned immediately. Conditions on Tyneside and in Scotland were even worse. In Great Britain as a whole 550,000 dwellings were ready for immediate demolition, and a further 350,000 had a life of not more than six years.

But most towns could point to a slum clearance programme, however modest; in the larger cities there were a considerable number of instances of quite dramatic development. Leeds, for example, had a long tradition of back-to-back houses: 30,000 built prior to 1844, 28,000 between 1844 and 1874, and another 12,000 by 1909. Between 1934 and 1939, however, a bold slum clearance scheme east of the Central Area Markets gave rise to an impressive project. This was the building of the Quarry Hill flats, 938 dwellings in all, in blocks of four to eight stories, with a shopping parade, communal laundry and other amenities on a compact 9 hectare (23 acre) site (6).

We have considered two aspects of inter-War housing: improved new houses in both public and private sectors, and the improvements recorded in housing conditions in the older parts of towns, although much still remained to be accomplished. A third aspect was the physical spread of towns caused by suburban expansion which was in its turn due to the absolute population growth and the dispersal of people from congested areas. In all towns and cities a common movement of population was recorded; densities in the centres declined and growth took place in the suburbs. Land was taken up by speculative builders for development. Demand seemed insatiable in the urge for new accommodation and for households to express social status, to secure a sound investment and to take advantage of good transport facilities. Above all, the new release afforded by the motor car encouraged even wider geographical spreads.

The inter-War years saw the further consolidation of various urban areas into recognizable amalgams. The pattern was cemented: 40 per cent of the population now lived in seven areas — London, Manchester,

Birmingham, West Yorkshire, Glasgow, Merseyside and Tyneside, and this group grew much more rapidly than the rest of the country.

THE GARDEN CITY

In the meantime the pressure groups for forms of planned residential development continued to voice their objectives. The monotony and visual dullness of average private housing areas, the innate horror of the large city with its social problems (the question of poverty continued to be a common investigation as we shall see), and the myth of the value of the self-contained small sized town, supported the search for radically different forms of development.

In 1920, Ebenezer Howard began his second Garden City at Welwyn, giving another fillip to the satellite town idea. The principles became enshrined in the conventional planning wisdom of the day, and while legislation was to be long delayed, the lobby in professional and political circles was a strong one. It is a useful reflection to pause on the ideas of one protagonist, C.B. Purdom (1921):

'The intention is that each garden city should be a distinct self-contained town of comfortable size — not too large to feel at home in, but large enough to contain a diversity of industries to occupy and provide for the people whose homes are there; furnishing that enlivening variety of interests and that mingling of classes so essential to a well ordered community, and thus to make possible real harmony and unity, the lack of which today so much retards progress and prosperity in all directions, not least in that of industry.

'In a huge city the sense of identity is apt to be lost, and in consequence the ordinary inhabitant often takes little interest in local government; but in a sizeable town, good to look at and with civic pride outwardly expressed in civic order, a man can feel that he is part of a definite community. Feeling a citizen of no mean city, he will take an interest in its good government, and his vision will not be bounded by the walls of his workplace.

'The garden city will advance healthy living, not only because the houses will be placed on the most suitable sites, with plenty of space all round to give free play to clean air and sunshine, but also because the gardens and surrounding agricultural belt will supply fresh and pure food and milk in place of the transit-soiled articles to which the average dweller in an ordinary city is condemned. Also, when working hours are short or in times of bad trade, the garden will afford a profitable outlet for energy. The absence of the permanent smoke-clouds of the large city will mean a purer atmosphere — curtains and clothes will keep clean much longer, and the house-keeper will save money on soap and be relieved of much harassing housework' (7).

Some of these sentiments might now seem quaint, but we shall find them expressed repeatedly for many years. Support for the general principles came from a number of sources. Once again the particular circumstances of London were to the fore. In the 1920s and early 1930s, the London County Council had spread over eighteen large estates, twelve within the county area and others outside it. Quite apart from the objection to this type of large, one-class suburb, lacking immediate communal necessities, the inadequacy of the administrative machine was apparent. Responsibilities for housing matters were shared between the L C C and the Metropolitan Boroughs and this overlapping was a serious obstacle to any idea of comprehensive planning. This was, therefore, an administrative argument for decentralized satellite towns where new, unified governmental machinery was possible.

In additon, the propagandist pointed to the health and social hazards of life in the inner areas of the big towns. Medical Officers of Health reported on infantile mortality rates where there were big differences between those of the central wards, the middle ring and the outer ring. It could be claimed that 'people died by the hundred in the crowded centres of London, Manchester, Newcastle, Glasgow and Edinburgh, who would have lived had they had good homes set in even moderately spacious surroundings' (8).

The correlation between bad housing and the incidence of disease and higher mortality rates was stressed. Gilbert McAllister made the point: 'Take people out of the crowded slums of the Hulme district of Manchester and place them in decent houses in the spacious planned satellite Wythenshawe and you cut the death rate by more than half. Place all the population of the country in well-planned areas similar to Wythenshawe, Letchworth, Welwyn, and you save more than a third of the people at present doomed to die because of bad conditions' (9).

This emotional lobby supported the national plea for comprehensive organization and planning to be applied to the growth of towns and cities. In considering alternatives to no action, Unwin's case, as early as 1921, was persuasive. In describing the tendency to concentrate industies in relation to one another and the means of transport, and to decentralize them in relation to London itself, he outlined the options: 'either we can allow these great movements to go forward haphazard, leaving each individual merchant to elbow his way into an advantageous office or warehouse in the centre, each individual manufacturer to seek out unaided some available spot on which to locate his industry, each individual tenant to scramble for the best tenement he can find in an overcrowded city; or, on the other hand, we can henceforth regard the development of our city as we should regard any other great enterprise, as one needing to be organized and directed towards producing the best results for the whole' (10). Unwin's master strategy was, therefore, to halt the further growth of the capital and to build self-contained satellites as expansion points beyond a green belt.

The satellite idea reached the pages of official reports. Raymond Unwin's *First Report* to the Greater London Regional Planning Committee in 1929 recognized the need for relief of overcrowding by means of satellite towns on the fringe of London, separated by a green belt. He wrote: 'It is of importance that the problem . . . . should be approached from the point of view of planning ample, though selected, tracts for building development on a background of open lands, rather than, as has hitherto been the case, from that of planning limited tracts of open space to be reserved on a background of unlimited potential building development'(11). His proposals were outlined in detail in the *Second Report* published in 1933.

The full context of the development of the green belt idea and related regional planning proposals has been sketched by David Thomas (12). For our purposes we should simply note the ever-increasing strength of this particular lobby, one that was not without success. In 1935, the London County Council green belt scheme was launched, extra enthusiasm perhaps being generated when the Labour Party gained control of the Council in 1934. In 1938, the Green Belt (London and Home Counties) Act was passed: 'an Act to make provision for the preservation from industrial or building development of areas of land in and around the administrative county of London, to confer powers for that purpose upon the London County Council and certain other authorities and persons, and for other purposes'. There were certain powers of acquisition, but the green belt was primarily intended to take shape through owners of land, local authorities and parish councils entering into covenants restrictive of users, and through local Authorities acquiring by agreement.

London was not the only instance of such thinking, at least as far as satellite towns were concerned. There were fourteen other regional planning reports in other parts of England and Wales which made references to or proposals favouring the provision of new towns, garden cities or satellites for the relief of congested areas. Legislation in various housing Acts and the Town and Country Planning Act, 1932, contained provisions for the establishment of garden cities. The 1932 Act, for example, enabled the Minister of Health to acquire land for garden cities on behalf of a local Authority or an authorized association.

In America similar interest was being expressed. The City Housing Corporation had been set up in 1924, a limited dividend company for the ultimate purpose of building an American Garden City. Early modest steps were taken in the development of the Sunnyside Community of Long Island. The Radburn experiment in 1929 failed because of the Wall Street collapse, but following a number of other community projects, Greenbelt Towns were authorized in 1935. President Roosevelt established the Resettlement Administration, and Greenbelt (Maryland, about 17 kilometres from Washington), Greendale (Wisconsin, about 9 kilometres from Milwaukee), and Greenhills (Ohio, about 7 kilometres from Cincinnati) followed as suburban imitations of the British idea (13).

In Britain, a Hundred Towns Association was formed and set out a national plan. A ten year programme for the migration of at least five million people to a hundred new urban centres of approximately 50,000 people each was proposed. This programme was part of a proposed national policy of remodelling existing towns, saving the countryside and properly co-ordinating industry and agriculture with urban developments.

TRANSPORT

Far reaching developments in transport took place in the inter-War period with important repercussion on town life. The 1920s and 1930s saw a marked loosening in the spatial aspects of urban structure as the

Tram transport in Sunderland in the 1930s. Overhead power lines and supporting poles, and fixed surface tracks for the tram which has now been superceded, create a very different highway from the kind to which we are now accustomed. The cobbled surface has largely disappeared to cater for the car instead of the horse.

possibilities for widening the distance between workplace and residence increased. In London and in one or two centres elsewhere such as Liverpool, Glasgow and Tyneside, electric traction augmented the steam railway in enabling the scatter of suburban development. In London, the underground railway with its high frequency of stations gave form and structure to the spatial arrangement of suburban estates.

The tram entered its golden age. A national route mileage of 4046 kilometres in 1913 achieved a peak eleven years later with 4225 kilometres. A rapid fall set in, and in 1933, only 2996 kilometres remained in service. As it was replaced by the motor bus, its rapid demise came to an end in the 1950s. The tram has its own part in urban history, contributing very definitely to the nostalgia of sounds and sights of bygone days. Charles Klapper reminisces: 'The sawmill grind of a Walthamstow car in full series slowly surmounting the railway bridge in Forest Road, after some evening excursion to the purlieus of Epping Forest, can be conjured up from over forty years back; the skirling of magnetic track brake gear mingling with church bells on some city's Sunday morning; the flutter of the petrol-electric drive along the Hasting's front; the measured tread of long wheelbase four-wheelers along the suburban roads of Sheffield or the smooth roll of cushioned wheel single-deck rail coaches on the front at Blackpool and the rather more exciting motion of a fast run on the sleeper track from Glasgow out to Airdrie . . .' (14).

It was with the motor car, however, that the most important changes occurred. The 1920s saw the development of the mass car market, assisted by the innovation of assembly line production, organizational improvement, amalgamations and price cutting. By 1929, the Austin Seven, for example, was selling for as little as £130 and the Morris Minor for £125; the first Hillman Minx (four doors, 10 hp) appearing in 1931 was £155. By 1935, Fords at their new Dagenham site had put their first £100 car on the market. By the outbreak of the Second World War, Britain had become the second largest producer of cars in the world.

The effective organization of the car industry demanded the mass market. William Morris, the car magnate, is said to have remarked in 1924: 'Until the worker goes to his factory by car, I shall not believe that we have touched more than a fringe of the home market' (15). The mass market needed little stimulation, and the potential and privilege of car ownership stirred the imagination of every sector of society. The car was accorded a prominent place in social values and the people's desire to own one became overwhelming.

As I have written elsewhere (16), the car became the new liberator in democratic terms; it was the new emancipator for the lower middle class and the new skilled worker. Position in society is reflected obviously enough with other possessions: one's house and residential area clearly reflect one's earning power and social status. But the car is different: the driver of one of today's typical family saloons is drawn from very wide sectors of society; his station to the casual observer is unknown and unknowable; the car is at once the concealer of his status and a herald of his stake in mid-mass. It is his passport to a social recognition formerly denied him. As a destroyer of old class barriers, it is supreme. The inter-War period first showed these symptoms and the history of towns entered a new phase of evolution.

Road improvement policies — widening and re-alignments, bridges and new roads — affected most of the larger towns at this time. There was an emphasis on the problems presented by long-distance through traffic and hence we have examples of new arterial roads such as the East Lancashire road to Liverpool or the London arterials, or bridges as at Kincardine over the Forth. But in towns there were spectacular new constructions too, the King George V Bridge over the Tyne at Newcastle, for example, or the Mersey tunnel at Liverpool.

In devising schemes for residential and other areas, planners gave detailed attention to the design of street systems, including the alignment and width of particular carriageways and the design of junctions. There was increasing concern that through-traffic should be deflected from the heart of neighbourhoods, but practical formulae for segregated layouts had to wait until after the Second World War. In the meantime planners looked with interest at Radburn, New Jersey, where the plan of Clarence Stein and Henry Wright incorporated the segregation of pedestrians from cars. Here, the main estate roads enclosed 'superblocks', areas of between 12 and 20 hectares (30 and 50 acres) within which were the houses and the culs-de-sac that served them. In the centre of the superblock was a backbone of continuous open space as a park towards which the houses faced; under-passes and footbridges across traffic roads linked the superblocks. In Britain, however, this new element in the planning of residential estates had to remain simply an idea for some years.

In the meantime the highway engineer continued to give great emphasis to innovations like the bypass, a spectacular addition to the urban scene, designed to relieve congestion and prevent through traffic from entering busy areas, a desirable objective subsequently prejudiced by permitting residential frontages with their own interruptions to free traffic flows. Additionally, ring roads, both inner and outer, became favourite measures in big cities for linking up radials and so completing the essence of a spider's web town lay out. On these ring roads the roundabout became a characteristic feature at major intersections.

An important figure in highway planning in the late 1930s was Alker Tripp, a commissioner of the London Metropolitan Police. In his *Road*

Traffic and Its Control (1938) he suggested a hierarchy of roads; arterial roads, 'roads from which all but motor traffic is excluded'; sub-arterial roads, 'roads open to all types of vehicular traffic and upon which the interest of vehicular traffic is to be predominant'; and local or minor roads, 'roads intended for local traffic only . . . as a means of access to premises'. The objective behind identifying these categories was to ensure that main traffic should be directed to the arterial and sub-arterial roads and should be restricted from 'the daily haunts of the populace' (17). We shall return later to this idea of segregation in the search for enhancing quality of urban environment (see page 176).

The rise in numbers in vehicular traffic began to point inevitably to the need for new concepts in the planning of roads, and Tripp's proposals gained widespread approval. But in many ways damage had already been done, and a popular outcry was directed against ribbon development, the exploitation of the frontage of main roads leading out of towns for housing purposes. Years of agricultural depression encouraged landowners and farmers to sell off land on the outskirts of towns; sprawl along main highways with development in depth at the rear postponed perhaps for many years, became an urban feature, particularly of course around the large cities and especially London. Authorities had had powers since 1909 (Development and Road Improvement Funds Act) to acquire land up to 203 metres depth on either side of a new road. But only a very few Authorities ever took advantage of this power; Manchester was one example in laying out their system of parkways on the Wythenshawe Estate. In an attempt to control a situation that was already out of hand, legislation in 1935 (Restriction of Ribbon Development Act) required all development within 68 metres of the middle of a classified road, and the formation of any new access to a classified road, to have the approval of the highway Authority.

INDUSTRY AND EMPLOYMENT

The nature of industrial development in towns and cities during the inter-War period stems from two underlying factors, both interrelated: change in Britain's industrial structure and change in the regional distribution of population. The population of London and the Home Counties increased by 18 per cent between 1921 and 1937; that of the Midland Counties increased by 11 per cent; that of the West Riding, Nottinghamshire and Derbyshire by 6 per cent, the Lowlands of Scotland by 4 per cent, and that of Lancashire by less than 1 per cent. The population of South Wales declined by 9 per cent, and that of Northumberland and Durham by 1 per cent (18). Depression in coal mining, textiles and heavy industries was associated with this population drift; the South East boomed with its new light industries.

The inter-War years saw important expansions and contractions in certain industrial groupings. Between 1911 and 1931 the working population of England and Wales increased by 16 per cent, but this rate of growth was not common to all industries. Clothing, agriculture, personal service and textiles actually decreased. On the other hand, substantial increases were recorded by those industries which reflected a good deal of the social history of the time: the functions of government had expanded; transport services had developed; millions of houses had been built; the range of domestic gadgetry had widened; consumer goods and entertainment services absorbed the rising standard of living. During the 1930s, large employment gains were recorded in the manufacture of electrical apparatus, entertainment services, vehicle construction and building; only small gains were noted in coal, textiles, clothing and iron and steel.

Associated with these changes in employment groups, prolonged mass unemployment became the feature of certain underprivileged regions. In the 30 years before the First World War, the national unemployment rate was about 4 per cent (as far as it is possible to tell, that is, from trade union returns — the only data available); in the worst years it may have doubled to 8 per cent. But, after 1920, unemployment rates were higher, with the North, Scotland and Wales heavily hit because of their reliance on depressed industries such as coal, ship building, heavy engineering and textiles. Before 1914 these areas had the lowest unemployment rates, with London a relative blackspot as a labour market. Between the wars these relative situations were reversed.

Unemployment, 9 per cent in 1924, did not fall below that again during the decade. In 1930 it shot up to nearly 20 per cent and reached a peak in 1933 with three million (23 per cent of insured people) out of work. The figure stabilized at 1.75 million between 1937 and 1939, as world trade picked up again and the volume of production rose. But chronic concentrations of jobless persisted. In 1935 more than 60 per cent of the insured workers of Merthyr Tydfil, and more than 70 per cent of those in Jarrow were out of work. Moreover, unemployment was of crippling length: in 1936 nearly three-quarters of the unemployed in Crook, County Durham, and half those in the Rhondda, South Wales, had been without a job for more than five years (19). Amalgamations and the closing down of unremunerative plant could have disastrous social consequences. Old iron and steel centres at Mossend in Scotland and Dowlais in Wales were shut down. At Jarrow the shipyards were closed and Ellen Wilkinson's march of the unemployed to London seared into the conscience of a nation. For her readers, Jarrow became *The Town that was Murdered* (1939).

This is the background situation to a period in which industrial changes affected the course of urban development and the very appearance of some industrial quarters of our towns and cities. In this context we might point to three factors: the rise of the industrial estate with different locational requirements from those of before; the search for a well designed industrial environment; and the disparity in employment prospects between regions of unequal opportunity. At the same time we should note the loosening bonds of industrial location through the availability of electric power. By 1924 nearly half the total power consumed by all branches of British industry was electrically generated. The formation of the Central Electricity Board in 1926 and the commencement of the National Grid System overcame the multiplicity of small generating plants, the use of different voltages and frequencies — obstacles in the electricity supply industry which had slowed down the adoption of electrical power in Britain's industries (20).

It was during the late 1920s that industrial estates first began to be important, particularly in London (21). A development company might provide factories for sale on the lines of a speculative housing estate; alternatively it might sell the land in plots or build factories for let. The choice of location depended on a number of factors. In the case of the Chase Estate, Park Royal, in north-west London, it was the sale of Government land and buildings of a wartime munitions factory that provided the nucleus in 1928. Within ten years a speculative factory estate had expanded to more than 190,000 square metres of floor space.

Rail and perhaps even canal-side facilities were still considered important for new industrial premises, but increasingly good transport facilities by arterial road were sought after (a nearby labour supply was still, of course, essential). In London, important new roads built in the 1920s included the Great West Road, Western Avenue and the North Circular Road, and the publicity value of taking sites on such frontages helped in the steady rise of land prices in these areas. Various London by-passes such as at Sidcup, Barnet, Croydon and Kingston, attracted similar attention.

These industrial estates were the natural home for the new 'light' industries that expanded so enormously between the wars, catering for and stimulating the consumer goods industries, electrical goods, chemicals and a range of service industries. They were ideally located in conveniently shaped buildings designed for new processes and had transport facilities geared for regular contact with a growing local market. Because of their lack of dependence on obvious sources of power such as coal, and because of their new architectural form, these new factories were much more acceptable in the urban scene than had previously been the case, even as residential neighbours. Inter-War planners were keen to stimulate this trend: 'well designed works and factories, planned in orderly surroundings, where efficiency in production is combined with comfort for employees, are a sign of good citizenship as well as of good business', concluded T. Alwyn Lloyd in 1935 (22).

New industrial development of this nature was a comparative rarity on any scale outside London and the Home Counties, although the first industrial estate of any size in Britain was developed at Trafford Park, Manchester, as early as 1896. This had been a speculation on 486 hectares near the Ship Canal. There was considerable expansion in London, particularly in the north west sector and there were large enterprises, particularly at Slough and centres such as West Thurrock. The London area was particularly sought after by American investment: between 1930 and the outbreak of war, more than one half of U S manufacturing units established in this country located their factories along the Great West and North Circular Roads and at Slough.

The Slough Trading Estate started in 1920 as a private speculative venture. A private company constructed a road and rail transport system and laid out the area, providing services and standard factories to let. Later, through co-operation with the Buckinghamshire County Council, a social centre and welfare and sports facilities were provided (23).

Because of the reversal of economic fortunes in other regions of the country, most towns outside London and the South East and parts of the Midlands saw industrial investment at a very low ebb. Their manufacturing plant and the visual appearance of industrial areas remained to all intents and purposes the same as before the War. The events of the 1920s, and particularly of the early 1930s, led to a growing recognition of the trends in national re-distribution that had developed and of the inherent dangers which were presented. The idea of economic planning grew, and symbolically there was the inauguration of P E P (Political and Economic Planning) in 1931. A national industrial location policy took shape and we begin to see, for the first time, the role of planning as a force of economic intervention in town development, acting either as an intended brake on growth or as a spur to industrial progress. The industrial history of towns took on a new phase.

The first steps were negative — to encourage labour to move out of depressed areas. In 1928 the Industrial Transference Board was set up, and from August 1928 to mid-1937 nearly 150,000 men and 40,000 women were transferred by the Board of Trade. Voluntary migration was on a more substantial scale and between 1932 and 1938, some 400,000 people moved from the North East and South Wales alone

(24). The slow growth or even stagnation of towns in these areas have to be seen in this context.

More positively, the Special Areas Act of 1934 made £2 million available for creating employment in depressed areas and encouraged the setting up of Trading Estates as a means of providing local employment to stop the steady drain of out-migration from areas of high unemployment, namely Central Scotland, the North East, South Wales and West Cumberland. Before 1939, the Team Valley Estate in Gateshead, the Hillington estate in Glasgow and Treforest near Pontypridd attracted a good deal of interest, both as instances of advanced planning layouts and examples of an interventionist policy designed to secure more equitable opportunity for the economically depressed parts of the country. By 1939 about 12,000 people were employed in factories in Special Areas owned by the State.

The Hillington Industrial Estate, Glasgow, was established in 1937 and was contemporary with the Team Valley Estate, Gateshead, and the Treforest Estate, South Wales. Notice the regular layout and the attention paid to space standards and amenity considerations.

The spirit of intervention developed quickly. Sir Malcolm Stewart, Commissioner for the Special Areas (England and Wales) recommended in his *Third Report* (Cmd. 5303, 1936) that 'an embargo should, subject to certain exemptions, be placed on further factory construction in the Greater London area; such exemptions would probably include small manufacturers, the distributive industries, retail trades and public utility undertakings, and also the manufacture of any particular product that could only be carried on successfully in that area. This embargo would involve the exercise of Government control over the Greater London area together with a system of licensing for new and for the extension of existing factories.'

A Royal Commission was promised and in July 1937 the Royal Commission on the Distribution of the Industrial Population, under the chairmanship of Sir Montague Barlow, was appointed. Its terms of reference were: 'to enquire into the causes which have influenced the present geographical distribution of the industrial population of Great Britain and the probable direction of any change in that distribution in the future; to consider what social, economic or strategical advantages arise from the concentration of industries or of the industrial population in large towns or in particular areas of the country; and to report what remedial measures, if any, should be taken in the national interest.'

This, then, was not to be an enquiry solely into industrial location but it was properly widened to relate to urban affairs as a whole. The evidence which the Royal Commission received was voluminous and covered every view of planning and the state of Britain's towns at that time. For a synthesis of the various lobbies of the day and the common attitudes to the social and economic problems of the 1930s, the submitted evidence makes fascinating reading. Some of it appears today heavily exaggerated, but the fact that it was repeated in so many different quarters suggests that it did represent an acceptable position. This is not the place to give details of the evidence to the Barlow Commission, but the following extracts from the Memorandum submitted by the Town Planning Institute are particularly revealing:

'A fact which is almost universally applicable at the present time is that continued development on the fringe promotes and encourages the concentration of high buildings in the old centres of towns. It is well known that this, in turn, so increases land values in the centre that large expenditure is necessary in order to remodel the central core to enable it to function. The streets in the town centre become dark and gloomy by reason of being hemmed in by tall buildings whose rooms are inevitably ill-lighted and ventilated; the streets become crowded beyond their capacity resulting in public safety being endangered; the air becomes heavily polluted by noxious fumes and smoke; transport facilities become overcrowded and congested; the population suffer from minor ailments — colds, chills, influenza, gastric trouble — and increasingly from neurasthenia and other nervous disorders; and recreational facilities are pushed further and further away from the people.'

Later: 'Excessively large centres of population deprive the individual of the "full and balanced life" which is necessary for his general welfare and health. In the smaller town the individual is, quite consciously, part of the town and its social structure; in the large town or city he is a nonentity — a cog of such minute size in the great machine that he feels himself entirely unessential to the working of it' (25).

There was considerable stress on the social and economic disadvantages arising from concentrations of industry or of the industrial population in large towns or in particular areas of the country. Strategic disadvantages were also seen in view of the likelihood of air attacks in the future. Many bodies made very similar statements. As far as solutions were concerned there was agreement that existing legislation was inadequate and there was a good deal of heart searching for an ideal machinery of government.

The Commission came to a number of far reaching conclusions. Essentially they accepted the arguments about social and economic disadvantages: 'associated with, and to some extent a cause of, the present disadvantages of the large towns in the matter of health are slums and over-crowding; the absence of adequate provision for open air recreation and games; a lack of proper and regular contact, especially in the case of the young, with the resources and amenity of country life; smoke and dirt, fog and general absence of sunlight; and noise. Not least grave of the social disadvantages is transport congestion, which in the case of the worker travelling long journeys to and from his work . . . often involves serious loss of time and money and probably some impairment of health. The economic disadvantages were noted too, consisting 'largely, if not mainly, of such obvious features as congestion of traffic, involving delay in the transport of goods, and serious economic and financial handicaps for the workers; smoke, pollution of the atmosphere, and noise, which are not only injurious to health but also involve economic loss; and high values of land and buildings' (26).

The Barlow Report was delayed by wartime conditions but was eventually published in 1940. It represented a new peak in thinking about British planning, setting certain directives which have since formed the cornerstone of national policies concerning economic development. In a very direct way, therefore, it had a bearing on the course of urban history, particularly on the size and the growth of towns. The objectives of suggested national action were threefold: the continued and further redevelopment of congested urban areas where necessary; decentralization or dispersal, both of industries and industrial population, from such areas; and the encouragement of a reasonable balance of industrial development, so far as possible, throughout the various regions of the country, coupled with appropriate diversification of industry in each region. We shall see in a later section how far these aims have been adopted, with what success, and with what consequences.

TOWN DEVELOPMENT

In the central areas of towns and cities certain trends which we have noted previously were consolidated during the inter-War period. In particular there was the increasing commercial importance of town centres from the point of view of shopping and employment in offices and service industry. The development of multiple-shop retailing continued with the rise of the variety chain store. Michael Marks had already established the Penny Bazaars in the North before the turn of the century, and the first British branch of F.W. Woolworth was opened in Liverpool in 1909, additional to the 600 branches already in the United States at that time. There was rapid growth in inter-War years, the number of variety chain stores rising from 300 in 1920 to 1200 in 1939 (27).

In residential areas the inter-War parade of suburban shops became a feature along main highways, especially at road junctions. A new wave of church building commenced and a range of community facilities included schools set in their own playing fields, new libraries and swimming baths. Petrol filling stations increased rapidly in numbers.

As the entertainments industry was revolutionized, new public buildings were added to the urban scene. The cinema was a prominent example. There were over 3000 cinemas in pre-War Britain, but in the 1920s came the first burst of conversions of theatres and music halls into cinemas. Once the first boom had subsided, the invention of 'talkies' brought a revival featured by the building of huge luxury cinemas. By the early 1930s aggregate weekly attendances at London cinemas amounted to one-third of the capital's population (28).

The Super Cinema era of the 1934—39 period provided distinctive buildings. The many Odeons afford good examples. Oscar Deutch, the son of a mid-European refugee, who had settled in Birmingham and operated as a dealer in non-ferrous scrap metal and rabbit skins, and whose initials went to provide the title 'Odeon', began to erect cinemas in the Birmingham area around 1930. By the end of that decade there were 250 Odeons in Britain, luxury cinemas that conformed to the same architectural pattern, incorporating vertical towers and sweeping corner entrance curves. To the designs principally of Harry Weedon, the Birmingham architect, there were ten to fifteen completions every six months in the boom years.

Popular urban leisure took on other new patterns. Additional pastimes to mark the urban scene between the wars produced the greyhound track and the dance hall. But the new mass medium of the 1920s, radio broadcasting, still served to emphasize the importance of home-based leisure.

A principal feature of inter-War cities in Britain was expansion at the periphery. But these years also saw the first halting steps towards policies of intervention whereby local government attempted to control the appearance and development of urban areas for reasons beyond those simply of public health. We have noted that the 1909 Town Planning Act provided the first steps in this direction: the years between 1918 and 1939 saw additional ones. Town planning became an accepted medium for shaping and guiding the physical growth of towns. It developed into something much more than street planning, and covered a wider field than that indicated by the contents of statutory town planning schemes.

The 1909 Act permitted the Local Government Board to authorize town planning schemes. Up to March 1915, 74 local Authorities had been authorized to prepare 105 schemes. The first complete scheme was the Quinton, Harborne and Edgbaston scheme in Birmingham, followed by the East Birmingham scheme and the Ruislip — Northwood (Middlesex) scheme; but many were never completed. There was further legislation in the 1920s and the Act of 1925 consolidated previous legislation. The emphasis remained on scheme preparation and, therefore, town planning became, for a time, heavily standardized as a process carried out in conformity with definite rules of procedure and with the recommendations of the Ministry of Health (having replaced the Local Government Board) in the form of model clauses. Particular attention was paid to density and the segregation of principal land uses: this was positive intervention to determine spatial structure. In addition, street systems were laid down, with roads to follow specified alignments and widths.

In the meantime, attention was being given to regional planning. The Town Planning Act of 1919 made the first provision for Joint Town Planning, as a result of which regional plans were prepared under the authority of joint committees. South Wales and Doncaster were two early areas selected, followed by West Middlesex and Manchester. By 1930 there were 105 Joint Town Planning Committees at work — mostly advisory, but a number engaged in preparing statutory joint schemes (29).

The Town and Country Planning Act of 1932, represented a definite advance in local government intervention in the shaping of urban structure. The general objectives, as given in Ministry of Health Circular 1305, were 'to control development; to secure proper statutory conditions — amenity and convenience; to preserve existing buildings or other objects of architectural, historic, or artistic interest and places of natural interest or beauty; and generally to protect existing amenities'. There was an important extension of powers additional to previous legislation, namely that land might be zoned for building, temporarily reserved from such development, or subject to compensation, permanently so reserved. There was the first promise here that land might be kept permanently free from building on account of certain criteria. This was a major step forward in assuming real control over forces that moulded the evolution of urban form. But compensation was to prove a major stumbling block: in order to avoid payment of compensation, local Authorities zoned vast areas of land for building purposes, and the possibilities of meaningful control were spurned.

Another advance of the 1932 Act concerned advertisements. Previous legislation had referred to rural areas, and apart from local Acts, general legislation prohibiting the display of certain advertisements did not apply to towns. The 1932 Act remedied this, giving powers to planning authorities to deal with advertisements and hoardings which seriously injured the amenity of land specified in a scheme.

ATTITUDES TO URBAN AFFAIRS

"'This sceptred isle; this earth of majesty, this something or other Eden . . . this blessed plot, this earth, this realm, this England".

'Nina looked down and saw inclined at an odd angle an horizon of straggling red suburb, arterial roads dotted with little cars, factories, some of them working, others empty and decaying; a disused canal; some distant hills sown with bungalows, wireless masts and overhead power cables.'

"'I think I am going to be sick," said Nina.'

This passage from Evelyn Waugh's novel *Vile Bodies* (1930), typified the growing reaction to England toward the end of the inter-War period. The untidy appearance of towns and the inchoate sprawl of the major cities contributed to a significant feeling of dissatisfaction about Britain's towns and cities. This feeling was reinforced by other aspects of town life which also caused concern, including poverty, poor housing and the unsatisfactory conditions for an adequate community life.

The years of unemployment had acted as a trauma. Belief in economic progress had been shattered. Two Labour Governments had come and gone and the socialist millenium was further away than ever. Scenes of working class life and the poverty of the masses made disturbing reading. The London School of Economics carried out studies of poverty in provincial towns and began a new survey of 'London Life and Labour'. In 1935, Seebohm Rowntree repeated the York investigation of 1899, and other surveys took place in Bristol, Birmingham, Tyneside and Southampton. Apart from York, the social survey of Merseyside (1928–34) was the most extensive. A national picture of poverty emerged. Probably one quarter of working class children were being born into families that could not afford the British

Medical Association minimum diet. In Rowntree's York, 31 per cent of the town's working men and their dependents were living in poverty (30). All this was in spite of the fact that the middle class was widening and the working class contracting, compared with pre-War days. Take, for example, the increase in salaried population: in 1911 less than 1.7 million were salaried, but in 1931 the figure was 2.7 million, a social phenomenon of great importance (31).

The publication of these many accounts of unemployment and poverty stimulated the Report urged by Dr Temple, the Archibishop of York, published in 1938 as *Men Without Work.* In the same year there was R.M. Titmuss' *Poverty and Population* which revealed once again the higher mortality rates in northern industrial areas of poor housing. In this way the dissatisfaction of the inter-War years concentrated attention on the environmental poverty and poor housing of the older parts of towns, especially in the North. A popular novel of the 1930s was called *Love on the Dole.* Set in Manchester and Salford, it described the effect on a family when depression hit the local engineering works.

There was no lack of popular description of the situation. George Orwell in *The Road to Wigan Pier* (1937) wrote: 'As you walk through the industrial towns you lose yourself in labyrinths of little brick houses blackened by smoke, festering in planless chaos round miry alleys and little cindered yards where there are stinking dustbins and lines of grimy washing and half-ruinous wcs. The interiors of these houses are always very much the same, though the number of rooms varies between two and five. All have an almost exactly similar living room, ten or fifteen feet square, with an open kitchen range; in the larger ones there is a scullery as well, in the small ones the sink and the copper are in the living room. At the back there is the yard, or part of a yard shared by a number of houses, just big enough for the dustbin and the wc. Not a single one has water laid on.'

Orwell's description of poor housing covered Sheffield and Barnsley as well as Wigan, and leaves one in no doubt as to what is implied by terms such as 'back-to-back' or what reality lies behind statistical data concerning unfit housing. Barnsley was taken to task for building a Town Hall when the money could have been used for providing 2,000 new working class houses and public baths. All this encouraged or articulated a general sense of deep dissatisfaction with things as they were. Moreover, any radical change seemed unlikely.

The face of Britain, however, both urban and rural, was changing; but here again there was the feeling that something had gone wrong. Progress towards better things was not inevitable. The professionals pointed to a failure which was only too readily recognized by laymen. The planner Thomas Sharp confessed the failings of the age, with his target the exploding city: 'so universal suburbia sprawls drearily on. Loosely (through sincerely) it was conceived: loosely and even still more loosely it develops. At bottom a social and an aesthetic ideal . . . it displays even more deeply as it grows the fundamental falsities of its inspiration. The "Town" part of it is but a straggling disorderly alternation of unrelated buildings and unrelated vicinities. The "Country" part is a childish sham where a privet hedge and a root of Michaelmas daisies pitifully symbolize the now all too absent beauties of the countryside. With its formula of "one plus one *ad infinitum*" it results in the covering of the greatest possible space with the least positive aesthetic result. Vague, wasteful, formless, incoherent, it slobbers over the counties' (32).

Using even less sedate language, Howard Marshall, in a collection of essays edited by the architect Clough Williams-Ellis in 1938, declared that 'we are making a screaming mess of England', and wrote of destruction spreading like a prairie fire. 'The jerry-built bijou residences creep out along the roads. Beauty is sacrificed on the altar of the speeding motorist. Advertisements and petrol stations and shanties ruin our villages. The electric grid strides across the hill-sides. A gimcrack civilization crawls like a gigantic slug over the country, leaving a foul trail of slime behind it' (33).

In the same collection of essays a popular philosopher of the day, C.E.M. Joad, confirmed that 'the towns are throwing their ever lengthening tentacles of brick and mortar over the country; round every corner pops up a perky new villa, and the green face of England's landscape comes out in an inflamed rash of angry pink. In fifty years' time there will, in southern England, be neither town nor country, but only a single dispersed suburb, sprawling unendingly from Watford to the coast' (34).

The dissatisfaction that was being expressed with our older towns and the way in which suburban expansion was progressing encouraged many attitudes which were to help determine the course of urban history over the next generation. There was a renewed interest in planning and in positive interventionist policies: the question was no longer *whether* we should plan, but *how* we should plan. The debates revealed at the time of the Barlow commission about machinery of government have to be seen in this context. Fundamental alterations to the environment were known to be necessary, and there was now an increasing demand for these to take place against a background of orderly and comprehensive planning.

There was also concern for the countryside, manifest in the desire to put an end to the blur between town and country. This was the time when attention was paid to the culture of the body; hiking, rambling and cycling were popular. Joad spoke of our being enriched by 'the feeling of the air upon the skin, of the sun upon the face; the tautening of the muscles in our legs as we climb; rough weather to give us strength, blue skies and golden horns of sunlight'. And then in a relapse to a determinist philosophy, the essence of which had been said in relation to towns over the last century: 'Let a boy grow to manhood among beautiful sights, harmonious sounds, and just institutions, and his soul will give forth beauty, harmony and justice. Let him grow up in the midst of brutality and violence, among squalid sights and ugly sounds, and he will be unjust and violent in his dealings, his soul will give forth ugliness, and he will not know how he came to terms with gentleness and beauty' (35). Small wonder is it that the 1930s began to pin so much faith in the virtue of restraint on city size and in the creation of satellite communities in order to allow for the proper planning of the countryside too.

The visual aspects of our civilization were also the target for many observers. As an example, the Year Book of the Design and Industries Association (36) offered telling photographs of poverty of environment in town and country, but also some pointed to what could be achieved. The factory of the Shredded Wheat Co at Welwyn was suitably compared with a 19th century huddle of factory buildings; the clean lines of a new Underground Station with an untidy, poster-spattered Railway Office; the aggressive individualism of a normal shopping street with a planned parade of one architectural conception, and so on. The tirade of evidence against pollution, ugliness and the disgrace of city slums continued to affect opinion and shape common policies for city reconstruction.

Another strong feeling in the 1930s concerned the community aspect of town life. Great reliance was put on the fostering of the community spirit which was likely to be thwarted in too small a town and dissipated in the formless suburbs of the big city. T.S. Eliot stirred the intellectuals with his poem *Choruses from 'The Rock'* (1934):

> 'And no man knows or cares who is his neighbour
> Unless his neighbour makes too much disturbance,
> But all dash to and fro in motor cars,
> Familiar with the roads and settled nowhere.
> Nor does the family even move about together,
> But every son would have his motor cycle,
> And daughters ride away on carnal pillions.'

The first community centres were being built, and planners set ideals of urban structure round the neighbourhood concept. A new social awareness of man's interrelationships affected how people viewed the potential of town life. An interesting novel of the period was Winifred

Holtby's *South Riding* (1936.) This concerned the affairs of a fictitious South Riding County Council, and interwoven in the plot was a scheme to rehouse slum dwellers living in Kingsport (an imaginary town resembling Hull), in a rural part of the South Riding. In a new found understanding and love for the South Riding, one of Holtby's characters reflects: '"Take what you want, said God: take it and pay for it"... Yes, but who pays? And suddenly she felt that she had found the answer. We all pay, she thought; we all take; we are members one of another. We cannot escape this partnership. This is what it means — to belong to a community; this is what it means, to be a people.'

George Orwell expressed the concern over loss of community identity when settlements were engulfed in inter-War sprawl. In *Coming up for Air,* the narrator returns to his home town and: 'The first question was, where *was* Lower Binfield? I don't mean that it had been demolished. It had merely been swallowed... All I could see was an enormous river of brand-new houses which flowed along the valley in both directions and half way up the hills on either side...

'Where was the town I used to know? It might have been anywhere. All I knew was that it was buried somewhere in the middle of that sea of bricks.'

But if there was doubt about the existence of Lower Binfield as a recognizable entity and a community in its own right, there was even more doubt about the value of some of the newly built settlements as a worthwhile setting for community life. Slough, for example, incurred the satire of John Betjeman:

Come friendly bombs and fall on Slough,
It isn't fit for humans now,
There isn't grass to graze a cow
Swarm over, Death!

Come bombs and blow to smithereens,
These air conditioned, bright canteens,
Tinned fruit, tinned meat, tinned milk, tinned beans,
Tinned minds, tinned breath.

Mess up the mess they call a town —
A house for ninety-seven down,
And once a week a half a crown
For twenty years.   (*Slough*, 1937)

Four years later the bombs did fall and created the first opportunities for reconstruction based on ideals and objectives which the inter-War period had so strongly thrown up. Substantial development for the better had taken place during these twenty years, but chronic problems remained. The solid prosperity of growing towns in the South and the Midlands had to be seen against the continued problems of overcrowding and poor housing everywhere. While in 1939 40 per cent of Britain's families were living in dwellings built since 1911, the fact remained that 7.5 per cent of the population were still living at more than two to a room and that over half a million houses were scheduled for slum clearance (37). After the hiatus of another war, the next two decades were to see striking changes in these and other aspects of urban life.

References

(1) Rodgers, W.T. and Donaghue, Bernard, *The People into Parliament,* Thames and Hudson, 1966.

(2) Young, Terence, *Becontree and Dagenham,* Becontree Social Survey Committee, Samuel Sidders and Son, 1934.

(3) Simon, E.D., Inman, J., *The Rebuilding of Manchester,* Longmans, Green, 1935.

(4) Abrams, Mark, *The Condition of the British People,* Victor Gollancz, 1945.

(5) *Op cit* Abrams, Mark.

(6) Fowler, F.J., *Urban Renewal, 1918–1966,* in 'Leeds and its Region', British Association for the Advancement of Science, Leeds, 1967.

(7) Purdom, C.B., *The Building of Satellite Towns,* Dent, 1925.

(8) McAllister, Gilbert and Elizabeth Glen, *Town and Country Planning,* Faber, 1941.

(9) *Op cit.,* McAllister, Gilbert and Elizabeth Glen.

(10) Unwin, Raymond, *Some Thoughts on the Development of London*, in 'London of the Future' (Ed.) Sir Aston Webb, T. Fisher Unwin, 1921.

(11) Lloyd, T. Alwyn, *Planning in Town and Country,* George Routledge and Sons, 1935.

(12) Thomas, David, *London's Green Belt,* Faber, 1970.

(13) Stein, Clarence J., *Towards New Towns for America,* The M.I.T. Press, 1957.

(14) Klapper, Charles, *The Golden Age of Tramways,* Routledge, 1961.

(15) Turner, Graham, *The Car Traders,* Eyre & Spottiswoode, 1963.

(16) Cherry, Gordon E., *Town Planning and the Motor Car in Twentieth Century Britain,* High Speed Ground Transportation Journal, Vol. IV, No 1, January 1970.

(17) Tripp, Alker, *Road Traffic and its Control,* Edward Arnold, 1938.

(18) Marwick, Arthur, *Britain in the Century of Total War,* The Bodley Head, 1968, Pelican 1970.

(19) *Op cit.,* Rodgers, W.T. and Donaghue, Bernard.

(20) Goss, Anthony, *British Industry and Town Planning,* Fountain Press, 1962.

(21) Martin, J.E., *Greater London: an Industrial Georgraphy,* G. Bell & Sons, 1966.

(22) *Op cit.,* Lloyd, T. Alwyn.

(23) *Op cit.,* Goss, Anthony.

(24) *Op cit.,* Goss, Anthony.

(25) *Minutes of Evidence,* Royal Commission on the Geographical Distribution of the Industrial Population, Memorandum submitted by the Town Planning Institute, 1938.

(26) *Report of Royal Commission on the Distribution of the Industrial Population,* Cmd 6153, HMSO 1940.

(27) Jeffreys, James B., *Retail Trading in Britain 1850–1950,* Cambridge University Press, 1954.

(28) *Op cit.,* Marwick, Arthur.

(29) Adams, Thomas, *Recent Advances in Town Planning,* J. & A. Churchill, 1932.

(30) *Op cit.,* Abrams, Mark.

(31) *Op cit.,* Marwick, Arthur.

(32) Sharp, Thomas, *English Panorama,* J.M. Dent & Sons, 1936.

(33) Marshall, Howard, *The Rake's Progress,* in 'Britain and the Beast', (Ed) Williams-Ellis, Clough, J.M. Dent & Sons, 1938.

(34) Joad, C.E.M., *The People's Claim,* in 'Britain and the Beast', (Ed) Williams-Ellis, Clough, J.M. Dent & Sons, 1938.

(35) *Op cit.,* Joad, C.E.M.

(36) *The Face of the Land,* Year Book of the Design and Industries Association, 1929–30, George Allen and Unwin, 1930.

(37) *Op cit.,* Abrams, Mark.

8 The post-War years

The ideals sustaining the practice of post-War planning were largely formulated between the wars, especially during the 1930s. They were the ultimate sublimation of the work and ideas of men from that and previous generations: reformers, visionaries, experimenters, engineers, architects and builders who had reacted in various ways to 19th and 20th century urban manifestations. To meet the problems of size and disorder there was a measure of control over land use and the disposition of buildings; new architects' schemes explored the art of town building; social considerations encouraged community builders; and national economic problems led to proposals for population and employment distribution on a countrywide scale. The questions about the state of Britain's towns and cities (and the countryside in which they were set) had been fully explored before the Second World War; the issues had been identified, and in informed circles the answers had been given. In the trauma of war there had been urban devastation, but this only served to renew a determination to work towards a new social order and to rebuild our cities to a new pattern.

Thomas Sharp, in a popular book of 1940, summarized how our urban environment might be considered: 'Our towns have been repulsive and inefficient for a hundred years and more — for so long, in fact, that most of us have become almost inured to their badness' (1). This was an acceptable standpoint for many. On the one hand it was easy to eulogize those towns of pre-industrial days which were fine essays in large scale architectural composition. On the other, it was easy to relapse into a vilification of Victorian towns, evoking popular images of slums, bye-law streets, factories and smoky chimneys. An additional object of derision was the mass flight to the suburbs where individual domesticity in thousands of little units had destroyed any concept of collective social life. Suburbia was decried, visually and from the point of view of its social sterility. Formless urban sprawl was abhored, and with it the economic waste associated with lengthy journeys to work. In short, escape into romanticism, rejection of the heritage of the industrial town, and despair at the architectural and social deserts of suburban Britain, summarized the contemporary attitude.

It does not matter at this stage that many of these considerations were overdrawn and expressed in emotive terms, even by professionals;

the main point is that these views were extremely influential at a time when plans for Britain's reconstruction were being laid. Positive intervention in the form and shape of cities comes about when there is a strongly held view about the nature of a particular problem. The reconstruction years were notable for almost a consensus of what was wrong and what might be done to rectify a lost opportunity. In particular, there was the condemnation of individual action against the common good, and suburban expansion and rural despoilation were seen in these terms. Thomas Sharp, for example, wrote of people escaping to suburbia 'caring nothing for the general public effect of what they do, not even considering overmuch the ultimate long-term effect on their happiness. They are like an unorganized army of prisoners breaking gaol with no definite plans for what lies before them, concentrating all their thoughts on the escape itself' (2). Remarks like these seem dated now, but at the time strengthened the conviction that new forms of town life were desirable.

The 'alliterative unpleasantness of barricades in Becontree and ghastliness of Gosforth', as Sharp put it, indicated the national dilemma extending in scale from East London to Tyneside. In this total context, the idealist was a powerful source of inspiration. Sharp continued: ' . . . the town *can* be beautiful, it *can* be healthy, it *can* be efficient, it *can* be a utility for the living of a full and happy life, if only we have sufficient care to make it so. The town can be as full of poetry as the countryside, as full of romance, as packed with beauty'. Such stimulating challenges suggested to Sharp the nature of the towns Britain might build: 'Planned for light and air and good living. Built for beauty as well as convenience. Fine sheer towns that will make their inhabitants proud to live in them. Streets of serene houses with an occasional tower of houses lifting into the air. A sufficiency of trees and grass swards and public and private gardens to emphasize their urbanity by contrast; but not so much as to reduce them to suburbanity. A combination of concentration and openness. Towns of a new order, organic, vital, clear and logical'.

Thirty years later we can review just how far this dream has been realized. Planning ideas have certainly contributed to the shaping of our towns and cities, but there have been many other powerful influences on the changing pattern of urban development. To give an indication of the complex situation, we might begin with the example of London where the proposals for restraining metropolitan growth were so actively prepared. This initial focus can be readily justified, for here the urban spread was most in evidence and the important long-range plans, prepared in the war-time years, served as models for provincial centres elsewhere.

THE EXAMPLE OF LONDON

By the outbreak of the war, London had grown to a city of 8.7 million people with another 5.9 million living in an encircling regional ring. The concentration indeed was such that the conurbation accounted for one-fifth of the population of England; more than one-third lived in the South East Region as a whole. This situation was the consequence first of inter-regional migration in the country between the wars, resulting in a substantial net gain for London and the South East, and secondly of intra-regional movement within the London area itself, whereby the County of London lost nearly half-a-million population. Marked changes in geographical distribution of population were taking place. At the centre, the City of London, containing 130,000 people in 1850, and 27,000 in 1901, had only 9,000 in 1937; on the other hand, suburban London and the encircling regional ring registered dramatic gains.

The physical damage of war meant that immediate planning proposals were needed. London, with one-sixth of the country's housing stock, bore the brunt of the wartime destruction. In the County of London nine out of ten houses suffered damage of some kind; in Bermondsey, the proportion extended to 96 out of a hundred. New houses were required, and decisions had to be taken as to where they were to be built.

We may recall at this point that the Barlow Commission had encouraged the idea of decentralizing large urban areas, and this period was notable for a number of groups active in preparing a variety of plans for a reconstructed London. The Royal Institute of British Architects set up a London Regional Reconstruction Committee which prepared a plan. The Royal Academy had a planning committee chaired by Sir Edwin Lutyens and exhibited plans in 1942, 1943 and 1944. The Modern Architectural Research Society (MARS) produced radical proposals with a redevelopment based on an east-west spine across London, with urban blocks at right angles to it.

There was a distinct spirit of optimism about this rash of plan-making. The debate as to whether planning was necessary already belonged to the past. Meanwhile, the perplexing question as to what machinery of government could be devised to accommodate this plan-making was being answered. Once again, the event of war was crucial: what many had thought impossible was, in fact, being achieved because of necessity born of emergency. After 1941, the British economy was controlled and managed on a grand scale (3). Agricultural production was directed in a way that made nonsense of the pre-War rural decline. The coal industry was controlled, railways were run as a uniform concern, and labour forces, in certain industries like engineering and chemicals, were expanded. It is in this context of success in planning as a form of economic intervention that there was renewed speculation about the possibilities of town and country planning as a panacea for urban ills.

In October 1940, Lord Reith was appointed Minister of Works and Buildings, a newly created Department of Government. Initiative and enterprise was unleashed in many planning directions, and in March 1941 he asked the London County Council and the City of London Corporation, separately, to prepare plans for post-War reconstruction. The L C C appointed Patrick Abercrombie to work as consultant with the Council's architect, J.H. Forshaw. Their report was submitted and published in 1943 as *The County of London Plan*.

They recognized four major defects in the organization of London: traffic congestion, depressed housing, inadequacy and maldistribution of open spaces, and the jumble of houses and industry in what they called 'indeterminate zoning'. Their proposals were based on a civic survey which enabled them to make a number of suggestions for the future planning of London, considering the capital as a community, as a seat of Government, a cultural and commercial centre and as a machine of transporation. A Plan was submitted 'designed to include the best of existing London, to enhance its strongly marked character, and to respect its structure and spheres of activities, but at the same time, and drastically if need be, to remedy its defects' (4).

Meanwhile, in the summer of 1942, Abercrombie was also appointed by the Minister of Works and Planning (the Department having by this time a new designation) to prepare a plan for the development of Greater London. This report was submitted in late 1944 and published in 1945 as *The Greater London Plan*.

Abercrombie offered this Report as a direct extension of the County of London Plan. Both were dominated by the community idea: 'It is not satisfactory to build millions of houses, even if good ones, if they are in the wrong place; if they are too far from work; if they perpetuate overcrowded conditions; if they are not grouped into convenient units; if they are not provided with social or shopping centres; if they needlessly usurp the best farmland' (5). The need for planning on a strategic scale, which had been a popular call during the 1930s, was now even more strongly emphasized, and Abercrombie's Plan was the best opportunity yet for a concerted policy framework linking industry, residence, preservation of the countryside and the need for convenient transportation.

As Abercrombie wrote in his personal foreword: 'There is now a chance — and a similar one may not occur again — of getting the main features of this programme of redistributed population and work carried through rapidly and effectively, thereby reducing overcrowding and locating industry in conjunction ... Give a man and his wife a first-rate house, a community, and occupation of various kinds reasonably near at hand, within a regional framework which enables them to move freely and safely about, to see their friends and enjoy the advantages of London; add to these a wide freedom of choice, and they will not grumble in the years immediately following the war.'

The administrative need for metropolitan planning was long over-due. Greater London, covering 673,400 hectares (2,600 square miles), had 143 local Authorities, and nearly every one had a planning scheme prepared, or in the course of preparation, independently of its neighbours. There had been a lamentable failure to achieve any co-ordination, and Abercrombie's Plan was to provide the first overall master plan. Its wider importance was that it provided a strategic planning model which was to serve as the basis for urban and regional planning for twenty years.

Abercrombie envisaged a simple basic structure for the London Region, with a number of concentric zones overlain by a revised communications system. The first was an inner ring where a reduction in population densities was necessary as well as an out-movement of industry. The second was a suburban ring which needed no intervention in the way of receiving either population or industry. Then followed a green belt ring, stretching up to ten miles beyond the outer edge of London. Here, the growth of towns already within would be curtailed, and further growth of London prevented. Lastly there was an outer country ring, containing existing communities set in an agricultural background, where the general character would be preserved, but overspill population with accompanying industry would be introduced in eight new towns.

Essential to this plan were the proposals to reduce densities in the congested inner areas and to move employment and up to one million people to outlying areas in communities of relatively small size beyond a green belt. This would effectively end the type of suburban expansion that occurred between the wars. This was grand strategy indeed, and we can warmly agree with Donald Foley, an American observer, who, twenty years later, commended this interlocking web of constructive ideas as 'creative social invention of high order' (6). The green belt idea had been endorsed during the war by the *Report of the Committee on Land Utilization in Rural Areas* (the Scott Report, 1942). The Committee considered that where a town had reached a maximum or optimum size it should be limited by this zone of open land, where building development should not be allowed. Abercrombie was quick to confirm an increasingly popular idea.

The plan for Greater London was based on certain assumptions. It was assumed, for example, that little new industry would be admitted to the region, and that both industry and worker would be redistributed internally within the area. Both these assumptions demanded planning powers and a machinery of government that did not yet exist. Equally, the questions of planning control and compensation and betterment demanded new powers. Perhaps the major assumption was that the overall population of the region would decrease slightly, with the implication that the solution to overspill and finding sites for additional population was a 'once and for all' business. This was not to be.

THE GENERAL BACKGROUND

Planning in post-War years was largely based on the Abercrombie ideal. Nearly a hundred advisory plans for urban areas and half a dozen regional plans for metropolitan areas were prepared throughout Britain by 1951. Almost all had a common outlook. As an ideal, a circular form of town maintained a strong hold on the imagination. (It did this in spite of alternatives such as the linear city suggested long ago by the highway engineer, Soria y Mata, who conceived a small prototype near Madrid in 1894, and more recent attempts by Russian designers in Stalingrad in the late 1920s.) In practice, an approximately circular shape with concentric rings of development included a green belt as a limit of suburban sprawl. Physical design went hand in hand with social policy. A common aim was the dispersal of people to be achieved through density control at the centre and the creation of new satellite towns beyond. The green belt itself had a popular appeal, and there is perhaps no term more widely used (though often used wrongly) by the general public in planning matters. Conservation groups, particularly the agricultural lobby, were influential supporters.

In the meantime, there were important events during the war years in the creation of the governmental machine for planning. Barlow's recommendation that there should be a central planning agency was implemented by the establishment of the Ministry of Town and Country Planning in 1943. In the same year, the Town and Country Planning (Interim Development) Act extended interim development control to areas where, as yet, no planning schemes were in preparation. In the next year, the Town and Country Planning Act, 1944, provided planning powers in respect of areas of extensive war damage or bad layout and obsolete development. Machinery for intervention was being strengthened.

This was a prolific period for plan making. In some cities the blitz had released the energies of the civic designers, but everywhere there was interest in the possibilities of reconstruction. The 'now or never' approach won the day and teams of considerable expertise were assembled to produce lavish reports for a number of towns, cities or regions. The *First Planning Report* of the City of Glasgow (March

1945) typified the spirit of boldness; on its cover it quoted the challenge 'The voice of time cries out to man — ADVANCE!'

The Middlesbrough Survey and Plan (1946), directed by Max Lock, was a remarkable compilation of a vast array of survey information, and, as such, exemplified the approach of many consultants' reports at this time. *Conurbation* (1948), a survey of the West Midlands by the West Midlands Group, also brought together a range of information on land use, resources and facilities, which presented a new understanding of the social geography of a large built-up area.

These and other consultants' reports at the time received a good deal of attention. Thomas Sharp's *Exeter Phoenix* (1946), and Lutyens' and Abercrombie's *Plan for Kingston upon Hull* (1943) and R. Nicholas' *City of Manchester Plan* (1945), were examples of plans which dealt with problems of reconstruction following bomb damage and problems associated with the need to impose a new conscious order on the course of urban development. The plans incorporated the accepted canons of planning faith: decentralization, planned dispersal and a re-ordering of basic land uses, with schemes for civic dignity in commercial centres.

After the War, the Government devised further machinery for national planning. This was concerned with employment, new towns, land use and national recreation. The Distribution of Industry Act, 1945, began the control of industrial location by the system of industrial development certificates (IDCs) issued by the Board of Trade, necessary for new industrial floor space above a certain size. Detailed planning control powers were provided by the Town and Country Planning Act, 1947. A severely reduced number of local planning Authorities (the County Boroughs and the Counties) were now obliged to carry out surveys of their areas and prepare Development Plans. They were given extended powers to compulsorily acquire land, to preserve historic buildings and trees and woodland. A comprehensive framework of development control powers was provided whereby land use could be rigorously regulated. Provisions were made for compensation and betterment, based on a 100 per cent development levy. The New Towns Act, 1946, provided for the setting up of satellite towns. The National Parks and Access to the Countryside Act, 1949, set up the National Parks Commission which embarked on a programme of national parks for outdoor recreation.

The urban situation, as perceived by Abercrombie, changed, however. For example, with regard to demographic considerations, a projected future of steady or even declining numbers of people was to prove quite false. Population increased, and between the mid-1950s and later 1960s, there were forecasts of still greater increases by the end of the century, although these have since been appreciably amended. The continued growth of the population of cities meant that any static approach to redistributing people to a number of set overspill sites and in maintaining a rigid green belt soon broke down. In fact, green belts (they were not specifically requested by Government until a Ministry circular in 1955) by and large have been resolutely protected. But pressure has been intense and the protection has not stopped further suburban spread at the peripheries of cities, nor the continued growth of settlements in the outer ring. In the event, therefore, overspill was not a 'once and for all' affair, but a continuing process demanding flexibility in locational strategy. Together with increasing numbers of people there was a changing household-size distribution. The average size of households decreased, demanding an even greater number of dwellings for accommodating a given number of people.

The schemes of the early 1940s have been prejudiced in other directions. The car phenomenon, for example, has continued to encourage both suburbanization and wider dispersal in metropolitan areas. In addition to this, relative economic stability, prosperity and full employment compared with the inter-War years have given stimulus in a period of rising standards of living to the demand for new and better housing in areas of suburban distinction.

As far as central areas are concerned, the prospect of large scale redevelopment brightened considerably in the 1950s. In the larger cities, London in particular, a new employment boom ensued with office development. Prospects for employment dispersal were set back. The Barlow Report had been concerned with industrial employment and its distribution, but the post-War years gave rise to important developments in other sectors of employment (jobs in offices, not factories), and a very different situation had arisen.

This, then, is the post-War background to Britain's changing cities. The post-War years saw planning come into its own in affecting the course of urban development. Plans have been made at all levels and power provided for their implementation. But the twenty five years have also seen a quickening of certain economic and social trends which have themselves considerably affected town growth. New towns have been created, some towns dramatically expanded; the appearance of towns has changed through clearance and redevelopment; and a new potent factor has emerged: the car — the destroyer and creator of cities.

NEW TOWNS

The New Towns lobby had strengthened during the 1930s. The national mood in the formative years of reconstruction strongly favoured the need for purposive direction, and there was a renewed determination to create towns of acceptable quality. It was the homes for heroes debate all over again. The propogandist, F.J. Osborn, was particularly prominent during this period. His book *New Towns After the War,* published in 1918, was re-issued in 1942 and was followed by *Green-Belt Cities* in 1946.

His New Towns programme was revised. In 1918, Osborn demanded a national target of 100 towns of 40–50,000 people; by 1942 the specification was reduced to 50 towns for two million people. But his formula had not altered; the basic prescription was unchanged. The ideal was twofold:

'(a) A town should be of a population large enough to allow for efficient industrial organization and full social activity; but no larger. The urban area should be limited to a size requisite to house this population well, and should be surrounded by a zone of open land large enough to possess a distinctively rural and agricultural character.

(b) The whole of the land, including the urban area and the rural zone, should be owned and administered in the interest of the community' (7).

Attempts made to apply this formula during the first half of the 20th century held fast to a remarkably constant view about the form that garden cities and New Towns should take. Osborn wrote in 1918 and 1942: 'There is little doubt that a population of 30,000 to 50,000 would be ample for most normal industrial purposes; on the present average scale of manufacture it would permit a very considerable diversity of industry within the town'. The town would have an urban area of 800 hectares (2,000 acres) and be 'roughly round in shape, would have a radius of about a mile, which would enable all its industrial workers to be within walking or cycling distance of their work, of the town centre, and of the open country, and an extensive rural community to have easy access to the markets and social attractions of the town' *(op. cit.)*. These expressions have been quoted at length in order to emphasize the consensus of professional and lay opinion about the requirements and design of New Towns. Not until the late 1950s was there any serious divergence of view about the satellite ideal. Then there was a greater awareness of the loose spread of towns. Interrelationships between towns were leading to the emergence of larger scale city regions, and the first questions were raised about the actual practicability of containment and dispersal as a regional strategy.

We shall say more about this in the next chapter, but in the meantime we should stress again the almost fanatical belief in the system of New Towns as a social panacea. 'What an impulse it will give to the solution of the major problems of society!' wrote Osborn. 'If a great number of town dwellers secure the inalienable advantages of comfort in their houses, beauty and grace in their surroundings, sunlight, fresh air, health, and a share of civic power; if many more rural workers have access to the social pleasures and opportunities of lively towns; if to a greater extent people of all classes or functions in town and country are brought together and come to understand the interests of each other; then vital political issues will be immensely clarified, and the rise of numerous groups of alert and responsible citizens will quicken national progress in every sphere' (*op. cit.*).

Abercrombie's recommendation of satellite towns for Greater London secured Government acceptance in principle; and, in Ocober 1945, Lewis Silkin, the new Minister of Town and Country Planning in the first post-War administration, appointed Lord Reith to chair an Advisory Committee 'to consider the general questions of the establishment, development, organization and administration that will arise in the promotion of New Towns in furtherance of a policy of planned decentralization from congested urban areas; and in accordance therewith to suggest guiding principles on which such Towns should be established and developed as self contained and balanced communities for work and living'. Three reports were issued in nine

Orchard Croft, Harlow, 1957. Mixed 3-storey flats and 2-and 3-bedroomed terraced houses in a landscaped setting, capturing scenic interest in an essentially low density development.

months. The first dealt with the choice of agency for building a town; the second with the legislation that was needed; and the third with the principles on which a new town should be built and the organization for implementing the plan. Legislation was being prepared even while the Committee was still sitting, and the New Towns Act received the royal assent in November 1946. Only a week later, an announcement proposed the building of a new town at Stevenage.

Between 1946 and 1949, eight New Towns were designated for Greater London, exactly the same number as Abercrombie had proposed, but only two of the sites were the same. The New Towns, in order of designation, were Stevenage, Crawley, Hemel Hempstead,

Harlow, Hatfield, Welwyn, Basildon and Bracknell. In 1950 there followed Corby. Meanwhile in the North East, Newton Aycliffe (1947) and Peterlee (1948) were designated; and in Scotland, there was East Kilbride (1947) and Glenrothes (1948), and in Wales, Cwmbran (1949). These were the 'Mark I' New Towns, and after 1950 there was a pause in this form of enterprise. The designs had a certain similarity from the point of view of their neighbourhood structure and reliance on low density development; strictures calling the designs 'prairie planning' came in later years.

Cumbernauld (1955), a New Town for Glasgow, swung the design fashion to higher densities, taken up in the 'Mark II' New Towns. These

Lower Meadow, Harlow. Industrialized housing to a layout emphasizing pedestrian circulation. Notice the careful attention to landscape and the children's play feature in the pedestrian area.

Bishopsfield, Harlow, showing recently built flats which complement the urban variety in the New Town. The harshness of the concrete and brickwork contrasts strongly with Orchard Croft and Lower Meadow.

Harlow town centre. New Towns have had a reputation for advanced ideas in design and layout and Harlow is a good example of the result of careful attention to detail in a New Town development. In Broad Walk (*above*) note the surface texture, the litter bins and shrubberies. In the Market (*below*) the personal touch is preserved.

were in England, Skelmersdale (designated in 1961), Dawley, later Telford, (1963), Redditch, Runcorn and Washington (1964). Milton Keynes (1967) was designated with others in a new phase of larger New Towns, which incorporate extensions to sizeable existing towns, such as Peterborough (1967), Northampton and Warrington (1968) and central Lancashire (1970). Proposals for Ipswich were not proceeded with. In Scotland, Livingston was designated in 1962 and Irvine in 1966; in Wales, Newtown was designated in 1967. Proposals for Northern Ireland stem from the *Belfast Regional Survey and Plan*, 1962, and the following designations have been made: Craigavon (1965), Antrim (1966), Ballymena (1967), and Londonderry (1969).

This remarkable achievement has added a substantial chapter to the course of Britain's urban development. In spite of the persistent lobby of the 1930s, and the courageous advocacy of Abercrombie, there was still considerable strength of opposition after the War, fanned by political hostility and caution at the local level. Legislation had to be

framed, local resistance overcome (the railway station name plates at Stevenage became Silkingrad as a gesture of defiance to totalitarian powers and, in particular, the work of the Minister for Town and Country Planning, Lewis Silkin), and economic doubts soothed. Admittedly the first post-War Government had embarked on far reaching social legislation, but in consideration of the country's economic and other problems at the time, we might well echo Frank Schaffer in thinking it a miracle that the New Towns programme ever got off the ground (8).

There is a large amount of available literature on New Towns, and in this book we can only look in passing at the main aspects of New Town development. They were important as planning laboratories where new experiments in building, layout and design, and in catering for social groups could be made. The neighbourhood structure for urban development was followed and strict land-use zoning applied. Each neighbourhood was carefully planned round its school and community facilities. Progress was made towards segregation of pedestrians and road traffic in both residential and shopping areas. In short, New Towns became models for other local Authorities to emulate.

Statistically there is an impressive achievement to record. Frank Schaffer summarizes as follows: 'Fifteen towns almost built: a dozen more started. Nearly 175,000 new houses; hundreds of new industries in 35,000,000 sq ft of modern factory space; 350 new schools with 150,000 school places; 4,000,000 sq ft of office space, 100 new pubs, scores of churches and public buildings, several thousand acres of park, playing field, and open space and a host of minor achievements too numerous to catalogue'.

But, on the other hand, of seven million new houses in Britain since the war, only 175,000 have been in New Towns. They have not stopped peripheral urban expansion. They are not self-contained and they have not put an end to dormitory town living, for industry has not moved as readily as people have. They are not necessarily meeting, directly, the social need for which they were established, in that only a proportion of the residents are drawn from the overcrowded conurbations they are meant to relieve. Any adherent to a crude environmental determinist philosophy must be disappointed to note the repetition of suburban neurosis in 'New Town blues', reported in the 1950s.

The balance sheet is not a straightforward one but there can be some confidence in claiming an overall success. Financially the New Towns are viable, and their contribution to the long story of town building has been noteworthy. Many are now being considered for expansion to sizes far in excess of original proposals. The all-pedestrian shopping precinct of Stevenage was an early trend-setter, and the centres of Crawley and Harlow have become equally renowned. The careful preservation of the old High Street at Crawley and the old village at Harlow are fine instances of improvement and incorporation with the modern. Peterlee in Durham and Glenrothes in Fife were brave examples of replacing a number of existing mining centres with a single new settlement. Basildon dealt with the redevelopment of 5,600 shacks and sub-standard dwellings in south Essex. Experiments in the abandonment of neighbourhood planning in favour of dense housing development connected by a footpath system to a compact town centre, begun at Cumbernauld, have been extended to Skelmersdale. New transport systems form the basis of development at Runcorn, Washington and Milton Keynes. Cumbernauld has a most striking shopping centre, crowning a hill top-site. In fact, every New Town can point to some aspect of advanced urban planning which mark them off from common-place development experienced all too frequently in towns and cities of all sizes throughout the country.

Old Harlow where the new is carefully incorporated with the old settlement. Notice the paving and surface treatment, unifying the two parts in one pedestrian area.

New towns were only one method in the public sector of redistributing urban people beyond a borough boundary, either those from the dense city cores or the additional households from an expanding population. They were certainly the most dramatic method, but in terms of dwellings provided the numerical contribution has been relatively small. At the end of the war a temporary expedient in London was the building of peripheral estates in and around the green

Left: Cumbernauld, a Mark II New Town. Unusual house design and an emphasis on pedestrian ways opening out into landscaped areas are particular residential features of the New Town. In this photograph, a comparatively bare hill-top site is being softened by extensive tree planting (notice the young trees in the middle foreground). In fact, 400,000 trees have been planted in the area in the last eight years. Note the openness of the countryside in the far distance: Cumbernauld is relatively isolated from Clydeside, the built-up region it has been planned to serve.

Below: This photograph of the Seafar district of the New Town shows the great care taken in design and layout. Cumbernauld itself is more compact than the earlier Mark I New Towns, but the best use is made of a hilly site. The terraced houses face west while the split levels in the foreground are staggered in such a way as to provide each with a view of the surrounding hills.

Above: Only one-fifth of the town
centre of Cumbernauld (shown in this
aerial photograph) is as yet complete and further phases will extend
the complex considerably. It already
provides a remarkable skyline.
Indoor shopping facilities add another
dimension to pedestrian life in this
very interesting New Town.

Right: The main shopping mall in the
first phase of the shopping development in Cumbernauld's town centre.

belt. About 150,000 people were housed in this way, but by the mid-1950s this particular programme had come to an end.

More importantly, when the first wave of New Towns came to an end, there was the Town Development Act, 1952. This legislation assisted existing small towns to expand voluntarily by absorbing the overspill population from the big cities. The export from London has naturally been the largest, and the effects of town expansion are seen best in the Home Counties, but the conurbations and some of the larger cities have also had town expansion programmes. We need not go into the complex financial arrangements between district council, county council and county borough which the Town Development Act implies, nor the stories of sour relations which have sometimes marked the operation of the Act. From our point of view, we should simply record that through this Act a significant redistribution of urban population has been achieved by the voluntary movement of people from major cities to smaller towns at a distance from them. Difficulties have been encountered in transfering jobs with people in an acceptable proportion, and many of the expanded towns are dormitory settlements in a regional context; 'self-containment' has proved to be an impossible ideal.

London's search for sites was wide and far flung, extending to Barnstaple, Devon, until its rejection following pressure from local residents. The best known schemes have been Swindon, Bletchley, Haverhill and Thetford. For the West Midlands, Tamworth, and other sites in Staffordshire, and Daventry have been the biggest examples.

Expanded towns and new towns were public sector attempts to redistribute population in an attempt to reduce densities in the inner rings of large cities and limit urban size to manageable proportions. There has also been redistribution in the private sector, whereby many hundreds of thousands of people have been relocated in smaller satellite towns. The availability and flexibility of personal transport, higher incomes which make possible increased commuting costs, and the attraction of living close to the countryside have all been factors in this movement.

The strategy of urban containment and planned dispersal of population was dependent on the green belt (10). The idea was familiar enough in London, but in the provinces there were only a few cities, notably Birmingham, Leeds and Sheffield, which, before the War, had bought or otherwise secured land beyond their boundaries to protect from building development. The Ministry of Housing and Local Government Circular 42 of 1955 finally defined the nature of green belts, recommending them in three ways. They could contain the growth of a large built-up area; they could prevent the coalescence of two neighbouring towns; or they could assist in the preservation of the special character of a town. The Circular indicated that a green belt should be wide enough to ensure a substantial rural belt, where (except in special circumstances) no new buildings or changes in the use of existing buildings were to be permitted. The appropriate uses were to include agriculture, sport, cemeteries and institutions standing in extensive grounds. A practical straight-jacket seemed to have been devised, but the subsequent history is one of delay in Ministerial approval of green belts and running fights between developers and local planning Authorities (and the Ministry on appeal) to prevent or localize 'nibbling' into green belt areas.

These, then, are some of the tools by which a certain redistribution of population has been effected: New Town, outlying estate, expanded town and green belt. The overall result has been a marked loosening in spatial distribution. Contributory forces have been the weakening of residential ties to workplace, the effect of the car, and different determinants of industrial location, all factors favouring dispersal.

While sub-regional, or perhaps even regional dispersal was going on, there was also intra-urban redistribution, and the process of suburbanization has been more marked in post-War years than ever before. Local Authority and private building in the suburbs has led to a relative emptying of the inner suburbs. This activity has been associated with a dramatic change in personal transport opportunities and preferences, whereby the private car has come into its own. This has complemented the underlying social dictates of suburban living, to which we have referred before.

TRAFFIC AND TOWNS

Colin Buchanan is a name strongly linked with town planning and the motor car, and his report *Traffic in Towns,* published in 1964, is one of the most important post-War planning documents. He was in no doubt of the magnitude of the new problem. For him, the development of the car 'marked the point at which many of our social and economic arrangements were diverted, gently at first, on to a new course; and time was to show that we had pulled in a Trojan horse more brutally destructive in some of its consequences than any that emerged from the original Wooden Horse upon an unsuspecting population' (11). The post-War transport revolution has affected patterns of social habits, as well as the very physical fabric of the urban environment (12).

The car revolution quickened after the interruption of the War. With rising incomes and a rapid extension of hire purchase facilities, the manufacture of new cars increased. In 1958, for the first time, one million vehicles were produced in Britain. Between 1950 and 1960, the number of vehicles in the country more than doubled, and in the 1960s, the dream of car ownership became a reality for a broadening section of the community. In 1969 there were 4.8 persons per car in the United Kingdom. This figure varied from a regional 'low' of 6.2 persons per car in Scotland and the North to 3.9 in the South West. But these figures concealed much higher car populations in particular localities, especially suburban areas of prosperous cities.

To review the issues which the car has raised in society is an entire subject in itself, but from the point of view of urban change we can usefully identify two factors. First, there is the impact of enhanced mobility with consequent repercussions on the spatial explosion of the city; and, second, there are the problems concerning the need physically to accommodate the car, both parked and in motion, in an urban fabric largely built up in the days before cars.

We have referred elsewhere to the centrifugal forces which are encouraging the outward dispersal of some important urban functions. We should simply emphasize here the importance of the car in this dispersal. One particular facet is the new phenomenon of commuter settlements on the fringes of metropolitan areas. Socially and physically they are new specialist additions to the urban scene. R.E. Pahl's study of townships in Hertfordshire drew attention to this. He found that through selective immigration, mobile, middle-class communities were attracted to live and work in distinct and separate social and economic worlds from the established populations. He felt that these settlements might be better understood as interlocking parts of a 'dispersed city' (13).

From the point of view of physically accommodating the car in towns, the major issues are concerned with provision for movement and parking. In towns with an old urban fabric, where only limited redevelopment is possible because of architectural or townscape value, the accommodation of the car is an immense problem. Elsewhere, where widescale redevelopment is not only permissible but desirable in order to clear unfit or outmoded buildings, striking highway improvements are now radically altering the urban scene. The urban motorway with its multigrade intersections is the 20th century equivalent of the railway in its uncompromising effect on the appearance of urban areas. There is the familiar land hunger, and vast areas of land, or surface area in the case of multi-storey buildings, are required to park the stationary vehicles. Visually and aesthetically the car is an inescapable challenge. The very nature of our contemporary urban environment is in question, and the pedestrian-vehicle conflict is both a daily hazard and an architectural problem. Physical danger, affronts to human sensitivity by sight, noise and smell and the threat to architectural gems of different architectural periods in a host of towns, all now pose new environmental problems.

The first solutions were essentially engineering in origin, and we have already mentioned the contribution of Alker Tripp in the 1930s with his approach to a hierarchy of roads, designed according to function. In the 1940s he built on this idea to think of precinct planning (14). He envisaged the creation of areas of local and minor roads devoted to different land uses, industrial, business, shopping or residential, each area being a precinct, no part of which should be more than about 400 metres from an arterial or sub-arterial road which carried a bus service. The idea was taken up by a Departmental Committee of the Minister of War Transport, whose report *Design and Layout of Roads in Built-up Areas* was published in 1946. It endorsed the principle of neighbourhood precincts and of shopping precincts where the interests of the pedestrian were predominant.

Relatively few towns and cities took up these ideas in the immediate post-War period. This was in spite of the fact that on the Continent there were positive experiments to emulate, such as the Lijnbahn, an early example of a shopping precinct in Rotterdam, or Vallingby, the Stockholm suburb which had a multi-level shopping and commercial precinct centred on a tube railway providing a link with the capital. In Britain also, there were some instances of a number of prominent experiments in design which met at least partially the challenge of producing an urban environment in the age of the car.

After bomb damage, Coventry's central area was replanned with a pedestrian precinct and peripheral neighbourhoods there, like Willenhall Wood, had segregated layouts based on Radburn lines (see page 141). In London, the Barbican redevelopment in the centre of the city was matched by other first class design ideas, both in outlying estates as at Roehampton and in redevelopment areas as at Stepney and Poplar. In the early New Towns neighbourhood planning advanced with the design of grouped dwellings in residential areas, and they frequently incorporated town centre pedestrian areas. In the 'Mark II' New Towns, Cumbernauld offered a new approach to coping with the car with its pedestrianized courts and elevated central shopping area. In Sheffield there was a notable experiment in a peripheral estate, Gleadless, where a whole township with three neighbourhoods, was planned on Radburn lines. The enterprise and ingenuity of the City Architect, Lewis Womersley, continued with a redevelopment site, Park Hill, where slab blocks gave a dramatic new skyline to the central city (15).

Examples such as these pointed the way to radically different forms of urban design. But they were relatively rare, and one can only conclude that the 1950s presented a decade of lost opportunity in this respect. Residential areas continued to be developed on accustomed lines where the estate road and the traditional street frontage were the key elements. Commercial areas were redeveloped but opportunities were lost to resolve the pedestrian/vehicle conflict and to experiment

with the new designs. In Sheffield, a 1½ kilometre shopping street, the Moor, was built up piecemeal, repeating a uniform street frontage. In Hull, first developments after the war damage spurred the chance to change from the traditional shopping street, and this was to be the case in Southampton, Bristol, Plymouth and Exeter. In Wakefield, early 1950 shopping development was centred on a roundabout. In Birmingham, as part of the Inner Ring Road, the Smallbrook Ringway was given a shopping frontage.

Above: Smallbrook Ringway, Birmingham; *below:* the central area of Sheffield. These two photographs indicate the emphasis on the car and the importance of the highway in post-War planning. Smallbrook Ringway is part of the Inner Ring Road in Birmingham and the conflict inherent in the traditional shopping street which was also a major thoroughfare has continued. The Sheffield photograph shows how pedestrians are funnelled underneath a roundabout at a major road junction in the city centre.

The situation improved in the 1960s. Architectural planning practice in both the private and public sectors became more enterprising in conceiving new forms of both residential and commercial development, and there were more clients willing to accept the non-traditional. An important motive force was Colin Buchanan who was asked in 1960 by the Minister of Transport to study 'the long term development of roads and traffic in urban areas and their influence on the urban environment'. His report was published in 1964.

Buchanan conceived only two kinds of roads: distributors designed for movement, and access roads to serve the buildings. He thought in terms of a hierarchical network of primary, district and local distributors linked in urban areas by an urban motorway system. The network permitted the concept of environmental areas. These were not 'precincts', as suggested by the idea of freedom from traffic; rather they were the rooms of a town, 'areas or groups of buildings and other development in which daily life is carried on, and where, as a consequence, it is logical that the maintenance of a good environment is of great importance'. These areas may be busy, of mixed uses and very different environmental standards might obtain, but the basic idea as far as traffic flow was concerned was that there was to be no extraneous traffic, 'no drifts of traffic filtering through without business in the area' (16).

The Buchanan Report represented a new dimension in thinking which linked the problems of transportation to the wider issues of town planning generally. Indeed we have since made little further progress conceptually. The disappointment is that advance in practice continues to be limited to very few examples. The theme of the Report was that 'there are absolute limits to the amount of traffic that can be

The approach to the motorway system in Newcastle's central area. The motorway goes underground. A pedestrian/vehicular segregation is aimed at throughout much of the central area.

accepted in towns, depending on their size and density, but up to those limits, provided a civilized environment is to be retained or created, the level of vehicular accessibility a town can have depends on its readiness to accept and pay for the physical changes required. The choice is society's'. Much of the remainder of the report falls into place because of this concern. There is the proposal that development plans for large urban areas should be supplemented by transportation plans designed to assess the main movement needs likely in the future and indicate how these are to be shared by various forms of transport, including the private car. As part of this transportation plan, there should be a comprehensive parking policy. There is emphasis on the attention which should be given to the development of public transport in order to keep a ceiling on private car traffic. The idea of traffic management was further fostered by suggestions as to the regulation of peak period flows. There was concern for special attention to be given to historic towns where the problem is not to retain simply a number of old buildings, but to conserve a wider historic and architectural heritage. But the focus was on environmental management and the scale of the primary roads. A new term, 'traffic architecture', was coined to convey the idea of buildings and the circulation systems which immediately serve them being designed together as a single comprehensive process.

Almost every town and city shows some attempts to segregate pedestrians and vehicles. Many of these were conceived or actually begun before the Buchanan Report was published, but post-Buchanan development has certainly been stimulated by the technical and political debate which followed. Some of the town centre examples we can point to are isolated, ranging from a host of small schemes to the massive Bull Ring Shopping Centre in Birmingham. Other examples are more comprehensive in nature, perhaps aiming at co-ordinated pedestrian circulation over whole city centres.

At the heart of the transportation problem and its impact on urban areas is the choice between public and private transport. Planning proposals for British towns and cities are heavily reliant on a workable balance between both forms. The Leicester Traffic Plan (1964) is a good example of an analysis of the alternatives that faced a provincial centre, and the comprehensive solutions that might be followed (17).

In Leicester, Konrad Smigielski argued from three assumptions: that the saturation level of car ownership will almost be achieved by 1995, that the population of Greater Leicester will grow from 475,000 to about 640,000, and that the present balance between land uses as traffic generators and the available traffic accommodation in the form of roads and parking, will have broken down by the end of the century unless measures on a formidable scale are undertaken.

The situation allows several possibilities, but the uninhibited use of the private car throughout the whole city was thought to have unacceptable consequences. It would necessitate the construction of an elevated Inner Motorway of sixteen lanes with enormous multi-level intersections; the historic environment would be destroyed; and the cost would total over £400 million. The recommended solution emphasized a balanced interplay of interchange car parks, a high capacity road network and public transport, including bus, monorail taxis, and pedestrian conveyer belts in the town centre and connecting the centre with the car parks. These measures were thought to reduce the cost to £135 millions and give considerable other benefits, including retention of the historic central area core, and the unlimited use of the private car outside the central area.

HOUSING

Significant changes in the appearance and structure of Britain's towns and cities have taken place since the War because of important developments in the field of housing. Rates of slum clearance and new building have achieved new peaks, and a programme of improving older housing is expanding. Vast tracts of suburban housing extend our towns further than ever before. New types of housing, both 'low rise' and 'high rise' have dramatically altered the urban townscape. Important changes have taken place in housing tenure. Owner occupiers now represent about half the households in the country. Local Authority tenants have also increased in proportion, but private tenants have sharply decreased. Some older housing stock is now occupied by social and occupational groups very different from those originally living in them, and many well-to-do Victorian or Edwardian residential districts have taken on new social characteristics. In some cities, late Victorian houses has formed reception areas for immigrants, to add a new demographic element to the urban scene.

To adequately identify and understand these urban changes, it is necessary at least to indicate the context of national housing policy which underlies the whole situation. Only the briefest review is possible, but fuller texts are readily available, such as those by Donnison (18) and Cullingworth (19).

During the War, 200,000 houses were destroyed, another quarter of a million were so damaged that they could not be lived in, and a similar number severely damaged. With an immediate shortage of dwellings, probably totalling 750,000, housing policies were directed towards the speedy provision of new houses. First experiments in industrialized building produced the 'prefab', rapidly shrinking numbers of which still remain in the urban scene. More importantly, emphasis was put on local Authorities to provide the necessary houses, and the Labour Government was quick to enlarge the dimensions of the standard three-bedroom council house from the 72 square metres of pre-War days to 86 square metres, plus 5 square metres of outhouse. National economic problems made it difficult for house building targets to be met and the standards of council housing were gradually reduced. But in the early 1950s the Government achieved an improved house building rate, and in 1954 a new record of 357,000 houses were completed in the United Kingdom. The private sector now began to expand, and building for owner occupiers became the dominant element after 1959. The later 1960s saw a renewed upsurge in local Authority building, but the private sector retained its prominence. Standards of local Authority houses were raised following the recommendations of the Parker-Morris Report, *Homes for To-day and Tomorrow*, published in 1961.

From 1954 onwards increasing attention was paid to slum clearance. The 1951 Census revealed the extent of unfit housing: one third of the houses in England and Wales had no bath, and over a million houses had no flush toilet. Following the Housing Repairs and Rents Act, 1954, slum clearance and rebuilding became a local Authority priority.

The slum clearance programme and the growth of owner occupation served to extinguish a good deal of privately rented property. This became serious for those who found themselves unable to buy a house because of inability to secure a mortgage and who could not obtain a council house because of impossibly long waiting lists. Competition for a dwindling supply of poor quality housing, largely in the privately rented sector, led to scandals of exploitation and homelessness in the 1960s. Combinations of social problems and poor housing in the inner ring of major cities, sometimes exacerbated by influxes of immigrant population, produced another era of social enquiry reminiscent of the 1880s and 1890s. The Milner Holland Report *Report of the Committee on Housing in Greater London* published in 1965, was particularly influential in its collection of objective data, but pressure groups such as *Shelter* continued to highlight the housing problems.

In the 1960s it became more and more important to improve old houses and avoid disrepair. Improvement policies were initially conceived largely in terms of single houses, but increasing attention was given to the improvement of whole areas. The Housing Act, 1969, proved a major landmark in this respect. Local Authorities now have power to declare General Improvement Areas, within which the aim is to help and persuade owner s to improve their houses through financial and other assistance, and to improve the general environment. There are millions of older houses and hundreds of thousands of older streets in this country. They are mostly neglected at the moment, but it is national policy to make them pleasant and comfortable places to live in.

Left & below: Recently photographed tenements in Glasgow; *bottom:* Rillbank Place, Leeds, 1960. *Opposite, top, left:* Scotswood, Newcastle, 1950; *top, right:* Newtown, Birmingham; *bottom:* St Ann's Nottingham, 1950. These photographs have been taken at different times in the post-War period. The dates do not matter. There is a depressing similarity about them all which indicates the poverty of living conditions for many while the backlog of unfit or inadequate housing remains. Conditions in Glasgow are eloquently described in both the street scene and in the rear view of the properties. The houses in Leeds are Victorian back-to-backs within two kilometres of the city centre; most of the houses in the foreground are now closed. Nineteenth-century houses were built at Scotswood close to the industries bordering the Tyne, in parallel streets at right angles to the river; the builders were seemingly indifferent to the gradient. The Birmingham properties are now demolished but are typical of many which are still standing. The Nottingham illustration is another reminder of the gloom and overpowering sense of enclosure which these courts provide.

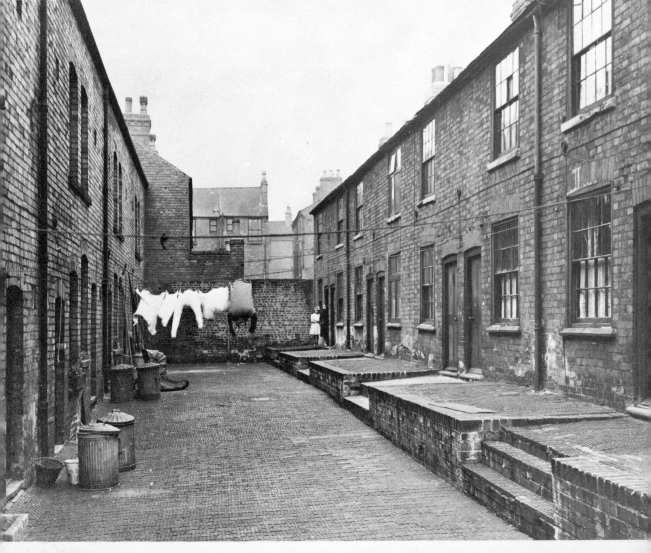

Private building has catered for a seemingly insatiable demand for owner occupied dwellings, and as prosperity increased, there have been higher and higher standards of accommodation. Central heating, domestic gadgetry and fittings and better garage provision are cases in point. The bulk of private building has been achieved by peripheral development, only limited sites for infilling being available elsewhere.

This private development in Sunderland shows how the private housing sector allows for individual treatment and variety around a standard theme of detached (or semi-detached) houses. The expansion of the owner-occupied sector in housing has been a remarkable feature of 20th-century Britain, and the social prestige associated with living in pleasant surroundings like this, is an important driving force in meeting housing needs.

While local Authority building has tended to be in terrace or tower block form, private building has held usually to the semi-detached or detached tradition.

As a result of these many developments the face of urban Britain has changed rapidly. Since 1953 there have only been two years (1958 and 1959) when fewer than 300,000 dwellings have been built annually in the United Kingdom; indeed, since 1964 the annual total has been just above or below the 400,000 mark. This represents an enormous physical change in the appearance of towns and cities, which has been associated with the redistribution of hundreds of thousands of people. Taking a longer term look at the scale of this development, we can see the rate of change over the last century or more. In 1851 there were 3.4 million houses in England and Wales; by the Census of 1901 the number had almost doubled to 6.7 million; by 1951 a rather slower increase gave a total of 12.4 million. But by 1966, the figure was 15.4 millions. This consistent trend, with an upsurge during the last fifteen years, is a most important aspect of recent urban history in this country.

Lee Bank, Birmingham, a mixed development built by the local Authority in the early 1950s. Notice the open setting and the incorporated play-area for children.

A more recent feature is the action taken on unfit houses. Since 1965 there have been between 60 and 70,000 houses demolished or closed annually in England and Wales alone. Most of the larger towns and cities can point to areas of temporary devastation. Socially we should remember that these figures represent the enforced movement of between 170 and 190,000 people each year.

College Road, Bradford, 1970, is a good example of the process of urban renewal. The new is cheek by jowl with the old; vertical development is replacing the horizontal street. Vacant land awaits landscaping or future building.

Nechells, Birmingham, 1966, illustrates the phasing of urban renewal. The rawness of a rebuilt district persists for many years as old communities are broken up and new ones form only slowly. Unfinished new highways are superimposed on an old street pattern. Long-standing industry is now oddly sited, clearly awaiting the next phase of rebuilding. Dereliction and vacant land abounds.

This brief survey permits us to draw attention to at least two important features about housing and the nature of present day residential districts. One is the condition of the existing stock of dwellings, and the other is the heterogeneous composition of our towns. In England and Wales in 1967, the age distribution of owner occupied dwellings was nicely spread: 38 per cent dated from before 1919, 31 per cent were constructed between 1919 and 1944, and a similar proportion were built after 1944. Those rented from local Authorities or New Town corporations, however, were largely modern, 64 per cent dating from 1944, and only 7 per cent from before 1919. Other tenures, largely privately rented houses, were imbalanced the other way: 77 per cent dated from before 1919 and only 7 per cent from after 1944. The implications of this age distribution are seen in their condition. Local Authority and New Town houses are largely fit (98 per cent of the total are classed this way) and owner occupied houses, more or less so (93 per cent), but one out of three of the other tenure group is unfit. This highlights an important feature of the

Left: Early post-War flats in Liverpool built by the local Authority. The aspect is of a harsh concrete world; the children's playground is fenced and the saplings are encased in protective netting.

Below: Roman Road, Tower Hamlets, London, shows urban renewal on a smaller scale and more sensitively handled than the examples of Bradford (see page 185) and Birmingham. Six 4-storey terrace blocks fit neatly into a site adjoining older properties and the intervening spaces are well landscaped.

Right: Metchley Grange, Birmingham. This development won a Ministry of Housing and Local Government award in 1967 and is a brilliantly handled design for high density two-storey housing. There is variety in the environment, it is designed to a human scale and any rawness is softened by the retention of substantial numbers of trees.

housing problem: privately rented houses are the oldest and most unfit.

The association of types of housing with social class and occupation groups gives a heterogeneous pattern to urban structure. Recent investigations such as Robson (20) and Edwards *et al* (21), in respect of Sunderland and Birmingham respectively, show how the technique of social area analysis can be a skilled tool in revealing this pattern. The usual picture in towns is a concentration of housing and social problems in the inner areas, particularly in the districts of larger Victorian houses which have been made into flats and are now multi-occupied. Here the housing problems are at their most severe.

Developments in post-War housing have influenced the urban scene in at least two other ways. One is the different style of building which has affected townscape; the other is the layout of houses in planned neighbourhoods.

Because of architectural fashion and an inconclusive end to a long debate about the need to save land because of agricultural needs, during the late 1950s and 1960s the tower block replaced the two-storey or tenement slum in inner areas. The nature of housing subsidies also encouraged this form of development. The need for high densities

Above: Lewey House, Tower Hamlets, London. A giant tower block makes a powerful intrusion into a residential area of old two-storey properties.

Right: Priory Road, Birmingham, was given a Ministry of Housing and Local Government award in 1969. It is a fine example of sensitive treatment of a mixed development of high and low rise housing. Again, the retention of trees helps to break up the landscape.

continued to be stressed, but design ingenuity began to achieve density targets without absolute reliance on the tall block. Improved housing layouts included mixed development of tall flats with two- and three-storey development associated with them. Visually the dramatic effect of the residential tower made a new impact on skyline and townscape. Sociologically they represented a new physical frame for a way of life which the elderly, the lonely and families with children found far from satisfying.

A principle of layout which characterizes a good deal of post-War residential development is that based on the neighbourhood. The planning reports of the middle 1940s and the early Development Plans put very great stress on the neighbourhood and its capacity to revitalize community life. The events of war helped to popularize the idea of the community, one that had been strongly developed in the 1930s. The threat of a common enemy and nightly trials like the continual bombing raids, created a feeling of civic unity and communion between classes.

Gleadless Valley, Sheffield, a brilliant neighbourhood design on an attractive and partially wooded hillside with mixed forms of housing in a strictly car-segregated layout.

The fervour for community is now a thing of the past, but community facilities are still provided on the basis of clearly defined neighbourhoods. This has resulted in a more convenient residential pattern than between the wars. It is conceded that there are clear limits to how far neighbourhoods of 10,000 or more people can, are, or should be self-contained, but there are a number of practical criteria which are commonly followed. Neighbourhoods have their own primary schools, open space, playing fields and groups of shops. On the other hand, the war time euphoria about community centres quickly died away as a general aim. In fact, the 'community spirit' literature of only twenty five years ago now appears as some of the most dated of all planning publications. In 1944, as part of the plan for Birkenhead, C.H. Reilly designed an intimate residential layout which became known as 'Reilly Greens', and this stimulated a lively national debate at the time. Belief in the value of cohesive living has taken new directions, but in the meantime it is true to say that the basic principles of neighbourhood planning expressed in design terms have helped to shape extensive areas of post-War housing.

CENTRAL AREAS AND COMMERCIAL DEVELOPMENT

A form of post-War development which is particularly striking is the commercial redevelopment of town centres. In the mid-1950s there

Market Street, Bradford, is a typical example of an uneasy relationship between Victorian and modern buildings. The difference between the architectural styles is striking, and the contrast is heightened by the blackened exteriors of the old properties.

St Sepulchre Gate, Doncaster, is a comprehensive redevelopment scheme in the heart of the town's central area. The attractive external appearance (*above*) is complemented by the two-level shopping mall within (*below*) offering a new sophistication to shopping with high standards of comfort and pedestrian circulation.

was increasing availability of capital for commercial projects. The replacement of war damaged sites was an obvious spur. Elsewhere, perhaps, the falling in of leases, let in Victorian times, triggered off redevelopment. Added to this was the demand for new forms of commercial property; different shop design, better utilization of floor space or new commercial functions such as the enormous growth of office employment. Virtually every town in the country prepared schemes of comprehensive development hopefully incorporating the latest symbols of commercial success: the supermarket, bowling alley, offices and perhaps hotel. It was through the efforts of property companies that substantial developments occurred.

Sometimes it was a case of extending shopping facilities in an area of unfit housing as in the Overgate scheme at Dundee. Elsewhere the occasion was the redevelopment of a non-shopping site embedded in a town centre, as with the Wulfrun Centre at Wolverhampton. At other times it was a case of an enterprising property developer buying up a piecemeal shopping frontage and making better collective use of available depth, as with the Chippendale Mall at Doncaster. There were many possibilities, but everywhere the package for the local Authority was increased rateable value, the possibility of additional car parking spaces and the prestige of progress.

The tall office block has been the most noticeable feature. The office employment boom in London earned the capital the title of the 'paper metropolis' and resulted in a call for planning powers to control office development, just as industrial buildings had to receive prior approval from the Board of Trade. Office Development Permits (ODPs) were instituted in 1965, but effected only a limited check. The fact is that in London and the larger cities there has been little dispersal of office development except to favoured London suburbs. In city centres office jobs have increased, aggravating the problems of journeys to work and central area traffic circulation.

There has been some dispersal of shops and suburban shopping centres have experienced stimulus for growth as part of a decentralizing trend. Solihull, for example, south east of Birmingham, has expanded greatly, and similar changes in fortune have been experienced round the London compass. There has been a good deal of discussion about planned out-of-town shopping centres on an American style, but little has actually been achieved in this direction. A proposal to establish such a centre at Haydock between Manchester and Liverpool failed to receive Ministerial blessing in 1963, but one imagines that a first major experiment is not far away, especially in an area where a motorway gives convenient access.

Distributive trades, previously tied to railway terminals and commercial zones in the inner ring of cities, are certainly tending to decentralize and motorway locations on urban peripheries are eagerly sought. The scatter of food warehouses near strategic highway intersections is particularly noticeable.

The actual process of redeveloping central areas in years after the War is one of the most spectacular episodes of town building in recent years. It is something which has occurred to some degree in every sizeable town in the country and, in the larger cities, whole townscapes have been transformed by comprehensive development for shops and offices. Town centres have been dramatically altered in the last twenty years. Victorian townscapes have been virtually erased in a fraction of the time they took to create.

The contrast with pre-War years is illuminating. In the 1920s and 1930s property development was prominent in the suburban parades of shops and, in the town centres, a certain uniformity was imposed as small local shops closed down and chainstores took their place. We might refer back to the rise of Woolworths (81 branches in 1919, 768 by 1939) and the variety stores.

Office building of major consequence had been confined to London and the larger cities. It is interesting to reflect how the pre-War control of London office building through the London Building Acts was to prove quite inadequate after 1945. There were two methods of control. First, a building could not be more than 25 metres high to the cornice, with another two storeys in the roof, making a maximum of 37½ metres. Secondly, the angle from the opposite pavement to the cornice of a building had to be in excess of so many degrees, usually 56 degrees, in order to ensure adequate daylight. In practice this promoted buildings featuring 'set-backs'. They edged backwards from the highway after a certain height, layer by layer, like a wedding cake.

After the War, a scheme of 'plot ratio zoning' was devised to replace this system. This worked on a relationship between the area of the site and the total floor area of the building. But it was not foreseen that developers would want to build as much on a site as the plot ratios allowed. In time, the ratios which had been conceived as maxima, were, in practice, being regarded as minima. Opportunities for the tall office block were presented, aided fortuitously by planning legislation itself. The Third Schedule of the Town and Country Planning Act, 1947, allowed for the enlargement of a building by up to 10 per cent of its cubic content. This may seem a minor point, but old Victorian office buildings with high ceilings and other wasteful aspects of space utilization had remarkably high cubic content and very different ratios of site to floor space could be obtained by new building.

Central area redevelopment has provided both new shops and offices. Very often they were linked in comprehensive schemes, but we might usefully separate the two elements to trace the main features of what Oliver Marriott calls the 'property boom' (22). He calculates that no less than 108 men and two women, who became extremely rich through property development between 1945 and 1965, 'must have made at least £1 million in this golden period'. With the end of building licences and restrictions on building in 1954, the flood gates were opened and high tide has not yet been reached. Finance, on an unimagined scale, became available through insurance companies, building contractors, merchant banks and the joint stock banks. A major shift in investment took place as the big investors left residential property to re-invest in commercial property. Local Authorities, sometimes suspicious at first, soon welcomed enquiries for redevelopment projects and many formed joint schemes with development companies, attracted by enhanced rateable value and the political prize of securing progress and new development, associated perhaps with the prospect of hotels, new shopping magnets or new entertainment including the bowling alley.

With regard to new shopping developments, the first provincial centres to secure any measurable redevelopment after the War were the blitzed cities, such as Plymouth, Exeter, Hull and Coventry, and the new towns. In this phase, between 1948 and 1955, Ravenseft was the prominent property company. After the mid-1950s they were joined by such companies as Arndale, Hammersons, Laings, Murrayfield and Town and City, and a large number of provincial towns were selected for schemes. All the sizeable property companies were run from London, but Arndale, founded in 1950, was based on Bradford. Their first big operation was at Jarrow in 1958, followed by the Crossgates Shopping Centre at Leeds.

Murrayfield developed an early interesting precinct at Preston, the St George's Centre, a triangular site between Friargate, Fishergate and Lune Street. This and many developments, were based on the new

requirement for segregation of pedestrians from vehicles and brought together a large number of standard shop units in attractive malls or precincts, with rear service for goods vehicles. The largest development was at the Bull Ring, Birmingham, which in its first stage accommodated 140 shops under one roof and on different levels. Adjoining the Inner Ring Road, an improved railway station and bus station, and incorporating a new market area, this was a remarkable technical achievement. Nor far behind the Bull Ring in scale, but not so commercially successful, was the Elephant and Castle in South London, a scheme accommodating 120 shops. There are so many successful schemes that it may seem churlish to mention some that went wrong. The Bargates Shopping Centre at Burton-on-Trent, the Duckworth Square precinct and the Castlefields Main Centre at Derby, and the Central Shopping Precinct at Doncaster, are all examples.

Birmingham City Centre from the GPO tower, looking south. The circular tower in the middle distance is the Rotunda, which overlooks the Bull Ring. Within twenty years, what was once a Victorian city centre has been transformed, both functionally and in appearance. The office boom has provided more floor space than in any other provincial city, and the central area skyline has changed dramatically. The cathedral (middle left in the photograph) is now dwarfed; compare the skyline of the city 200 years ago shown in the engraving on page 20.

Redevelopment in Plymouth, 1967. The complete restructuring of a central area is vividly illustrated in this aerial photograph. Within the confines of a roundabout-studded Inner Ring Road, Abercombie (acting as a consultant) and Watson (the City Engineer) laid out a simple grid on which to build after the Blitz. Wide streets, regular building lines and a unified architectural control have created a distinctive and attractive shopping centre. A hint of the pre-War housing densities in Plymouth is given in the bottom left-hand corner of the photograph.

Above: Shopping precinct, Coventry. The precinct is aligned with the spire of the old Cathedral church of St Michael. The vehicle-free area was developed in stages in a comprehensive redevelopment plan for the city centre. The circular Lady Godiva cafe, on the right of the precinct, was completed in 1959. A particular feature of the precinct is the two-tier shops which initially caused a great deal of controversy. This photograph, taken during the summer of 1971, shows the increasing maturity now afforded by the trees in the midst of the paved area. The precinct is only one axis of the pedestrian circulation plan, and the total vehicle-free area is now one of the largest expanses of planned pedestrian shopping of any city in Britain.

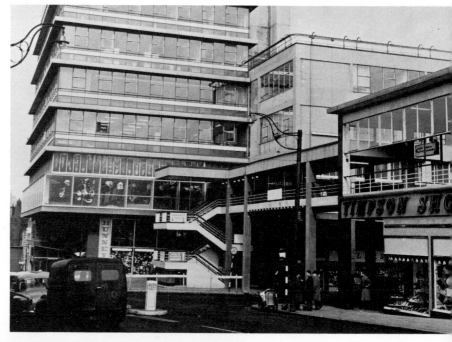

Castlehill Market, Sheffield, where pedestrian segregation has been effected by means of an indoor shopping mall. A complex of different levels (*above*) opens up in part to accommodate a new version of the old open-air market (*left*).

The Bull Ring, Birmingham. The traditional open market has not been lost. Although the Bull Ring Centre (*above*) provides a new indoor shopping area close to the old market site adjoining St Martin's Church (just visible on the extreme left in the photograph), the outdoor traders remain (*left*) to add a little vitality and human scale to an otherwise massive and rather overpowering context.

With regard to offices, London had an early achievement in the Barbican scheme. This northern area of the City was formerly the centre of the rag trade but was blitzed in December 1940. Surviving firms departed, and resurrection of the area came with comprehensive office development. But the most concentrated burst of office building took place in London during the period 1955 to 1960, on a scale that has not been matched anywhere else in the country. The total stock of office floor space in central London in 1939 amounted to 8,300,000 square metres. Bombing during the war had destroyed 900,000 square

metres, a deficiency that was soon more than made up. By mid-1962, there were 11,000,000 square metres, and by 1966, 13,300,000 square metres. In addition to this there was a remarkable suburban office boom in such areas as Wembley, Ealing, Kingston and Harrow. But the most spectacular boom was at Croydon where, by November 1964, 200,000 square metres of offices had been built in the town centre, a further 70,000 square metres was under construction and another 310,000 had been given planning permission, a scale of development out of all visual proportion to the surrounding suburban area (23).

The post-War transformation of Croydon is well illustrated in this aerial photograph. The new office blocks which now dominate the central area of the town rise dramatically from the surrounding suburban areas.

A view of the City of London from Tower Bridge looking up river. The old skyline of domes and spires has gone; the new commercial world predominates with its post-War tower blocks. This remarkable concentration of new buildings resulted from the office boom of the 1950s and 1960s.

London, by this time, had a new reputation for central area employment. Lack of control over office development compared with industrial building, which required the permission of the Board of Trade, was very noticeable. In November 1964 (hence the significance of the date for Croydon), a ban was put on any further office building in the area of the Greater London Council. Office Development Permits (ODPs) were required and this form of control was extended during 1965 and 1966 to Birmingham, and finally to all the South East, and the East and West Midlands. Relaxations have since

been announced.

As with the building of shopping centres, success did not attend all ventures, and the Monico dispute concerning the proposed redevelopment of Piccadilly showed how schemes could go wrong. A perspective sketch was released when the Minister's Inspector was considering the application for planning permission in 1960. It depicted a building surmounted by a crane and a large advertisement on the front main panel reading 'Snap Plom for Vigour'. A public outcry met this proposal and planning permission was refused.

OTHER CHANGES

In this chapter we have focused attention upon certain post-War developments which represent the more essential urban changes that have occurred. These have been the formulation of a coherent planning strategy centred upon containment of the larger cities and the dispersal of population and economic activity to satellites or districts beyond; the adoption of a new towns programme; the spectacular increase in road vehicles giving rise to urban congestion and the need for highway surgery; developments in housing, both from the point of view of new housing and slum clearance, which have led to marked suburban expansion and reconstruction of older areas; and significant changes in central areas, both visually and functionally.

Post-War developments have also taken place in many other directions with the overall result that during the last quarter of a century, urban change may be regarded as very extensive and far-reaching. In many ways we are living through a period when change is not so much piecemeal alteration here and there, but radical restructuring. There are shifts in land use to record, old buildings and their uses are disappearing and new ones being created; the very appearance of towns and cities is altering quickly and attempts at local government reform have been made. Underpinning much of these changes has been the fact that for the first time a comprehensive, purposive intervention in land use and community affairs has been attempted.

From the point of view of the changes in land use, major shifts have occurred. Fundamentally they concern an attempt to redistribute major activities, to segregate conflicting interests such as industry from housing, to define more tightly the extent of commercial areas, and to provide new open space, largely in the form of playing fields. In detail of importance locally, there have been other changes such as the decline in allotments and the change from cemetery land to crematoria.

With regard to buildings, changes in entertainment reflect losses and gains. The cinema, for example, reached a peak of 1,635 million national attendances in 1946 when 32 per cent of adult civilians went to the cinema at least once a week. But the number of admissions has fallen drastically resulting in cinema closures during the later 1950s and 1960s. A total of nearly 4,000 cinemas in 1958 in Great Britain had fallen to under 1,650 in 1968. The number of public houses has also changed. Since the Licencing Act, 1904, the number of 'on' licences has fallen from about 100,000 to rather more than 70,000 in England and Wales. There are now 15 licences per 10,000 population compared with 34 per 10,000 at the turn of the century. On the other hand, the number of registered clubs shows an opposite trend, and this general picture has been confirmed since the war. There have been new buildings for public entertainment: the bowling centre was of relatively short life, but the indoor sports centre, often of striking design, is likely to be more permanent. Swimming has gained in popularity and new swimming baths are a source of local prestige.

In commercial areas, shop unit design has altered and commodities sold have changed. The local street scene is often very different; a new uniformity of style has erased considerably older traditions. The education explosion has produced universities, polytechnics and other centres of higher education in many provincial cities. In every town new primary and secondary schools constitute an important element of post-War change, not only socially, but visually in the landscape. More than five million new school places have been created since the war in England and Wales alone. New hospital building has been less common, but where new hospitals have been provided, very differently designed

The Civic Centre, Newcastle upon Tyne. Designed by the City Architect, George Kenyon, and built during the 1960s, the Civic Centre replaces the old Town Hall in Newcastle as the local seat of government. Many people have seen it as part of the general resurgence of Tyneside and the North East.

City Hall, Belfast; Council House, Nottingham. Two examples of earlier seats of local government. City Hall, Belfast (*right*), built between 1902 and 1906, is similar in style to Cardiff's City Hall and reflects the imperial grandeur of the time. The Council House, Nottingham (*below*) built between 1932 and 1938, was one of the most imposing public buildings of inter-War Britain.

buildings form new landmarks. Local Authority rebuilding has provided the occasional new town hall or central library to replace out-moded Victorian buildings.

The appearance of cities has changed radically in many ways. The Clean Air Act, 1956, for example, met the objections of many decades of protest, and as the result of the combination of legislation and the move away from solid fuel heating, it is now possible to speak of relatively clean cities in contrast to the smokey atmosphere of the past.

Atmospheric pollution in Sheffield. Concern over clean air can readily be understood from this photograph showing the situation in the 1940s. The smokey atmosphere which polluted all the larger towns and cities was an important element in the argument for dispersal of urban population to smaller towns in green belt surroundings.

But as one pollutant disappears, another is created, and noise, smell and chemical poisoning are increasing environmental hazards. Another visual improvement concerns advertisements. Important provisions for their control were given by the Town and Country Planning Act, 1947, in addition to which the poster industry itself had done a good deal to put its own house in order. Great advances in advertisement design and lettering have added to the post-War improvements in the appearance of shopping streets.

These changes in the physical structure and appearance of towns and cities, are balanced by the conservation of buildings and areas of architectural importance. A number of our historic towns have been the subject of special analysis, and it is to be hoped that pressures for change can be contained to safeguard an invaluable heritage. The Civic Trust has played an important role in popularizing the idea of improvement or 'face lift' schemes as, for example, in experiments at Norwich.

London Street, Norwich, a thoroughfare in the core of a historic town before (*above*) and after (*below*) closure to traffic. The space between the buildings is once more fully used by people and appears as a unified architectural composition, not the point of division that the motor car made it.

On a wider scale, urban appearances can have altered as part of long term economic change. Professor S.H. Beaver (24), for example, has traced the landscape evolution of the Potteries, where bottle ovens, colliery spoil heaps, beehive kilns and marl holes, iron works, slag heaps, canals and derelict land produce a confused picture of both activity and dereliction. The rapidity of change in certain aspects of the picture has been marked. In 1939 there were over one thousand bottle ovens; in 1959 there were 500, and in 1964 only about 200 existed. Other broad changes in the landscape have taken place elsewhere in response to economic development; on the one hand closure of collieries and redundant plant can be melancholy, but, on the other, new industrial landscapes can be dramatic as in the plant of oil refineries and the petrochemical industry.

These many different changes are now being accompanied by changes in local government and in the planning system. Attempts have been made at the structural reform of administration. Local government boundaries increasingly became anachronistic as population and services spilled over old lines of local responsibility. In 1957, a Royal Commission on Local Government in London was appointed, and following the Local Government Act of 1958, a series of commissions were established to consider certain localities and, in particular, the problems of the English conurbations. The Greater London Council replaced the former London County Council, but the archaic situation in the conurbations was unresolved. Another enquiry, the *Report of the Royal Commission on Local Government in England* (the Redcliffe-Maud Report, 1969) made sweeping proposals, as were also made for Scotland (*Report of the Royal Commission on Local Government in Scotland,* the Wheatley Report, 1969) and for Wales (*Report and Proposals for Wales,* 1963). In 1971 new Government proposals were made and it is anticipated that new local government boundaries will be in force in 1974.

In the local government planning system, the statutory Development Plan has been of great importance in the post-War period. The Town and Country Planning Act, 1947, influenced urban affairs to a considerable degree. The Development Plans indicated in some detail the land use proposals for their areas and the major developments that were expected as a result of public or private sector operations, such as new highways, new buildings (for example, schools or hospitals), or areas of redevelopment such as slum clearance and rebuilding. Proposals for development were approved or refused permission largely in the light of the Development Plan provisions. Development Plans are now being replaced by Structure Plans, designed to indicate broad strategies rather than detailed proposals, but the planning process of development control continues against the backcloth of local and district plans.

An urban and industrial landscape in the Potteries. The photograph, taken in 1962, shows a landscape of conflict and exploitation. The main London-Manchester railways cut through from upper left to lower right, following the Fowlea Valley; Wolstanton colliery is middle left and the new Kaldo Steelworks are in process of construction in the middle distance. An old marl hole adjoins the railway in the lower right, and blast furnaces can be seen in the upper right. The huge conical shapes of spoil heaps are just visible in the far distance. Burslem town centre is located beyond Wolstanton colliery.

Canal-side industry in Birmingham, 1957. All too frequently, post-War Britain showed the industrial heart of the older cities to be virtually derelict. The remarkable canal system in the West Midlands has proved difficult to utilize and only recently have there been fleeting attempts to realize the new potential of surface water in urban design. Transport revolutions speeded urban decay in districts dependent on the canal and this run-down scene in Birmingham is a melancholy reminder of the industrial renewal that is necessary.

In short we can say that a substantial measure of planned intervention has been applied to the course of the post-War development. Fairly strict land-use zoning principles have been followed and perhaps the planners' zeal for order went too far. But it was not until the 1960s, when Jane Jacobs' *The Death and Life of Great American Cities,* published in 1962, achieved popularity, that land-use rigidity was seen as excessive. By and large, however, the success of local Authority intervention has been to see that development has occurred more or less at the right time and in the right places. Schools have been built in accordance with housing programmes; open space has been reserved; building in certain areas has been restricted; elsewhere it has been encouraged; unfit houses have been demolished and new ones built; shopping centres rather than ribbons have been created; the worst excesses of badly sited industry have been avoided. This represents a high point in public intervention in the shaping of an urban environment.

References

(1) Sharp, Thomas, *Town Planning,* Penguin Books, 1940.
(2) *Op cit.,* Sharp, Thomas.
(3) Marwick, Arthur, *Britain in the Century of Total War,* The Bodley Head 1968, Pelican, 1970.
(4) Forshaw, J.H. and Abercrombie, P. *County of London Plan,* Macmillan, 1943.
(5) Abercrombie, Patrick, *Greater London Plan,* 1945.
(6) Foley, Donald L., *Controlling London's Growth,* University of California Press, 1963.
(7) Osborn, F.J., *New Towns after the War,* J.M. Dent & Sons, 1918, revised and reissued 1942.
(8) Schaffer, Frank, *The New Town Story,* MacGibbon and Kee, 1970.
(9) *Op cit* Schaffer, Frank.
(10) *See* Thomas, David, *London's Green Belt,* Faber, 1970.
(11) Buchanan, C.D., *Mixed Blessing: the Motor in Britain,* Leonard Hill, 1958.

(12) Cherry, Gordon E., *Town Planning and the Motor Car in Twentieth Century Britain*, High Speed Ground Transportation Journal, Vol. IV, No 1, January 1970.

(13) Pahl, R.E., *Urbs in Rure*, in 'The Metropolitan Fringe in Hertfordshire', London School of Economics and Political Science Geography Papers No. 2, 1964.

(14) Tripp, H. Alker, *Town Planning and Road Traffic*, Edward Arnold, 1942.

(15) *See* Tetlow, John, and Goss, Anthony, *Homes, Towns and Traffic*, Faber, 1965.

(16) *Traffic in Towns,* (The Buchanan Report), Reports of the Steering Group and Working Group appointed by the Minister of Transport, HMSO 1963.

(17) Smigielski, W.K., *Leicester Traffic Plan: Report on Traffic and Urban Policy*, City Planning Department, Leicester, 1964.

(18) Donnison, D.V., *The Government of Housing*, Penguin Books, 1967.

(19) Cullingworth, J.B., *Housing Needs and Planning Policy*, Routledge and Kegan Paul, 1960.

(20) Robson, B.T., *Urban Analysis: a study of city structure*, Cambridge University Press, 1969.

(21) Edwards, J.R., Marshal, T. and Leigh, E., *Social Patterns in Birmingham*, Occasional Paper No. 13, Centre for Urban and Regional Studies, University of Birmingham, 1970.

(22) Marriott, Oliver, *The Property Boom*, Hamish Hamilton, 1967.

(23) *Op cit.,* Marriott, Oliver.

(24) Beaver, S.H., *The Potteries: a study in the evolution of cultural landscape*, Transactions, Institute of British Geographers, 1964.

Queenslie Industrial Estate, Glasgow, is a new post-War estate. It was developed as part of the drive towards decentralization and dispersal of population and industry in Clydeside.

$\mathcal{9}$ The process of change

We have described the main features of towns and cities at various stages, together with the main factors which have influenced change between particular periods. We have traced the continuity of the urban system as it evolves, its function, composition and characteristics constantly in flux. In this last chapter, we will now try to see urban development not as a series of snapshots in time, as in previous chapters, but in terms of an overall process and a complex of constantly changing functions. First we will look at the facts of urban growth through population statistics and remind ourselves of today's urban map. Then we will pay particular regard to social processes inherent in urban change, concentrating particularly on housing and residential cycles. Finally, with regard to urban function, we shall speculate on where modern trends are leading as the forces of dispersion threaten to disaggregate a formerly compact city structure.

URBAN SIZE AND CHARACTER

The pace of urban development over the last two hundred years, in this country as elsewhere, has been dramatic. The period has seen the unparalleled expansion of most towns and cities. It has witnessed the actual creation and subsequent growth of some towns and the relative stagnation and decline of others. Centuries of gradual evolution can readily be set apart from the decades of rapid transformation over the span of a few generations.

As an extreme, Birmingham reflects the changes which have occurred. In 1086, at the time of the Domesday Book, Birmingham was recorded as consisting of 'five villeins and bordars', occupying land to the value of twenty shillings. By the first quarter of the 14th century the manor had 75 tax-payers; in the County, Warwick and Coventry were both larger. By the 17th century its local industries had expanded and the town was an important source of swords for use in the Civil War. Industrial tempo quickened in the 18th century and from then onwards Birmingham became a regional and national centre for a great variety of trades, including iron, brass and copper manufacture and jewellery. The 20th century has seen the introduction of industries based on new technologies including motor vehicle manufacture and electrical machinery. A manufacturing base for the city has widened in the sense of the number of component trades undertaken, but a relative contraction is setting in as jobs in service industry increase.

The inner wards of the city now form the areas which were built up for houses and factories from 1820 onwards. The form of development was very high density with a tight network of streets and a complex mixture of land uses. In the late 19th and in the 20th century, suburban expansion has been of increasingly low density, and public and then private transport have assisted in the spread of the city. Successive boundary extensions could not contain what was, in fact, Birmingham. Centrifugal forces have replaced centripetal forces, but a good deal of commercial inertia continues to exert pressure for development in the city centre in the form of new shopping and office employment. The rail net of the 19th century was followed by an improved highway net in the 20th, and a city of more than one million people has arteries of communications which permit the daily passage of tens of thousands of city dwellers. The adoption of a 19th century fabric for 20th century patterns of living, proceeds alongside wholesale redevelopment in the desire for new forms of living, work and recreation. Like other cities, Birmingham is now at a fundamental point in its modern evolution. The forces which gave it birth are now not necessarily the same as those that sustain it, and the urban future holds out many interesting possible variations.

The essential feature of two hundred years of urban development in this country has been rapidity of growth and transformation of appearance and function. As part of this process there has been the population explosion of the country as a whole. The population of England and Wales and Scotland was 10.5 millions in 1801; it doubled in fifty years to 20.8 millions, and doubled again in the next sixty years to 40.8 millions in 1911. Slower growth followed, but a quickening increase has been noted since the 1940s. The 19th century was the major formative period, and while a growing proportion of the increasing population was absorbed by towns, there was a relative shift against the pull of London. In 1831, 10.6 per cent of the population of England and Wales lived in London. In 1891 the proportion was 14.5 per cent, not greatly in excess of what it had been in 1861 (14.0 per cent). In 1831, 5.7 per cent of the population of England and Wales lived in towns of over 100,000 persons; in 1891 the proportion was 17.3 per cent (1).

In this first stage of urban growth, the largest cities soon had increasing concentrations of population. This was particularly marked in Glasgow, which in 1801 contained one in twenty of the Scottish population, but by 1891 contained almost one in five. The century saw the growth of some very large towns indeed, and generally speaking those most prominent at the beginning of the century still occupy premier positions. Discounting London with 865,000 population in 1801, there were Manchester-Salford, Liverpool, Birmingham, Bristol and Leeds in the range 50–100,000 people; between 25–50,000 there was the Plymouth complex of Plymouth–Devonport–Stonehouse, and, also in the same range, Norwich, Portsmouth, Sheffield, Rochdale, Nottingham, Newcastle and Bath. In Scotland, Edinburgh and Glasgow were in the first range, and Paisley, Aberdeen and Dundee in the second.

In the early decades of the 19th century there were instances of very rapid rates of increase. The population of Manchester grew by 40 per cent between 1811 and 1821, and by 47 per cent between 1821 and 1831, a decade when Leeds also increased by a similar proportion, and Liverpool by not much less. In Glasgow the population increased by more than 30 per cent in each of the first four intercensal periods. Amongst the range of smaller towns, industrial centres were joined by spa and resort towns as well as ports which registered high rates of increase. For example, towns of less than 10,000 persons in 1801 but more than 25,000 by 1841 included Brighton, Merthyr Tydfil, Bradford, Cheltenham, Southampton, West Bromwich, Woolwich and Huddersfield.

In 1861, London had reached 2.8 millions and Birmingham had exceeded a quarter of a million. Towns of more than 100,000 now included Sheffield, Wolverhampton, Newcastle, Bradford, Salford and Stoke. Towards the end of the century rates of growth were particularly the features of suburban towns, especially those dormitory for London. The population of West Ham, for example, increased from 38,000 to 129,000 between 1861 and 1881. In the penultimate decade of the century, Leyton, Willesden, Tottenham and West Ham all recorded extraordinary rates of increase. Elsewhere in the country, the last twenty years of the century saw a number of towns with high rates of growth: Cardiff, Newcastle, Newport (Mon.), South Shields, Blackpool, Gillingham, Smethwick and Wallasey.

In the 20th century there is a change in emphasis from the continued rise of the established towns to the marked growth of towns adjoining the larger, established cities. This, of course, reflected the trend in population redistribution whereby the older districts lost people through reductions in overcrowding and a dispersal of population took place. This population movement was most prominent in the London area, but also extended to suburban towns for Liverpool, Birmingham and Manchester. In the inter-War period a number of seaside towns also grew quickly. But while these inward movements to certain towns were going on, there were net outward movements from some of the older industrial centres in the North and in Wales. Since the War, these trends have continued. In particular, the inner areas of cities have emptied while the suburbs have grown. Between 1951 and 1971 the population of England and Wales increased by nearly 5 millions, and the bulk of this was attracted to urban areas, especially the suburbs.

The artificiality of local Authority boundaries means that for recent decades the population of particular towns is of no great significance in measuring rates of increase. It is more important to emphasize the emergence of major areas of population, for which Patrick Geddes in 1915 strove to find the right term: 'Constellations we cannot call them; conglomerations is, alas, nearer the mark at present, but it may sound unappreciative; what of "Conurbations?"' (2). He identified Greater London, and areas he called Lancaston, West Riding, South Riding, Midlandton, Southwaleston, Tyne-Tees-Wear and Clyde-Forth. Not all these areas are now so recognized, but in order of population those granted recognition in official statistics are (by 1971) as follows:

	thousand population		*thousand population*
Greater London	7,379	West Yorkshire	1,726
West Midlands	2,369	Merseyside	1,262
South East Lancashire	2,386	Tyneside	804
Central Clydeside	1,728		

Both in and beyond these conurbations are now many large cities. The 1971 populations are given below with 1951 figures in brackets:

	thousand population		*thousand population*
England and Wales		Wolverhampton	268 (243)
Birmingham	1,013 (113)	Stoke-on-Trent	265 (279)
Liverpool	606 (790)	Plymouth	239 (226)
Manchester	541 (703)	Newcastle upon Tyne	222 (291)
Sheffield	519 (542)	Derby	219 (196)
Leeds	494 (505)	Sunderland	216 (206)
Bristol	425 (443)	Southampton	214 (190)
Teesside	359	Scotland	
Coventry	334 (265)	Glasgow	896 (1090)
Nottingham	299 (307)	Edinburgh	453 (467)
Bradford	293 (292)	Dundee	182 (177)
Kingston upon Hull	285 (299)	Aberdeen	182 (183)
Leicester	283 (285)	Northern Ireland	
Cardiff	278 (262)	Belfast	360 (444)

(Source: Census Reports)

The pier head and city centre, Liverpool. The illustration captures the
physical heart of Liverpool. Behind
the landing stage are the Liver
Building, the Cunard Offices and the
Dock Board Offices. Salthouse Dock
is on the right. In the top left of the
photograph is St George's Hall and
Lime Street Station; between these
and the waterfront is the City Centre.
For an idea of the social and cultural
side of the city read *Portrait of
Liverpool* by Howard Channon,
published in 1970.

The City Docks, Bristol. The old warehouses and the spires of the city skyline are reflected on the surface of what is now a commercial backwater.

Quite apart from the question of size in population terms, there can be other important differences between cities. Cities can be very different in economic structure and social composition, their populations being distinguished by differences in housing, education, social class and demography (3). A ready contrast can be seen between the heavy-industry towns of the North and those of the South where light engineering and service industry is prevalent. This modern distinction summarizes the effects of economic shifts of regional balance

Woollen mills, Bradford. The photograph suggests the industrial and cultural distinctiveness that springs from the dominance of a staple trade in a town.

The riverside, Sunderland. Wearside lacks a gantry skyline on the scale of Tyneside, Clydeside or Merseyside, but even here marine engineering is important in the affairs of the town. The vagaries of shipbuilding and a declining port trade have had their effect on the economic fortunes of Sunderland.

extending for over half-a-century.

Indeed, the modern town in its size, form, structure, appearance and cultural attributes reflects many influences of the past. We have noted in previous chapters the changing appearance of shopping streets, housing areas, factories and roads, the overall impression at any time being an amalgam of all these characteristics at various stages of their development. More subtly there is what F.M. Jones (4) has called the aesthetic of towns — the idea that buildings and urban complexes are 'the hardware of a social organism', the form and detail of which reflects the responses of that organism to its environment.

He has identified three aesthetic qualities which typified the 19th century industrial town, and we can reflect on the changes which have taken place since then, the importance these have had, and how far they are still part of some towns which might not have changed all that greatly. The three were noise, dirt and smell. Noise came largely from

Central pier, Blackpool. Fashions in recreation change, and the relative attraction of seaside resorts within Britain has altered considerably since the War. But Blackpool, with many others, continues to cater for mass recreation with its simple commodities — sand, sea, pier, promenade and entertainments.

the iron-shod hooves and wheels on hard-wearing road surfaces, and rattling of horse harness chains, shouting drivers, clanking railways and humming factories. Dirt featured horse droppings, muddy streets, airborn grit and chimney smoke. Finally, there was the smell of breweries, tanneries, dye-works and gasworks and, not least of all, unwashed people.

These three qualities give very clear clues to what cities were really like for their inhabitants in different periods. Cities change at different rates and are cultural expressions rather than just physical creations. Great variations can occur between the social characteristics of different cities in spite of the general uniformity of influence on urban change. Different aesthetic and cultural forms are fascinating reflections of urban life: C.E.B. Brett gives an insight into one extreme city of Britain, Belfast. He accepts that there are many miles of dreary, red-brick terrace housing, but because of the Ulster farmhouse tradition where houses are whitewashed once a year, thousands of sub-standard houses are painted in gay colours. This is an aesthetic detail of an urban fabric. Culturally there are other features which make up Ulster's history: 'the crude slogans, the primitive painting on gable walls of King William III on his white horse crossing the Boyne; the union jacks and tricolours; coarse comments on Paisley or the Pope; the lattice-work arches erected for the twelfth of July, the banners and bonfires and processions' (5). Belfast with its 265 houses of worship (mostly locked on weekdays), and 589 licensed houses (all locked on Sundays), crystallizes in its present form a turbulent and divisive history. But all towns portray their past, incorporating fragments from various periods; population size alone is just one indicator of a town, its size and characteristics.

The internal urban variety which both stems from and reflects successive stages of development is shown by a present day pattern which is built up of areas of very different physical and social characteristics. The use of census data, which from 1961 onwards has been available for small areas (termed Enumeration Districts) has helped in identifying the spatial distribution of a number of key features. These, typically, include 'dwellings without possession of certain household facilities', namely hot and cold water, fixed bath and flush toilet; also age structure of occupants, their country of origin and social class, all of which are important variables in social composition. From this census data areas of very different characteristics can be identified.

The land economist would argue that the structure of land use of an urban area is dictated by the competition among different land uses which gives a distribution of optimum efficiency. There has been a succession of theories developing this theme over the last forty years, largely from an American background, but equally relevant to the British situation.

The concentric zone theory was contributed by E.W. Burgess (6). He generalized the land use pattern of cities in terms of five rings:

(a)   The central business district, the 'loop'. Immediately adjacent is the area accommodating markets and the older wholesale and warehouse districts.

(b)   The zone of transition between residential and non-residential areas.

(c)   The zone of working men's homes.

(d)   The zone containing white collar workers and middle class communities.

(e)   The commuters' zone of middle class and upper income groups.

This simple structure had a dynamic component: as growth occurred, each inner zone invaded the next outer zone. Thus, with a growing urban area, zone (c), for example, would tend to progress outwards into zone (d). On the other hand, where no growth was taking place, the zones remained stationary, and the only spatial movement was that the inner fringe of the transitional zone receded into the commercial district.

Homer Hoyt (7) considerably re-fashioned this theory, basing his model on sectors. He explained the pattern of residential land use in terms of wedge-shaped sectors which were radial to the city along main transportation routes. He considered high grade residential areas as having a dominant influence on the direction of urban growth. He argued that they tended to develop along the fastest existing transportation lines, and from these sectors property values decreased in all directions. The growth process is more easily explained by Hoyt's theory than by that of Burgess: as high price residential areas move radially outward, previously fashionable residential districts are abandoned, and this certainly describes the situation as far as some twilight areas are concerned.

Both Hoyt and Burgess developed their theories around the concept of a single central core. But first R.D. McKenzie, (8) and later Chauncy Harris and E.L. Ullman (9), saw district centres originating in urban areas and persisting with different roles as urban growth took place. This is called the multiple nuclei hypothesis. Apart from the central business district other nuclei may be industrial or warehousing centres, shopping centres or suburban district centres, and recognizing them is a useful refinement of the sector theory.

Simple economic hypotheses see land-use patterns as the aggregate result of the interplay of the forces of supply and demand acting on the sum total of all parcels of land in an urban area. This is useful in explaining in broad outline the structure and functioning of the urban economy and the location of major land uses. But there are clearly other determinants of land use, and much of the sensitive detail is missing until the interrelationship of social and political factors is linked with the pattern of land values. To understand residential structure, we must turn to social theory and first of all, the idea of ecological processes.

Of particular importance has been the idea of invasion of areas by groups, with sequences of change brought by invasion and succession. 'Invasion' is the penetration of one population group by another; 'succession' occurs when the new population or use displaces as a dominant characteristic the former occupants or uses. This is a particularly powerful concept because it relates the process of change in social structure to changes in spatial patterns in the internal ordering of cities. As a development of the idea of invasion and succession, there is the concept of 'filter'. This holds that when new, quality housing in an expanding urban area is produced for higher income groups, dwellings released by these households become available for lower income groups. In this way filtering is an indirect process for meeting the housing demand of a lower income group.

The filter theory helps to explain the present-day situation in twilight areas in the inner city. As suggested above, an important aspect is the movement of population through the housing stock, which is the competitive market's way of making use of a durable but deteriorating inventory. In this way, the filtering down of old dwellings provides poorer houses for the lower income population.

A housing systems approach to understanding the dynamics of urban structure holds that a change in the composition of a community's housing demand sets in motion a series of systematic changes in the pattern of occupancy of the housing stock. The value in thinking in 'systems' terms is that we may see the urban community as a social system which is adaptive, in the sense of it being responsive to change. In inner urban areas, where housing and social problems tend to be concentrated, adaptation is difficult because of competition of resources, notably in the use of dwelling stock. In these districts the essential characteristic may be conflict and, it has been argued, it is against this background that the process of change takes place. The social environment is the result of conflict between those with different degrees of power over resources and the consequent ability to manipulate situations for their own benefit. The way in which this power is first of all assumed and then exercised determines the pattern of change; for example, whether succession follows rapidly upon invasion or whether the invasion is abortive. As one aspect of this, John Rex and Robert Moore dealing with the immigrant situation in Sparkbrook, Birmingham, used the concept of class struggle over the use of houses, concluding that this struggle is the central process of the city as a social unit (10).

This sociology of a zone of transition puts a new perspective on the understanding of twilight areas, and, thereby, the whole housing market. Professor Rex explains the position as follows: 'the persistent outward movement which takes place justifies us in saying and positing as central to our model that suburban housing is a scarce and desired resource. Given that this is so, I suggest that the basic process underlying social interaction is competition for scarce and desired types of housing. In this process people are distinguished from one another by their strength in the housing market or, more generally, in the system of housing allocations'. He goes on to say that 'this model ... assumes ... an inability to exercise power on their own behalf by disadvantaged groups and an aspiration to relatively detached family life in suburban conditions amongst all groups' (11).

We can now emphasize the major factors that have operated in the process of change in residential areas over a relatively extended time span. There are two features of particular significance. These are, first, suburban expansion, and second, marked shifts over lengthy periods of time in the use of housing stock by different social groups. As a consequence, the social characteristics of many housing areas have undergone substantial changes; social change, rather than stability, has indeed been the norm for most housing areas.

Urban growth in the 19th century was stimulated by migration from the country. Large towns attracted people from small towns. In London the scale of migration was enormous because of its great attractive power; in the words of H.J. Dyos, it 'sucked up provincial migrants because jobs were either better paid there or thought to be so; it also offered a more liberal array of charities, richer rewards for crime, a more persuasive legend of opportunity than could be found anywhere in the country' (12). In this way, net migration into London in the 1840s, for example, added 250,000 people; a relative fall was soon followed by a renewed surge in the 1870s when nearly 500,000 were added to the natural increase.

But the in-migrants did not occupy the slums of Victorian London; the slum dwellers were largely the second or later generation Londoners. Professor Dyos offers the view that London's Victorian slums 'are more properly thought of as settlement tanks for submerged Londoners than as settlement areas for provincial immigrants' (13).

Slums existed in Victorian London, and for very much the same reasons as today: decay of houses, absentee-landlordism, sub-leases and rack rents as part of the London leasehold system; housing improvements which had the effect of reducing the supply of working class houses; the disruptive effect of railway or street improvement schemes; and the prevalence of casual employment, meaning low and irregular income. But slum formation was part of a social process in which there were two paths, one leading upwards and outwards to the suburbs, and the other leading downwards, and frequently inwards to areas of older, poorer housing.

The downward path for some may have been violently induced or gradually effected. Rapid change has often been the result of a physical intervention of some form of new development. For instance, Hugh Prince has described how, following the building of the trunk line of the Great Central Railway to Marylebone between 1895 and 1899, 'In Marylebone several hundred familes, turned out of their homes, crowded into the congested neighbourhood of Lisson Grove. When new housing was offered to them, the rents were too high to attract any but well paid clerks and tradesmen. The slum dwellers were displaced, not re-housed. The new railway yards crossed the barrier between the stately Portman estate and the villadom of St John's Wood, but the elaborate precautions written into the Act saved their properties from any appreciable loss of amenity' (14).

The upward path has been the move to the suburbs, first by the upper middle classes and lastly by the working classes. Underlying this suburban movement has been a prevalent anti-urban outlook: the feeling that the inner city is unwelcome and that the social problems it presented could only be overcome by building afresh elsewhere. This has supported the activities of the Victorian and Edwardian suburban estate developers, the garden city protagonists, and the post-War suburbanites. The possibilities of living at greater distances from the inner city have been realized by successive transportation improvements: the tram and bicycle, steam train, electric traction and the internal combustion engine.

But the flight to the suburbs was also a personal reaction to evidence of unsatisfactory sanitary conditions. Dyos referring to the rise of Victorian Camberwell writes: 'The resulting squalor led those who could to recoil to the suburbs where they could breathe purer suburban air and drink cleaner water' (15). This sensitivity to environment has its counterpart today: the revulsion from domestic and industrial smoke, dangers of traffic, lack of open space and the sheer noise from high density living.

Personal decisions were taken in the light of social attitudes and aspirations current at the time. 'Social leap-frogging made the suburb one of the transit camps of modern society' (Dyos, *op. cit.*), and this was clearly to be one of the factors underpinning social change as the status of the Victorian estates altered. Suburban respectability was enshrined in the new suburbs until they were 'unbalanced by the emigration of its top people and the immigration of a different breed of newcomers from some inner suburb (*op cit.*). If we are to understand the condition of the present day twilight area, which perhaps began as an esteemed Victorian estate, then a recognition of past history is important, for the present situation appears to reflect what might be the terminal stages of a life cycle.

Evidence from all cities confirms the pattern of suburban expansion involving the movement of people from district to district. Referring to Birmingham, Asa Briggs writes: 'By 1860 business men were moving farther and farther from the centre. They would settle in a suburb, as they settled in Yardley from 1861 to 1871, and then move on again as the city expanded, leaving better paid working men to come in' (16). The relatively simple outward growth from the centre overlaid a rural pattern, but the process displayed several phases. First 'merchants and manufacturers acquired substantial plots for their suburban houses on agricultural land or in the grounds of country houses; in their turn the large suburban houses were surrounded by, or were demolished to make room for, smaller villa-type houses; and in some instances these villas were themselves removed and replaced by rows of small modern suburban houses' (17). There were of course local variations, the type and speed of change dependent on such factors as the fortunes and ambitions of the first families to inhabit the suburb, the proximity of a railway station, the influence of local builders and building societies and the terms of conveyances.

This process of suburban expansion had the result that major residential areas were laid out within a relatively short period of time and these now form the recognizable areas of older housing today. To refer to Birmingham again, today we can recognize a fragmented middle ring to the city, the largest continuous areas being Handsworth with the northern part of Aston, and the Alum Rock and Small Heath districts lying east of the city centre, with suburban communities developed particularly around railway stations, as at Stechford and Selly Oak. Today, these areas are much changed. Philip Jones writes: 'These important sections of our cities, with their vast expanses of later Victorian and Edwardian housing (neither very good or adapted to present social needs, nor totally inadequate), have lapsed into a state of neglect which has at its roots the facts of ageing — both of the dwellings and their resident populations. In Birmingham this zone has been the major reception area for its newcomers, and the unplanned manner in which this movement has developed has set in motion an accelerating process of decline in both actual living standards and environmental conditions' (18).

Next three pages: Chorlton upon Medlock and Longsight, South Manchester, 1851, 1901 and 1956/68. These are extracts from Ordnance Survey maps covering the same area of South Manchester at different periods of its growth.

In the first, the main Manchester-Birmingham railway has been constructed. Much of Chorlton and Moss Side is given over to suburban villas lying at a distance from the built up area of Ardwick.

In the second, the main road pattern is unaltered, following the principal radials to Stockport and Wilmslow. The Victoria Park area remains devoted to low density suburban villas. Whitworth Park has been laid out at Chorlton. Much of the rest of the area is developed for housing, the new street pattern faithfully reflecting old field boundaries and other demarcation lines to a remarkable extent.

In the third, full cycles of development have taken place. Poorer dwellings in Ardwick and north of Hyde Road have been cleared. A growing density round Victoria Park has left only a small area of the former villas. Belle Vue Entertainment Centre occupies a site adjoining Longsight Station. The Royal Infirmary has consolidated on a site across the road from Whitworth Park, and the University has expanded on its site to the north.

(Reproduced from the Ordnance Survey Maps with the sanction of the Controller of Her Majesty's Stationery Office; Crown Copyright reserved.)

The historical process of change in terms of variations in social status can be traced from local directories. From evidence of descriptions of householders for given years, interesting patterns are revealed of the changing composition of particular neighbourhoods. The story might record, for example, the gradual disappearance of the term 'gentleman', the reduction in proportion of merchants or manufacturers, the change in composition of professional and administrative workers from teachers and doctors to clerks, the stability of the shop-keepers and skilled worker element, or the incursion of the semi-skilled.

These characteristics suggest that the decay of a declining neighbourhood, once begun, tends to accelerate and the process to be self-reinforcing. The onset of decay within a lengthy process of change, stems from a complex range of factors. Fundamentally it seems to be associated with disturbance, consequent upon urban growth. This in turn leads to a process of redistribution whereby certain people replace others. Many activities may initiate the process of succession. From the physical point of view there might be the obsolescence of property, the impact of new highway construction, the effect of nearby industrial development or the repellent effect of buildings or development by virtue of noise, smell or dirt. On the social side it may be a case of invasion by different population groups, particularly those of a lower class or different ethnic group.

These are some of the important elements in understanding the changing residential structure of Britain's towns and cities. The creation of the slum and the high class suburb is part of the same 'system', whereby there is a differential use of housing stock by different groups of the population over different periods. Neighbourhoods rise, decline and fall according to social and other dictates.

URBAN FUNCTION

During the last two hundred years the industrial and the post-industrial city has emerged. During successive stages of growth, cities have performed certain important functions. Some of these functions have changed, and at the present time important shifts of emphasis are taking place as centrifugal replace centripetal forces. In this section we examine these forces and their consequences.

There are many overlapping stages in the process of change that has marked British urban development. Towns today accommodate many areas, activities and buildings which exist almost as fossils in a townscape of different age. Indeed, the composition of the whole urban scene might be described as a palimpsest where relic features record activities of the past. Sometimes these features reflect very different social histories. G.H. Martin, for example, notes the distinction between old and modern seats of local government (19). He

Below: Castle Rock Gardens and Princes Street, Edinburgh; *opposite:* bridges over the Tyne. *On next three openings:* Coventry, an air view; Glasgow, an air view; Leeds, an air view. These photographs reflect stages in the evolution of particular cities.

makes the point that until the 19th century our town halls were usually not impressive buildings; until 1835 the English borough was governed and managed by something like a private club and it consequently housed itself in a private, informal and domestic manner. The Mansion Houses at York and Doncaster, for example, 'were built as places in which the mayor could live and dine and entertain, not rule and administer' (Martin, *op cit*.). But when the new corporations built they did so in quite a different manner, and their new buildings had to mirror a new civic order with a complex of public rooms and offices. This is just one example of how buildings are designed to reflect their purpose, and how they may be retained in the urban scene from past ages.

The idea of the townscape accommodating a succession of past aspects of history can be especially appreciated when one particular feature has existed through a number of different stages of urban development. Take, for instance, the example of Queen's Gardens, Hull, the history of which does much to summarize two hundred years of commercial activity in the centre of the city (20). In 1778 a dock known as the Legal Quay was opened north of the walled city with access from the River Hull. Before this, Hull's peculiarity as a port was that the west bank of the river was completely occupied by ship owners, the east bank was occupied by the royal citadel and was difficult of access, and there was no room to establish a proper Legal Quay. The Commissioners of Customs put pressure on the city, and a

In Edinburgh the scene incorporates the Castle and the spire of the old Town as it followed and straddled the slope down to Holyrood. The dip in the centre was the site of the Nor' Loch, beyond which, on the right in the photograph, the New Town was built.

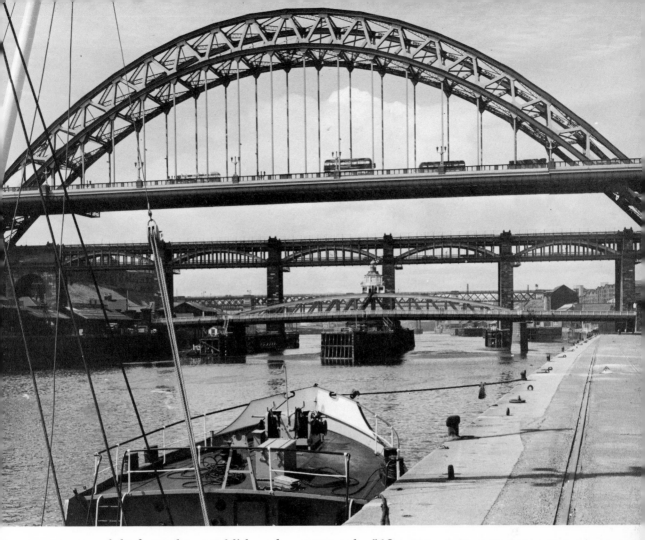

company was duly formed to establish such a quay, and a 519 metre dock capable of accomodating 100 square rigged vessels was built. Much later it became know as Queen's Dock in 1854, and the Dock Company built palatial offices at the western end as a reflection of its reputation.

But the Dock outlived its usefulness as the Humber frontage was developed for larger shipping which the River Hull could not accommodate. By the end of the century it was serving no purpose except for harbouring lighters and river craft. The Dock Company was bought out by the North Eastern Railway in 1893; later, in 1930, the Corporation purchased the Dock. Its filling in was completed in 1934 with a view to making an open boulevard and gardens. A third stage, therefore, began: having originally formed part of the city's defences, and later the source of its commercial power, it was to be renamed Queen's Gardens and became an important open space in the central area. To the design of Frederick Gibberd in the 1950s the Gardens are now the setting for a number of new public buildings.

In Newcastle the importance of communications in the growth of a riverside settlement is apparent. We are looking upstream, from the east, Gateshead on the south bank, New-castle on the north. The King George V Suspension Bridge (built in 1929) was the prototype for the Sydney Harbour Bridge. The High Level Bridge was built by Robert Stephen-son in1849; it has cast-iron girders on masonry piers and carries road and rail traffic on separate levels. Another railway bridge is in the far distance. The lowest is the swing bridge which opens to let river traffic through.

This air view of Coventry shows the Inner Ring Road almost complete, encircling a redeveloped city centre. The railway station is on the lower right in the photograph, and it was from this site that the drawing of Coventry in 1850, shown on page 81, was made.

The spread of Glasgow is suggested from this air view which focuses on the new Clyde Bridge. A bleak riverside frontage is backed on the north by the tower blocks of a housing redevelopment which is taking the place of existing tenements (visible in the middle distance).

The effect of new highways on the changing urban scene is dramatically illustrated in this air view of the central area of Leeds. Their own space-demands, and the vacant land awaiting redevelopment or in use as car parks, have contributed substantially to the emptying of the old housing ring which formerly adjoined the city centre. The scale of post-War reconstruction is suggested in comparison with the oval shaped Quarry Hill flats (top right of the photograph), themselves a noteworthy housing development of the 1930s.

More broadly, from the point of view of total urban function there are a number of important observations to make. Robert Lopez has given us the useful reminder that the original essence of the city was communication and togetherness, and indeed this characteristic obtained until recent decades. He writes: 'In the earliest handwriting that we can read, hieroglyphic, the ideogram meaning "city" consists of a cross enclosed in a circle. The cross represents the convergence of roads which bring in and redistribute men, merchandise and ideas . . . The circle in the hieroglyph indicates a moat or a wall' (21). Such a broad view of Britain's urban centres was relevant until the 20th century, but a fundamental divergence is now taking place which emphasizes dispersal rather then concentration and, because of new technologies, puts less store on central points of contact. Spatially this is reflected in the looser spread of built up areas in this century as opposed to the tight knit concentrations of previous years. This is more than a change in building styles and indeed is more than a simple reflection of the importance of means of private transport; it is a fundamental change in urban function whereby it is no longer necessary for many human activities to be conducted at traditional points of contact.

As with the very rise of the industrial city in the 19th century, these trends are universal. Whereas Britain was a trend setter in the first case, it is now America where new patterns can be seen more distinctly. There, the old form of urban cluster, the conurbation, is being replaced by 'megalopolis' — the loose coalition of a number of metropolitan areas into large regions. The north east seaboard region of the USA has been seen as an archetype of this development; the whole of north west Europe, of which south east England and the Midlands are part, is of a similar extent.

The important change is in function. Until the second half of the 19th century, a dominant characteristic of growing cities was the concentration of certain activities connected with the handling of goods in central areas: in short, the transhipment, trading and storage of raw materials and finished goods in a process which saw the working up of raw materials into manufactured articles. This purely physical function gave rise to forms of service industry, such as banking and insurance and an increasing range of activities which were carried on in offices and were not directly concerned with the handling of goods. About the turn of the century, this change speeded up as the handling of information became as important, and then more important than the handling of physical goods. As Peter Hall has written: 'The road to economic advance no longer lies in concentration on the brute processes of physical production, but rather in increased attention to research, to education, to better understanding of the organization of the production and the sales processes' (23).

In recent years technological developments have produced revolutionary advances in person-to-person communication and in the storage and processing of vast amounts of data. These changes in themselves have not necessarily lessened the concentration of activity in the centre of cities; indeed, innovations like the penny post and the telephone have almost served to centralize further. But it is likely that the displacement of certain activities will continue. Types of manufacturing industry, warehousing and some retail shopping and certain types of offices might increasingly be displaced to suburban or even extra-urban locations.

With these forces it is likely that much looser types of city regional development will occur in the future. Highly centralized and compact cities typified the last century but looser clusters will be typical of the next. Economic function is changing and there is no reason to suppose that communication patterns cannot change to accommodate quite different urban forms. A radial transportation system which has supported the old compact city might well change to one based on a rectangular grid. In this way urban areas will not have a setting of a green belt surrounding a circular, compact area, but they will be loosely dispersed with belts of open land between. Within this polyform type of area, not one but a number of central concentrations where specialist activities take place will be located at junctions of the circulation system.

The point to emphasize is that the British city is undergoing subtle but very important changes. A long established European idea of urbanism is breaking down. The first century and a half of industrial cities, which grew so dramatically upon the economic transformations of the Industrial Revolution, accepted and indeed emphasized the traditional urban culture, but new technologies and new forces do not. In Hall's view, the traditional concept of West European cities 'holds that during five thousand years of European civilization, cities have achieved a special position in fostering and housing that civilization; that cities, as ancient repositories of culture, should be protected from decay; that urbanity, in the strict sense, is a virtue that should be preserved by the planner; that cities are organically related to the agricultural hinterlands around them, and that this relationship, too, should be preserved; that the social contacts between men and their neighbours are a central feature of urban civilization and are to be jealously preserved' (23). But form is disintegrating and the city is vanishing as a central embodiment of collective art and technics. New systems of communication have exploded the centuries-old association between place and people. Suburban culture is quite different and a loose metroplitan form of cities will change the urban way of life.

These are prospects for the future to which urban populations will respond, and we might well reflect that ultimately a social response may be more important than economic pressures. In the past, the way in which urban populations themselves have viewed their cities and the satisfactions which can be derived from them, has been important. Carl Schorske has made the interesting point that there are three broad evaluations of the city in the past two hundred years: the city as virtue, the city as vice and the city beyond good and evil(24). There is ample evidence to show that both Victorians and men of the 20th century have had a love-hate attitude towards their towns, first being impressed and proud with their achievements, but then horror-struck at the unmanageability of them and the social problems which were thrown up. The Victorians selected industrial towns as venues for the British Association, and W.E. Lecky writing in 1865 expressed the urban faith thus: 'The country is always the representative of stability, immobility and reaction. The towns are the representatives of progress, innovation and revolution' (25). But there was always a contrary view, and by the 20th century, there was a substantial body of opinion that reacted against the big city. New designers began to conceive of alternative creations. In the words of le Corbusier: 'The city alone cannot contain urban man: the country calls him. The country is tomorrow's second city' (26).

Changing attitudes to the city are in part symbolized in the emphasis on suburban development. In pre-industrial cities status households lived in the town centre while lower status families were located along the periphery and perhaps outside the walls. This was a feature of late 18th century London and other centres where the new squares of estate development perpetuated areas of privileged living in the heart of built up areas. But the next century saw this pattern reversed in leap-frogging suburban development motivated by a complex of social and other aspirations. In the 20th century the forces continued unabated and were joined by a process whereby the lesser privileged of the community could aspire to valued suburban locations: the public sector developed its own peripheral estates side by side with areas of private occupation.

Those concerned with the conscious shaping of our towns and cities, either in part or as a whole, have conceived their strategies in the light of the assumed function of the cities with which they were dealing and broad social attitudes which were in evidence. Again, whatever the dissimilarities, country by country, a universally widespread movement has been created with the desire to give order to urban appearance and form. We are reminded by Francoise Choay that the terms *urbanization, urbanisme, town planning* and *stadtebau* were formulated for the first time during the second half of the 19th century (27).

She argues that until the Industrial Revolution the urban system was a unification of communication and information, where there was a close relationship with other social systems such as political power, learning, economy and religion. The citizen as he inhabited his city was integrated into the structure of a given society. But the Industrial Revolution radically transformed this situation. The city dweller was confronted with a spatial order devoid of its traditional richness of meaning: there was the virulence of the economic drive, the rapid inflow of immigrants and new systems of communication. The railway, daily press and telegraph gradually transformed the informative and formative role which space traditionally had. The argument is that cities began to be considered alien; urban dwellers no longer felt inside the process and determined by it.

In this situation an early aim of planning was to regularize the disordered city, to conceive new layouts designed to disentangle it from the chaos of the past. In this context there developed the process of governmental intervention in housing and public health and the search for standards of fitness. Theoretical treatises and practical experiments regarding the conduct of urban affairs had the same objective.

In the 20th century there has been a recognizable influence on the course of urban development as a coherent body of planning ideas and practice took shape. In previous chapters we have seen how a broadly interventionist philosophy supported attempts to manage the way in which new development might be carried out.

From matters of land use there was an interest in economic planning, fanned by the disasters of the inter-War years. From the evidence of Jarrow, Ellen Wilkinson concluded that 'the most obvious palliative is all that is implied in the shorthand phrase "the planned location of industry"' (28). A coherent strategy for the planned distribution of population and employment which was linked to a policy of containing the further growth of large cities was pursued. Planning then widened its scope to embrace a co-ordination of all related activities, including the linking of transportation to land use. The desire for community identification has ebbed and flowed and an old paternalist view of planning has lost ground. Search for order has gone hand in hand with a search for beauty and convenience. Architectural and design whims have changed but underlying objectives remain in the desire to raise urban achievements to a level which individual attempts in a market-place economy could never achieve. But the total influence of planning intervention has to be seen in even wider terms than the securing of order and a sense of rationality. Its greatest impact has been to act as a bolster to the traditional view of the West European city to which we have referred earlier. In this sense planning has been essentially a conservative movement, aiming to retain traditional ideas about urban society and urban functions.

A CONCLUDING VIEW

In this urban history we have referred particularly to a social context. We have seen that factors which made 19th or 20th century society are also the factors which made 19th or 20th century towns. Eighteenth century towns contained elegant town houses and squares, circuses and broad streets in the 'grand manner', but they also had hovels and overcrowded slums, reflecting the gap in society between the powerful and the powerless. Twentieth century towns have a much broader uniformity in .residential style and privilege, a reflection of the democratic changes which have taken place and a more obvious sharing of resources.

The history of towns and of planning needs this social interpretation. R.F. Jordan argues, for example, that without it we can easily distort a particular situation. He reminds us that 'the main contribution of the Victorian age to architecture is the slum. If the Town Hall in Manchester is really rather superb, there is also . . . the rest of Manchester' (29). Those interested in the history of towns have not only to bear in mind the buildings of the period and the physical nature of towns, but also the social attitudes of the people of the time. An interpretation of the Victorian city, for example, its achievements and the seeds it sowed for the future, is impossible without a recognition of the competitive struggle whereby people pushed their conspicuous consumptions to higher points. The commitment of the Victorian middle class to this battle to raise standards, to emulate the class above and differentiate themselves from the class below, is apparent in everything from the design, and the clutter of the drawing room to the rise of the exclusive suburb. These are comments on a Victorian situation; the same interpretation extends to our day.

Consider also the question of attitude to family size as a background to the way towns have developed. The average family size of couples married in mid-Victorian Britain was between 5.5 and 6 live children, but for those married in 1925—29 it was 2.2 (30). Birth control had been taken up with enthusiasm from the 1870s, although artificial methods had been known and available much earlier. The new determination was to maintain the rising standard of middle class life and secure higher standards of comfort. Put another way, of every hundred women who married in the years 1870—9, there were 61 who bore five or more live children; 17 bore ten, or more, and only 21 who bore none, one or two. But in the years 1900—9, only 28 out of every hundred women who married then, bore five or more children, one in a hundred bore ten or more, and 45 bore none, one or two. Family structure, household size and the desire for family-centred comfort underlie residential changes in urban development over the last century or more.

Social attitudes become part of socio-political values, which have an enormous influence on the development of towns. Lewis Mumford, for example, has commented on the importance of the shift towards capitalism and the growth of the commercial city. He argues that the speculative ground plan became the new feature of development in the 19th century and later, in association with public transport systems. 'The city from the beginning of the 19th century on, was treated not as a public institution, but a private commercial venture to be carved up in any fashion that might increase the turnover and further the rise in land value. The analysis of this condition by Henry George, and its bold rectification by Ebenezer Howard in his proposals for the new Garden City, which would corporately hold all its land, marks a turning point in the conception of both municipal economics and municipal government' (31).

My view is, therefore, that we might conveniently and with benefit, view towns at any given time as concomitants of societal systems: the course of urban development might best be seen interrelated with social and other broad movements. Town plans should be interpreted in terms of the values and characteristics of the society that produced them. The design and layout of the great estates of 18th-century London can be distinguished from, for example, the ground plan of mid-19th-century Middlesbrough, or Hampstead Garden Suburb in the early 20th century, or Cumbernauld at the present day. In the same way, the distinction between planned towns and unplanned towns can be demonstrated, not solely in the light of changing architectural fashion, but in a political context, that of the degree of concentration of power and capacity for decision making. The greater the executive power that is in the hands of a particular body or élite, the more imposed and dominant will be the nature of a plan because it is the consequence of a few persuasions and not many. The more devolved the political power, the more fragmented will be the plan because many decisions are exerting influence. In this way we can begin to appreciate the reasons for the difference between Robert Owen's New Lanark, the creation of one man, or Titus Salt's Saltaire, the creation of a paternalist and his architects, and Milton Keynes, created by a Corporation though avowedly representing the wishes of many representatives of the community. Against these might be set any 19th- or 20th-century town development, the result of little or no conscious plan, a collection of disparate parts representing a myriad of uncoordinated choices and decisions.

The social and political objectives of a particular town planning scheme should be reflected in the nature of the development carried out. One might compare the New Towns of Edward I and of Lord Reith. Edward's advisers during the Autumn Parliament of 1296, held at Bury St Edmunds, were ordered 'to elect men from your wisest and ablest who know best how to devise, order and array a new town to the greatest profit of ourselves and of merchants'. Compare this desire for profit with a more contemporary one for social balance. Reith's New Towns in 1946 were to be 'devised, ordered and arrayed' on the basis that 'If the community is to be truly balanced, so long as social classes exist, all must be represented on it. A contribution is needed from every type and class of person; the community will be poorer if all are not there, able and willing to make it' (32).

With these general conclusions in mind, we can see that the results of two hundred years of urban development have been gains and losses. Health and housing standards have vastly improved. Unprecedented ease obtains for the majority of the population. As much, if not more comfort, warmth and convenience is built into a simple article of personal conveyance, the motor car, than was given to the wealthiest residents in their houses a century ago (a cold water tap was still the height of luxury in 1840; flush toilets did not come into use in even wealthy homes until this time; and the fitted bath did not become common for the wealthy until the 1870s). People have been liberated from chores by an unceasing array of inventions. A widening of an employment base for society gives choice in ways of living. Cities concentrate a range of cultural, educational, recreational and civic amenities on a scale which has never been available before.

On the other hand, there are constraints on opportunities; regulations and uniformities make a mockery of freedom of choice. There are new strains in daily living stemming from sources as varied as traffic conditions on a journey to work, or loneliness because of a breakdown in social communications. New housing has not removed all problems as the family difficulties in high rise buildings, as just one example, testify. Environmental pollution has occurred in different forms, more malignant than before. Social problems in the city remain and indeed multiply; eradication of poor housing has not meant the elimination of social casualties in the community, and the plight of underprivileged groups is as marked now as it ever has been. Accordingly protest literature about urban affairs shows no signs of abatement.

The city as a setting for human life remains broadly neutral. As a mechanism for sustaining human contact, or for inspiring human aims and ideals, it remains tantalizingly indifferent. Thinking of cities as 'social systems in action' rather than simply physical creations, seems to be supported by this historical review. Certainly the last two centuries provide an absorbing opportunity to reflect on the nature of town life, aspects of social change and the course of urban development.

References

(1) *See* Ashworth, William, *The Genesis of Modern British Town Planning,* Routledge, 1954.

(2) Geddes, P., *Cities in Evolution,* London, 1915.

(3) *See* Moser, C.A. and Scott, Wolf, *British Towns,* London, 1961.

(4) Jones, Francis M., *The Aesthetic of the Nineteenth Century Town,* in 'The Study of Urban History', (Ed.) H.J. Dyos, Edward Arnold, 1968.

(5) Brett, C.E.B., *Buildings of Belfast,* Weidenfeld and Nicolson, 1967.

(6) Burgess, Ernest W., *The Growth of a City,* in 'The City', (Ed). Park, R.E. *et al,* University of Chicago Press, 1925.

(7) Hoyt, Homer, *The Structure and Growth of Residential Neighbourhoods,* in 'American Cities', Federal Housing Association, 1939.

(8) McKenzie, R.D., *The Metropolitan Community,* McGraw-Hill, 1933.

(9) Harris, Chauncy D. and Ullman, Edward L., *The Nature of Cities,* Annals of the American Academy of Political and Social Sciences, November 1945.

(10) Rex, John and Moore, Robert, *Race, Community and Conflict: a study of Sparkbrook,* Oxford University Press, 1967.

(11) Rex, J.A., *The Sociology of a Zone of Transition,* in 'Readings in Urban Sociology', (Ed.) Pahl, R.E. Pergammon Press, 1968.

(12) Dyos, H.J., *The Slums of Victorian London,* Victorian Studies, Vol.XI, No. 1, September 1967.

(13) *Op.cit.,* Dyos, H.J.

(14) Prince, Hugh C., *North West London, 1864—1914,* in 'Greater London', (Ed.) Coppock, J.T. and Prince, Hugh C., Faber, 1964.

(15) Dyos, H.J., *Victorian Suburb: a study of the growth of Camberwell,* Leicester University Press, 1961.

(16) Briggs, Asa, *History of Birmingham,* Vol. II, Borough and City, 1965—1938, Oxford University Press, 1952.

(17) Elrington, C.R. and Tillott, P.M., *The Growth of the City,* in 'A History of the County of Warwick, Vol.II, The City of Birmingham', Oxford University Press, 1964.

(18) Jones, Philip N., *The Segregation of Immigrant Communities in the City of Birmingham, 1961,* Occasional Papers in Geography No 7, University of Hull, 1967.

(19) Martin, G.H., *The Town as Palimpsest,* in 'The Study of Urban History', (Ed.) Dyos H.J., Edward Arnold 1968.

(20) Alston, H.F., *Queen's Gardens, Kingston upon Hull,* Journal Town Planning Institute, March 1959.

(21) Lopez, Robert S., *The Crossroads Within the Wall,* in 'The Historian and the City', (Ed.) Handlin, Oscar, and Burchard, John, Cambridge, Mass. 1963.

(22) Hall, Peter, *The World Cities,* Weidenfeld and Nicolson, 1966.

(23) Hall, Peter, *The Urban Culture and the Suburban Culture,* in 'Man in the City of the Future', (Eds.) Eells, Richard and Walton, Clarence, Macmillan, Toronto 1968.

(24) Schorske, Carl E., *The Idea of the City in European Thought: Voltaire to Spengler,* in 'The Historian and the City', (Ed.) Handlin Oscar and Burchard, John, Cambridge, Mass. 1963.

(25) Lecky, W.E., *Rise and Influence of Rationalism in Europe,* London, 1865.

(26) Le Corbusier, *Vers une Architecture,* Paris 1923, Trans. F. Etchells, 1927.

(27) Choay, Francoise, *The Modern City: Planning in the 19th Century,* Studio Vista.

(28) Wilkinson, Ellen, *The Town That was Murdered,* Victor Gollancz, 1939.

(29) Jordan, Robert Furneaux, *Victorian Architecture,* Penguin, 1966.

(30) Ryder, Judith and Silver, Harold, *Modern English Society,* Methuen, 1970.

(31) Mumford, Lewis, *The City in History,* Secker and Warburg, 1961, Pelican 1966.

(32) Cherry, Gordon E., *Influences on the Development of Town Planning in Britain,* Journal of Contemporary History, Vol. 4, No. 3, 1969.

Picture credits

General Index

Place index